Royal Messages by the Wayside
Historical Geography of the Asokan Edicts

Royal Messages by the Wayside
Historical Geography of the Asokan Edicts

Dilip K. Chakrabarti

Aryan Books International
New Delhi

Royal Messages by the Wayside:
Historical Geography of the Asokan Edicts

ISBN: 978-81-7305-411-2

Published in **2011** by
ARYAN BOOKS INTERNATIONAL
Pooja Apartments, 4B, Ansari Road, New Delhi - 110 002 (India)
Tel.: 23287589, 23255799; Fax: 91-11-23270385
E-mail: aryanbooks@vsnl.com, aryanbooks@gmail.com
www.aryanbooks.co.in

Computer Typeset and Printed in India at
ABI Prints & Publishing Co., New Delhi

For

Nayanjot and Kishore Kumar Lahiri

Preface

This book discusses the geographical implications of the locations of Asokan edicts and is based on field-studies of many of these locations. The Asokan studies have largely been based since their inception on the issues of language, script and grammar, and one hopes that the studies of this kind, which are important ingredients of Asokan scholarship, will continue to be undertaken. However, textual scholarship and grammatical rules do not necessarily lead by themselves to historical or geographical knowledge. By studying in detail the geographical locations of the Asokan edicts, the present book has tried to understand some of the geopolitical factors operative in Mauryan India. This has also tried to identify ancient Tosali and the place where the battle for Kalinga was likely to have taken place. Among other things, this has argued that the Mauryan art, instead of being so-called 'imperial' and 'courtly', was much more broad-based than is thought and effectively foreshadowed some basic elements of the later 'Sunga art'.

Dr. R.N. Singh of Banaras Hindu University, who was a Smuts Visiting Fellow at Cambridge in 2009-2010, kindly obtained for me a copy of a paper on Magan Diwana hill near Ahraura. Dr. Rakesh Tewari kindly sent me photographs of the Surya image from Khairadih which still bears traces of being sculpted out of a Mauryan column. Dr. Tewari obtained these photographs from the Lucknow museum which owns their copyrights. He was also kind enough to read some portions of the manuscript.

This book is dedicated to Mr. Kishore Kumar Lahiri and his wife, Professor Nayanjot Lahiri. On two occasions in the 1980s, they financially supported my Union Territory of Delhi and Chhotanagpur exploration works. In the mid-1980s, when I was subjected to unwarranted and vicious attacks by a section of my colleagues in the work-place, they were steadfast in their support for me. When, several years later, I faced a similar situation in a different work-place, Mr. Lahiri, advocate, Supreme Court of India, gave me the benefit of his legal assessment. I must also put on record that they have been remarkably hospitable to me and my family during our stays in Delhi since 1990.

Beyond the personal level, this dedication is also in acknowledgement of the significance of Professor Nayanjot Lahiri's *The Archaeology of Indian Trade Routes up to c. 200 BC: Resource Use, Resource Access and Lines of Communication* (Delhi 1992) in Indian archaeology. A work of dependable and well-assimilated scholarship, the book has built up a full picture of how raw materials of all types were procured and traded throughout the sub-continent and how the lines of their movement conformed to some of the arterial routes of Indian history. Her analysis, although not based on any laboratory work, will stand the test of time.

Contents

List of Illustrations

By the Same Author

AUTHORED BOOKS

1. *The Antiquities of Kangra* (with S.J. Hasan). Delhi 1984: Munshiram Manoharlal
2. *A History of Indian Archaeology from the Beginning to 1947*. Delhi 1988: Munshiram Manoharlal
3. *Theoretical Issues in Indian Archaeology*. Delhi 1988: Munshiram Manoharlal
4. *The External Trade of the Indus Civilization*. Delhi 1990: Munshiram Manoharlal
5. *Ancient Bangladesh, a Study of the Archaeological Sources*. Delhi 1992: OUP
6. *The Early Use of Iron in India*. Delhi 1992: OUP
7. *Archaeology of Eastern India: Chhotanagpur Plateau and West Bengal*. Delhi 1993: Munshiram Manoharlal
8. *The Archaeology of Ancient Indian Cities*. Delhi 1995: OUP
9. *Copper and Its Alloys in Ancient India* (with Nayanjot Lahiri). Delhi 1996: Munshiram Manoharlal
10. *Colonial Indology: Sociopolitics of the Ancient Indian Past*. Delhi 1997: Munshiram Manoharlal
11. *The Issues in East Indian Archaeology*. Delhi 1998: Munshiram Manoharlal
12. *Bharatvarsher Pragitihas* (in Bengali). Kolkata 1999: Ananda Publishers
13. *India – An Archaeological History*. Delhi 1999: OUP

14. *Archaeological Geography of the Ganga Plain: The Lower and the Middle Ganga*. Delhi 2001: Permanent Black
15. *Archaeology in the Third World: A History of Indian Archaeology since 1947*. Delhi 2003: D.K. Printworld
16. *The Archaeology of European Expansion in India, Gujarat, c.16th-18th Centuries*. Delhi 2003: Aryan Books
17. *The Archaeology of the Deccan Routes, the Routes which Linked the Ganga Plain with the Deccan*. Delhi 2005: Munshiram Manoharlal
18. *The Oxford Companion to Indian Archaeology*. Delhi 2006: OUP
19. *Archaeological Geography of the Ganga Plain: Upper Ganga (Oudh, Rohilkhand and the Doab)*. Delhi 2007: Munshiram Manoharlal
20. *The Battle for Ancient India: An Essay in the Socio-Politics of Indian Archaeology*. Delhi 2008: Aryan Books
21. *Globalization and Indian Archaeology, and Other Essays*. Banaras 2009: Banaras Hindu University
22. *The Problem of the Sarasvati River and Notes on the Archaeological Geography of Haryana and Indian Panjab* (with Sukhdev Saini). Delhi 2009: Aryan Books
23. *The Ancient Routes of the Deccan and the Southern Peninsula*. Delhi 2010: Aryan Books
24. *The Geopolitical Orbits of Ancient India, the Geographical Frames of the Ancient Indian Dynasties*. Delhi 2010: OUP

EDITED BOOKS

1. *Essays in Indian Protohistory* (co-editor D.P. Agrawal). Delhi 1979: B.R. Publishing
2. *A Source-Book of Indian Archaeology* (co-editor F.R. Allchin), 3 volumes (Delhi 1979, 1997, 2003): Munshiram Manoharlal
3. *Indus Civilization Sites in India: New Discoveries*. Mumbai 2004: Marg Publications

1

Introduction

I. THE PURPOSE OF THE PRESENT VOLUME

The locations of the Asokan edicts, the publications available on each of them, their current stage of preservation, and the importance of these locations, if any, in the annual cycle of the local religious life have all been recently documented meticulously by Harry Falk in his comprehensively illustrated and mapped *Asokan Sites and Artefacts* (Falk 2006). In the Asokan studies, this book will serve as a major archaeological source-book for a long time to come.

It may be noted that some of the details which Falk could observe around the edicts have not always been there. In 1960, when I visited the small cave containing the minor rock edict on an isolated hill, in the outskirts of Sasaram, it was a desolate place devoid of any structure. The white-washed building that one can see in the relevant picture in Falk's book is, apparently, a later addition. One certainly agrees with him in the belief that Asoka had his edicts set up in places where there would be large congregations of people, at least at certain appointed times of the year. Whether these congregations were in honour of the mother-goddess or other cults, the presence of which is somehow visible at many of the edict locations, or were simply meant for people gathering in annual fairs which are still held at many of these sites, is a question which cannot be readily answered, but there may be an element of truth in both cases. We need not believe, however, that these spots also marked the places where the *Samajas* or the apparently festive assemblies of people, which were frowned upon in the RE-I, were held. There is no conceivable reason to accept Falk's idea that the *Samajas* of the Asokan time provided occasions for 'orgies'.

What one cannot hope to know is why a particular inscription was located where it was located. The individual circumstances of the location of an edict may be more varied than we can assume. Mother-goddess or other cult spots might have been the focal points, but which assurance do we have that such cult-spots were not post-Asokan developments? It is the mother-goddess temple outside the main cave of Karle and not the famous cave itself, which draws these days pilgrims in their hundreds, if not in thousands, to the site, but how does one prove that this cult predated the presence of the Buddhist monks at the spot? In view of the general continuity of sacred spots or cult spots in the Indian landscape, it may be considered a reasonable inference, but, then, it also remains beyond the level of any 'proof'.

The problems of ancient Indian historical geography, in so far as they can be related to the locations of the Asokan edicts, are not among Falk's concerns, nor have they been the focus of attention of those who devoted some attention to the location of these edicts. *The concern of the present work is precisely this, i.e. to elaborate how some of these locations can be considered parts of major routes of communication of the sub-continent and how some of them can throw light by themselves on the geographical nuances of Asoka's political domination.*

In this connection, I shall also comment on the identifications of various places and groups of people mentioned in the edicts. Similarly, I shall try to locate where the battle for Kalinga was likely to have been fought.

II. ASPECTS OF ASOKAN STUDIES

This approach is somewhat different from what has gone on so far in the field of Asokan studies. Its beginning in AD 1834-1838 when James Prinsep (cf. 1834, 1835, 1836, 1837a, 1837b, 1837c, 1837d,1838a, 1838b, 1838c) published most of his translations of Asokan inscriptions, along with a study of some of their historical issues, was closely related with the discovery of Buddhism itself (cf. Turnour 1836, 1837a, 1837b, 1837c, 1838). The knowledge of the existence of living Buddhism in many sections of Asia and the concomitant interest in the myriads of Buddhist texts, especially the two famous chronicles of Sri Lanka – the *Dipavamsa* (the first quarter of the 4th century AD) and the *Mahavamsa* (6th century AD) – brought about a renewed understanding of ancient India in which the figure of Asoka loomed increasingly large (for an early note on the beginning of

Buddhist studies, Wilson 1856a). By 1877, the study of Asokan inscriptions made considerable headway and was reflected in Alexander Cunningham's *Corpus Inscriptionum Indicarum Volume I, Inscriptions of Asoka* (Cunningham 1877). This volume was also helped by the manifold advances in the archaeology of early historic India, which had taken place under the leadership of Cunningham himself. Cunningham's edition of the Asokan inscriptions bears the signs of a close familiarity of the author with the basic terrain of their locations. By the time E. Hultzsch published his identically titled volume (Hultzsch 1925), they came to constitute almost a self-contained area of scholarship. It was not a matter of surprise because these inscriptions are still the most dependable category of evidence for the reconstruction of the history of Asoka. Vincent Smith, for instance, considered these the most dependable source and ascribed little validity to the various literary traditions regarding his reign:

> ... attempts to reconcile scientific inferences from ascertained facts with traditional dates, whether those of the death of the Buddha, the accession of Asoka, or of any other event, are, in my humble opinion, waste of time (Smith 1901a, p.499)

Throughout the second half of the nineteenth century, there were many publications on various aspects of Asoka and Buddhist texts, including the possible significance of Buddhist legends for the evaluation of his reign and its position in the history of India. The testimony of the Sri Lankan chronicles was favourably discussed in this regard by Cunningham (1877), among others. It may be noted that Vincent Smith's attitude to the Sri Lankan evidence regarding early history of Buddhism was very different (Smith 1901b). Smith suggested that there could be no dependable history of Sri Lanka on the basis of her Buddhist chronicles before the reign of Dutthagamini (c.160 BC).

The date of the *Parinirvana* of the Buddha had to wait for critical examinations of the relevant sources till the early years of the twentieth century (Fleet 1904, 1909a, 1909b, 1909c). It was also by the beginning of the twentieth century that the third king of the Maurya dynasty was given a historical personality of its own. In 1901 V.A. Smith published his *Asoka, the Buddhist Emperor of India* (2nd edition in 1909; 3rd edition in 1920). This was published in conjunction with his volume on a translation of the Asokan edicts (Smith 1909b). The interest of Asoka's 'story', as Smith points out, "is mainly psychological and religious, that is to say, as we read it, we watch the development of a commanding personality and the effect of its action in transforming a local Indian sect into one of the leading religions of the world."

> That interest is permanent, and no student of the history of religion can ignore Asoka, who stands beside St. Paul, Constantine and the Khalif Omar in the small group of men who have raised to dominant positions in religions founded by others (Smith 1909a, p.21).

Dharma of the edicts meant, according to Smith, "the rule of life for each man as determined by his caste and station, or, in other words, the whole duty, religious, moral and social, of a man born to occupy a certain position in the world" (Smith 1909a, p. 29). There is nothing to contradict in this matter, and Smith also understands that when "Asoka speaks of the toleration of other men's creeds, he is not thinking of exclusive, militant religions like Christianity and Islam, but of Hindu sects all connected by many links of common sentiment".

> Asoka, therefore, was in a position which enabled him to realize the idea that all Indian denominations were fundamentally in agreement about what he, from the practical point of view, calls 'the essence of the matter', all of them alike aiming at self-control and purity of life; and he thus felt fully justified in doing honours in various ways to Jains and Brahmanical Hindus as well as to the Buddhists (Smith 1909a, p.61).

Asoka of Vincent Arthur Smith was "both monk and monarch at the same time", retaining the position of the 'Head of the Church and Defender of the Faith' throughout his reign. On the model of the Sri Lankan and Burmese monastic vows, he points out that the Buddhist ceremony of full admissions to the order 'does not convey indelible 'orders' or involve a life-long vow' (Smith 1909a, p. 38).

In the context of the opinion which appears in print from time to time that the antiquity of the Brahmi and Kharosthi scripts was not much earlier than Asoka, what Smith calculates on the basis of the general distribution of the edicts, is decidedly interesting.

> I think it likely that the percentage of literacy among the Buddhist population in Asoka's time was higher than it is now in many provinces of British India.

In Oudh and Agra of his time, the number of literates per 1000 of population were 57 males and 2 females. Judging by the situation in Burma where the Buddhist monasteries were in a flourishing condition, the corresponding figures of literates per 1000 of population were 378 and 45.

Smith's book offered a clear starting point of the discussions on various historical issues of Asoka's reign: chronology, legends as a historical source of his reign, the importance of the two Sri Lankan chronicles, the issue of grammar, language and textual contents of the inscriptions, and observations on the locations of a few edicts.

The Asokan inscriptions themselves carried clues to their chronology, and in absolute terms, nothing is more important than their reference to several contemporary Hellenistic kings from the Hindukush to north Africa and the Mediterranean. The identifications of these monarchs and their chronology were pinpointed by Prinsep himself, and that was in line with what was already understood about his grandfather Chandragupta Maurya's chronology in the light of his mention in the Classical sources. It must be understood that like most other chronological issues of ancient India, the chronology of the Mauryas, of whom Asoka was the third king, cannot be established with pinpoint precision. In 1951, H.C. Raychaudhuri, a noted political historian of ancient India, wrote that Asoka's coronation "must have taken place between 277 and 270 BC", and ignored the temptation of putting a specific date on it (Raychaudhuri 1951). The uncertainty of a few years is, however, insignificant in the broad chronological scheme whose foundations may be said to be beyond reproach.

The second major field of Asokan scholarship has been the detailed study of the references to Asoka in the Sri Lankan chronicles, in the light of what can be gleaned from the edicts. Despite Smith's strong criticism of the historical veracity of these chronicles, most of the scholars have made use of them. This is also intertwined with the problem of Asoka's date in relation to what has been stated about it in these chronicles. The major points here are the inferred date of the death of the Buddha and the number of years inferred between this date and the accession of Asoka to the Magadhan throne. The issue is by no means settled. Alexander Cunningham made a detailed study of this problem in his edition of the Asokan inscriptions in 1877 (Cunningham 1877) and pointed out that in the light of Antiochus II's succession to the throne of Syria and his contemporary Alexander II's succession to the throne of Epirus, the Sri Lankan (and Burmese) chronology for the death of the Buddha (c.544 BC) had to be shortened by sixty-six years. The Sri Lankan sources add that Chandragupta Maurya came 162 years after the death of the Buddha and Asoka came after 218 years. If one accepts the Sri Lankan and Burmese date of the death of the Buddha at 544 BC, going by the testimony of the same sources, Chandragupta would begin his reign in 382 BC (544-162) and Asoka in 330 BC (544-218 = 326 BC; to this one has to add 4 years because of the 4 year gap between Asoka's accession and coronation, and thus one gets 330 BC). Cunningham further pointed out that an error of 66 years was also manifest in the estimate of the date of the Sri Lankan king

Mutasiva, who supposedly ruled 176 years after the Buddha's death, in the Sri Lankan sources:

"By applying this correction of 66 years to the date of Mutasiva, we get 176-478=302 BC for his accession, which would make his second son Devanampiya tissa, a contemporary of Asoka" (Cunningham 1877, iii-x for his chronological discussion; also, Cunningham 1852, pp. 47-48 of 1960 reprint).

Nothing, of course, is certain in such matters. Cunningham justly criticises the date of 544 BC for the death of the Buddha in the Sri Lankan and Burmese sources but does not hesitate at the same time to accept their estimates that Chandragupa and Asoka began their rules, successively, 162 and 218 years after the death of the Buddha. Thus, there is always a subjective element in these issues of chronology.

It may be noted at this point that the *Dipavamsa,* the chronicle of the island of Sri Lanka, a historical poem of c. the first quarter of the 4th century AD (Law 1959), contains some amount of material relevant to the early Buddhist and Asokan chronology. First, there is reference to the times when the first three Buddhist Councils were held. The first one, where a group of 500 elders gathered 'at the entrance of the *Sattapanni* cave at Giribbaja of the Magadhas', took place soon after the *Parinirvana* ('on the 4th month of the *Parinibbana*). The second one took place during Ajatasatru's 24th year, about 100 years after the *Parinibbana* and "was finished in 8 months in the pinnacle hall in the excellent city of Vesali" (Law 1959, chapter 5, page 162). The Third Council took place 118 years later than the Second Council under the aegis of Asoka 'in the monastery called the *Asokarama* built by king Dhammasoka' at Pataliputra and was finished in 8 months. The Magadhan succession beginning with Chandragupta (*Candagutta*), who ruled for 24 years, is clear: the son of Bindusara, 'the greatly famous prince Asokadhamma reigned for 37 years', Bindusara having ruled for 28 years.

The succession of the keepers of the *Vinaya* or the 'Book of Discipline' or *Vinayapamokkha,* is also clearly mentioned till Mahindra (Mahinda), the son of the king Asoka, made the island of Lanka (*Lankadipam*) 'full of faith': Upali who was in that position till 30 years after *Parinirvana,* Dasaka who held the position for 50 years, Sonaka who fulfilled the role for 44 years, Siggava who kept the *Vinaya* for 55 years, and Moggaliputta Tissa who did so for 68 years. However, regarding this *Achariyaparampara* or the succession of the *Acharyas,* Wilhelm Geiger (1912) notes that 'the dates must not be considered altogether authentic' and points out that the list of the patriarchs, according to the Northern tradition, is quite different from what we get in the *Mahavamsa*. In the Northern tradition, the succession of the keepers of the *Vinaya* is as follows: Kasyapa, Ananda, Sanakavasa, Upagupta, Daitika/Dhitika, and Kala. Thus, trying to date the *Parinirvana* on the basis of the years ascribed to a succession of *Vinayapamokkhas* who came after the Buddha is unlikely to yield any indisputable result.

Regarding Asoka, the *Dipavamsa* testifies that he was crowned king 218 years after *Parinirvana* and that 'the wheel of his strength rolled in the great kingdom of Jambudvipa'. The grandson of Chandragupta, the son of Bindusara, *Priyadarsi* (*Piyadassi*) was of great fame and served as a prince in charge of, successively, Ujjayini and Vidisa. At the latter place he married Devi, a *Sresthiduhita* (the daughter of a merchant/banker). Asoka ruled Pataliputra, the best of towns (*Pataliputte puruttame*), and three years after having been inaugurated a king, he had faith in, or was pleased with, the religion of the Buddha (*abhisitto tini vassani pasanno buddhasasane*). Mahinda, his son, was born 204 years after *Parinirvana* and he was 10 years old when Asoka reputedly killed his own brothers. He spent 4 years in ruling *Jambudvipa* and reputedly killing one hundred brothers. Asoka was made the ruler in the 14th year of Mahinda.

Devanampriya Tissa, the Sri Lankan king – 'the lord of *Tambapanni*' – who was contemporary with Asoka was crowned king 236 years after *Parinirvana*. He sent jewels to Asokadhamma as present and Asoka sent jewels to the coronation of Tissa along with various other items which included a fan made of yak's tail.

The *Mahavamsa* is dated in the 6th century AD and is considered equally important as a historical source. Wilhelm Geiger (1912, p. xi) regarded it "as a conscious and intentional rearrangement of the Dip. as a commentary to the latter". In the introduction to his translation of the text, Geiger (1912) dwells at length on the date of the Buddha's *Mahaparinirvana*. That Asoka was consecrated king 218 years after *Parinirvana* was a plausible and acceptable statement to him, and he also argued that the chronology 'current in Ceylon, Burma, Siam' which started out from the middle of the year 544 BC as the date of Nirvana was wrong and contained an error of roughly 60 years. He also drew attention to J.F. Fleet's opinion that this reckoning was not based on a continuous tradition. He further observed that the tradition of 'dotted record' in Canton where the number of dots added each year after *Parinirvana* amounted to 975 in AD 489, took the date of *Parinirvana* to 486 BC. The point to note is that Asoka's historical context was not a difficult one to settle as more and more data became available on Buddhism, especially the Sri Lankan early Buddhist testimony.

Although the *Piyadasi* inscriptions had been known since the 1830s, and as early as 1856, the director of the Royal Asiatic Society, H.H. Wilson, published an analytical study of "Buddhist inscription of king Piyadasi – translations and observations" (Wilson 1856b), it was only in 1901 that "the authorship of the Piyadasi inscriptions" and "the identity of Piyadasi (Priyadarsin) with Asoka Maurya" were discussed threadbare by Smith (1901a, 1901b).

The different aspects of the legends about Asoka, some as late as the Tibetan sources, form another major focus of 'the Asokan studies (cf. Biswas 1967, Strong 1983). The extent to which these legends can be accepted as an unimpeachable historical source also remains on the level of subjective preferences of individual scholars.

Equally, if not more, important is the establishment of the clear formulation of the texts which have gone on virtually since the very inception of the Asokan studies. A recent example of this kind has been furnished by P.K. Andersen (1990) who has prepared both an inventory and concordance of the Minor Rock Edicts. While reviewing this volume, K.R. Norman (1991, p. 245) admits that "there is, of necessity, a great deal of subjective judgement in determining the reading of these inscriptions". The difficulty has been explained by Norman (1991, p. 246) in the following terms:

> Although we should never try to see "what ought to be there", since there is no guarantee that what ought to be there was in fact there, nevertheless, when there is ambiguity or doubt, we should give thought to what ought to be there to see whether this helps us to postulate the correct reading.

Scholarly disagreements are abundant when it comes to the matter of details. The question of language and grammar is of paramount importance in this field. Again, there are a lot of scholarly disagreements over the minutiae of language and grammar. A recent example of hair-splitting over such issues, although not leading to any tangible historical conclusion, is J.C. Wright's commentary on "Asoka's 256-night campaign" (Wright 2000). The point to note is that the individual scholars' understanding of the relevant grammatical rules or their interpretations of various terms in the texts in the light of similar terms in other Asokan inscriptions or the general range of ancient Indian inscriptions may be very learned but they seldom lead to clear historical knowledge.

The scholarly disagreements have been manifest almost since the days immediately after Prinsep. The concordance of the texts of various inscriptions, published by A.C. Woolner (1924) was no doubt a major step forward, but the problems have not been over. As Smith wrote, "the time for declaring the interpretation of every phrase in the inscription of Asoka to be definitely settled has not yet come" (Smith 1909, p.6)

The question of translations into English also continues to cause problems. To give a convenient example, Vincent Smith rendered *Devanampriya raja* not as 'the king, beloved of the gods' but as 'His sacred majesty'. He was followed in this by R.K. Mookerji (1955). The point is that "His sacred majesty" carries with it the aura of 'divine kingship' which is hardly the case here, although in the context of Smith's opinion that he was both a monk and monarch at the same time, this translation makes sense.

The final major issue in this field is the interpretation of various terms used in the inscriptions in the light of the ancient Indian literature, which is bound up with the assessment of Asoka as a monarch in the light of the ancient Indian literary ideal of kingship. Related to this field is also the question of Asoka's relationship with Buddhism and the Buddhist ideals and attitudes reflected in his inscriptions. Possibly the most ambitious attempts in this field are those by D.R. Bhandarkar (1911) and B.M. Barua (1946), but basically all the scholars writing on his inscriptions could not avoid discussing the issue in one way or another.

We have mentioned earlier in this chapter that the mid-19th century advances in the early historic archaeology of the country led to a better understanding of the historical position of Asoka. Our current understanding is that the development of early historic India was accomplished roughly between 800 and 500 BC. By c.500 BC, all parts of India may be said to have entered the early historical fold. Thus, in the mid-3rd century BC, it was not imperative for Asoka to administer to the needs of a political territory which encompassed different stages of technological and economic development. In other words, Asoka preached tolerance for others as a crucial element of his philosophy not because it could bring about harmony between different techno-economic groups of his subjects but because this was good in itself.

III. THE SCOPE OF THE PRESENT VOLUME

The scope of the present volume does not include the minutiae of the Asokan scholarship. The outline of this scholarship is clear enough, although confusions based on some straight subjective readings of the edicts and their equally subjective interpretations will always remain. That Asoka was firmly in the throne in the middle of the third century BC is clear from his contemporaneity with the Mediterranean region kings whom he mentioned in RE-XIII, and a sharper focus has possibly been obtained by the testimony of the Sri Lankan texts that he came to the throne 218 years after the *Parinirvana* in c. 486 BC, although these 218 years are likely not to include the earlier four years during which he ruled but was not anointed the king. 268 BC + 4 years (272 BC) seems to be a straightforward date to opt for his coming to the throne, and according to the Sri Lankan evidence again, he ruled for 37 years. Again, this possibly does not include the earlier four 'unanointed' years. Further precisions are possibly not called for or even obtainable.

To some extent, the present volume is about the possible geo-political aspects of the locations of Asokan edicts. The first and foremost necessity in this connection is a personal familiarity with these locations, and where circumstances beyond control prevent from acquiring such personal familiarities, the only alternative is a close study of the geography of the area concerned and its links with the other areas. Equally significant is an understanding of the significance of such links in the wider geo-political setting of the relevant region.

In 1872, while trying to identify the places mentioned by Fa-xian in the early 5th century in Magadha, A.M. Broadley justified his exercise by writing the following:

> A constant residence of many months in the midst of the places visited by the pilgrim and consequently a very familiar acquaintance, not only with the ruined temples, topes and cities themselves, but with the geography of the surrounding country, must be my apology for publishing my notes, differing as they do with the former identifications of these spots. I maintain that no satisfactory identification can be made without a lengthened stay in the neighbourhood of the places in question, and a careful survey of the ruins themselves. No amount of antiquarian knowledge, however profound, can compensate for an imperfect or second-hand acquaintance with the places professed to be identified (Broadley 1872: 18).

As "Assistant Magistrate in charge of subdivision Bihar in Patna" (modern Biharsharif sub-division), Broadley was eminently qualified to undertake the task. What he writes of the problem of the identification of historical places is equally true of virtually all issues related to historical geography. Interestingly, soon after Broadley wrote, Smith made a mess of the identifications of Sravasti (Smith 1900) and Kusinara (Smith 1901c), placing them well in the interior of the Nepalese tarai, by his overzealous reliance on the textual evidence of Xuang Zang and Fa-Xian.

A personal familiarity with the terrain in question and its place in the history of the country is necessary at every step. Alexander Cunningham, with whom Broadly differs on many points regarding the identification of ancient places in Magadha, possessed this knowledge in ample measure in the context of the sub-continent as a whole, and that is the reason why he could contribute so much to the historical study of ancient Indian landscape without trying to put his knowledge in a 'dictionary' or 'atlas' of ancient Indian historical geography, as scholars like N.L. Dey (1983 reprint, original edition 1899), B.C. Law (1954) and others (cf. Bhattacharya 1991) had done later. Due attention must be given, in the more recent context, to the two volume catalogue of archaeological sites in Tamil Nadu by K. Rajan and his associates (Rajan, Yathees Kumar and Selva Kumar 2009). Although this 'catalogue' shies away from a specific landscape-oriented interpretation of the Tamil Nadu archaeological sites, the authors' close and detailed familiarity with the ground puts it in a class apart. Similarly, attention may be drawn to Vinay Gupta's recent detailed enumeration of archaeological sites (Gupta 2010) in the Mathura area, linking them to the various lines of communication which still retain their significance and orientations. In fact, one of the ways to infuse a pattern into any archaeological site-distribution is to find out if that falls in line with any major avenue of communication. This does not have to be the case always, but very often the alignments traced over large segments of the map offer insights into how history was related to the land.

My concern in this book is only with the distribution of the different types of Asokan edicts from south Afghanistan to southern Karnataka, with discussions on the locations of some uninscribed but possibly Mauryan pillars and capitals. More specifically, I am concerned only with the significance of these locations in the general context of ancient Indian history. A significant amount of scholarship has been built around Asoka over the last two centuries. Most of it is a combination of both literary and epigraphic material. The textual world of the Asokan legends and the epigraphic dimensions of the various internal aspects of Asoka's reign are not our concerns here, although there may be occasional references to them. We shall only look at the sites of the epigraphs and deduce whatever we can about the way in which the different segments of the Mauryan kingdom were linked and what the locations of the relevant epigraphs can tell about the historical geography of India of the third century BC.

2

The Minor Rock Edicts

A clear way to discuss the locations of the minor rock edicts (MRE) is perhaps to group the related ones together. The Sasaram, Gurhupur/ Basaha and Ahraura edicts were all located in a particular segment of the road which went from Rajagriha and Pataliputra to Varanasi and its adjacent areas. Beyond Varanasi, a route went to central India and the Deccan via Rupnath and Panguraria, both MRE sites. These two sites could represent two separate lines of more or less the same route alignment to the Deccan. There is virtually a cluster of MRE locations in parts of Karnataka and Andhra. The geo-political frame of the region where this cluster occurs, calls for discussion. From Delhi to Bairat there was an ancient route, and the locations of the Delhi and Bairat MREs merit attention in that context. From the ancient city of Ekachakra near Etahwa, a route went to another MRE site, Gujarra, from where the route to central India and the Deccan along the Betwa valley was open.

I. THE SASARAM-GHURHUPUR/BASAHA-AHRAURA SECTOR

Sasaram lies at the foot of the Kaimurs. Any land-route to the Varanasi region from Pataliputra or from Rajagriha had to pass through the Kaimurs. The points which are important at the approach to the Kaimurs from both these places were Sasaram and Bhabua. From Pataliputra one followed the Son valley up to Bikramganj, and from there one could go directly to Bhabua. However, one could also come first to Sasaram before proceeding to Bhabua. From the Rajagriha side, Sasaram lay directly on the Kaimur approach. The ancient alignment was Rajagriha-Gaya/Bodh

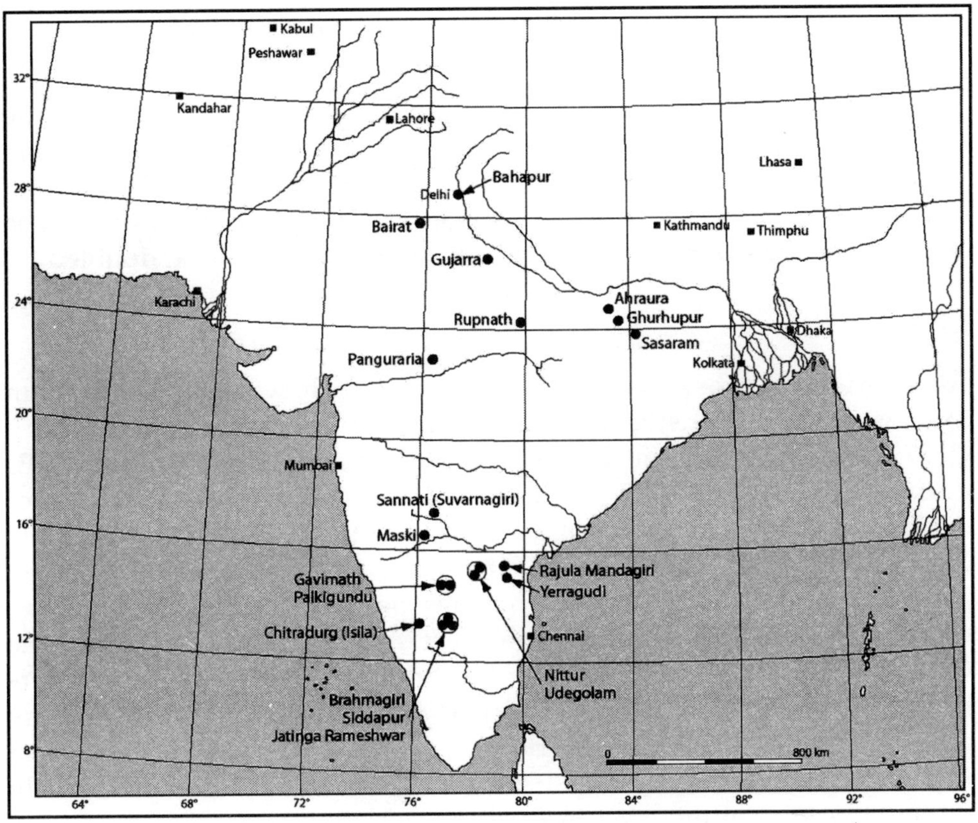

Map 1. Major sites mentioned in Chapter 2.

Gaya-Sasaram. Gaya could be approached from Rajagriha/Rajgir either via Kurkihar or through the Barabar hills. Although famous for its Mauryan period rock-cut caves, the Barabar hills are also said to contain a major settlement site, whereas Kurkihar, both a monastic and a settlement site, can be easily approached from Rajgir. The modern communication alignment is Hisua-Kurkihar-Gaya. Kurkihar has yielded both Black-and-Red Ware and NBP, and thus there is no doubt about its position on the ancient Rajgir-Gaya alignment. Kittoe (1847: 276-278) reported a number of sites in the vicinity of Gaya, which, although no longer traceable, underline the general significance of the Gaya region as a major focus of ancient routes. For instance, a high mound was noted at Chillor on the bank of the Murhar river:

> ... this mound is the site of an ancient city of great extent; a quarter of a mile to the south are several mounds of earth and bricks; two are very conspicuous; one seems to been a Dagope, the other has lately been opened

for the bricks and several Buddhist idols of beautiful workmanship found (Kittoe 1847: 277).

The whole of the Kaimur stretch up to Sasaram and Gaya on the south is an important archaeological zone where the history of settled life goes back to the late third millennium BC (cf. Senuar, and Taradih at Bodh Gaya). This region is full of BRW, NBP and later historic sites as well. The antiquity of the Gaya-Sasaram-Bhabua alignment cannot be doubted.

I.1. Sasaram

Although reported as early as 1839 by E.L. Ravenshaw (1839), the Sasaram MRE was comprehensively discussed first by Alexander Cunningham (1877: 20-21), although he was inclined to assign it, like all other MREs discovered up to that date, to Dasaratha Devanampiya, the grandson of Asoka, "as these inscriptions give only the title of Devanampiya". The Maski MRE, which mentions Asoka by name, was discovered much later. The location of the Sasaram edict has been described in detail by Cunningham: this lies in a cave with 4 feet high opening, a little below the Chandan Shahid shrine or a Muslim Pir shrine in an outlier of the Kaimurs in the outskirts of Sasaram. The text of the edict figures in many publications, but the following from E. Hultzsch's *Corpus Inscriptionum Indicarum*, volume I (Hultzsch 1925: 171) gives an idea of the currently accepted version of the edict in English translation:

(A) Devanampriya (speaks) thus.
(B) ... years since I am a lay-worshipper (*Upasaka*)
(C) But (I had) not been very zealous.
(D) A year and somewhat more (has passed) since ...
(E) And men in Jambudvipa, being during that time unmingled with the gods, have (now) been made (by me) mingled with the gods.
(F) (For) this is the fruit (of zeal).
(G) .... Cannot be reached by (persons of) high rank alone, (but) even a lowly (person) is able to attain even the great heaven if he is zealous.
(H) Now, for the following purpose (has) this proclamation (been issued), (that) both the lowly and the exalted may be zealous, and (that) even (my) borderers may know (it), and (that this) zeal may be a long duration.
(I) And this matter will (be made by me to) progress, and will (be made to) progress even considerably; it will (be made to) progress to one and a half, to at least one and a half.

(J) And this proclamation (was issued by me) on
(K) Two hundred and fifty-six nights tour (had then been) spent on tour (in figures) 256.
(L) And cause ye this matter to be engraved on rocks.
(M) And where are stone pillars here (in my dominions) there also cause (it) to be engraved.

The much-discussed historical issue of this edict is whether the words/ numerals "two hundred and fifty-six" towards its end (line K) refer to 'nights' or 'years after the death of the Buddha'. It was the latter interpretation which was put forward by Cunningham (1877) and G. Buhler (1877). Much later, A.K. Narain (1977) also expressed the same opinion. It is interesting to note that, according to Hultzsch (1925, p. 171, note 3), the term *lati* or night was read in this inscription by F.W. Thomas in 1910 whereas the scholars for the preceding 35 years failed to find it. As students of Asokan inscriptions know, not all the meanings or even words attached to the inscriptions are beyond doubt. This is a classic example. Buhler, whose competence as a palaeographer and epigraphist cannot be doubted, is positive that the MREs of Sasaram, Bairat and Rupnath "absolutely fix the length of time which elapsed between Buddha's *nirvana* and Asoka". He goes on to add that "their data, together with the information of the Greek historians, prove Buddha's *nirvana* to have taken place between the years 483-82 BC and 472-71 BC".

Buhler further argues that Asoka's strenuous exertions during a year and a half "made the inhabitants of Jambudvipa abjure the gods in whom they believed formerly". According to Buhler, Asoka then quotes a "passage in favour of exertion from a sermon", adding that "this sermon was delivered by the *vivutha*, the Departed, two-hundred and fifty-six years before". In Buhler's interpretation, the Rupnath version of the MRE adds that Asoka remained an *upasaka* for thirty-two-and-a-half years and that "during the period of exertion, testing upwards of a year, he was a member of the Sangha or of the community of ascetics." According to him, the Rupnath edict also contains the following section: "256 years from the departure of Sata, the Teacher". One of the conclusions reached by Buhler in this context merits a close reading:

> We now hear for the first time that Asoka's zeal for the Buddhist faith produced towards the end of his reign something like bigotry. His boast that he caused the people of Jambudvipa to abjure their ancient gods, which probably must be taken to mean only that he did his best to bring about such a result, stands in strange contrast to his earlier toleration. The

> change finds its explanation partly in the increasing age of the monarch, and the domestic difficulties which, both according to Buddhist and Jaina accounts, he had with the queen whom he married after Asandhimitra's death, and partly by his turning ascetic (Buhler 1877, p. 154).

Buhler's interpretation is no doubt based on his reading of the text of the Sasaram edict, and to highlight the different nuances of his translation and Hultzsch's later translation of the same edict, it may at this point be worthwhile to quote here Buhler's translation:

> The Beloved of the gods speaketh thus: (It is) (more than thirty two) years (and a half) that I am a worshipper (of Buddha), and I have not exerted myself strenuously. (It is) a year or more (that I have exerted myself strenuously). During this interval those gods that were (held to be) true gods in Jambudvipa have been made (to be regarded as) men and false. For even a small man who exerts himself can gain for himself great rewards in heaven. Just for this purpose a sermon has been preached: both small ones and great ones should exert themselves, and in the end, they should also obtain (true) knowledge. And this spiritual good will increase; it will even increase exceedingly; it will increase one (size) and a half, at least one (size) and a half. And this sermon by the Departed Two hundred (years) exceeded by fifty six, 256, have passed since; and I have caused this matter to be incised on the hills 'or where these stone pillars are, there too I have caused it to be incised (Buhler 1877, p. 156).

If one closely compares Hultzsch's translation of the MRE-I with George Buhler's translation of the same, the difference becomes obvious. The difference is on two major counts. Buhler clearly implies that during the period of Asoka's strenuous exertion on behalf of the Buddhist church, there was conscious preaching against the non-Buddhist gods, thus ascribing an element of bigotry to Asoka's policy after he had spent 32 and a half years as a lay person in the service of the Buddhist church. In Hultzsch's translation, there is no reference to' 32 and a half years'. Instead of imputing any element of bigotry to Asoka, Hultzsch writes that due to Asoka's exertion over a period of "a year and somewhat more", men in Jambudvipa, i.e., his subjects, who were previously 'unmingled with the gods' became mingled with them. This apparently is an allegorical claim: the gods themselves came down to earth or Asoka's subjects became devout or holy enough to be considered gods on earth. If Buhler's attribution of bigotry to Asoka is harsh, Hultzsch's thought that he imparted godly qualities to his subjects as the result of his exertions seems too much of a hyperbole. Secondly, Buhler has no doubt that there is a clear reference in the MRE-I to the *Parinirvana* of the Buddha 256 years before the promulgation of the edict whereas, according to Hultzsch, this particular edict was promulgated after the king had been on tour for 256 nights.

The discrepancies are serious enough, and there is perhaps no point in extolling the merits of any particular study of the textual matter at the expense of another. Both the scholars were trying to be true to what they could read on the rock. The fact that the lines on the rock were too frequently full of gaps stretched their power of scholarly imagination to the extreme.

Sasaram is locationally significant not only for its position on the Rajgir-Gaya-Bhabua alignment or even Patna-Bhabua alignment, it is important also for the route which goes from it to the area of Rohtasgarh fort which, although primarily associated with the sixteenth century power of Sher Shah Suri and the Mughals after him, was politically important from the seventh century onward, marking, as it did, one of the furthest points of the kingdom of the seventh century Gauda king Sasanka. The area commands the Son Valley as the river comes out of the central Indian table-land to flow through Bihar and also overlooks the Palamau sector of the Chhotanagpur plateau. Further, the fort guards the route which comes from Bhabua to Sasaram via Rohtas. Although there is no geographical difficulty to reach Bhabua from Sasaram, the location of the Rohtasgarh fort suggests that there was a secondary route between these two places. The idea of this secondary route is also reinforced by the location of the seventh century AD Mundesvari temple, which does not lie directly on the Bhabua-Chakia alignment but on the route linking Bhabua with Rohtas. The Mundesvari temple lies on the top of a Kaimur peak, and there are also reports of many painted rock-shelters in this general area.

That Bhabua of the modern Bhabua-Chakia alignment is an ancient place is evidenced by the finds of silver punch-marked and later coins in the area which is known to have yielded both stray coins and coin hoards (Anand 1995: 19). If the idea that the silver punch-marked coins from Bhabua are exclusive to this area on the basis of their variety and form (Anand 1995) is true, one may assume that the place formed part of an ancient political unit of the pre-Mauryan period.

That there was an ancient city in the sector between Bhabua and Chakia is shown by the site of Nindaur. This sector has been described well, on the basis of Francis Buchanan's records, by Robert Montgomery Martin in his *The History, Antiquities, Topography and Statistics of Eastern India*.

> There are in this division some considerable remains of the Suir, and the most remarkable is called Patana, from having been a capital city, or

Nindaur, from its having been the residence of a Nindu Raja of the Suir or Sivira tribe. It is also often called Srirampur Patna, from a village of the former name, that now occupies part of the ruins. From the name and appearance of the place, there is some reason to suspect that this may have been the abode of the supreme chief of the Sivira tribe. The chief ruin is a mass of rude stones, broken bricks, and earth, extending 780 feet from east to west, and 1080 from north to south. This is composed of five unequal masses, very irregular in height, but in most parts from 40 to 50 feet above the level of the plain. At the distance of three and a half miles, it has the appearance of a small hill. There is no appearance of a ditch, nor of any other fortification. East from this great mass is another nearly of the same length, but narrower, and not near so high. Its south end is called the Charmar Toli, or shoe-makers quarter. On its north end are two ruinous mud castles, built by late Zemindars, but now decayed. Northeast from this a little way is the village called Patana, or the city, from which we may perhaps infer that the town was in that quarter; but, consisting merely of huts, has left no traces. Under a tree near this village a Lingga has been placed, and surrounded by a wall, within which have been collected some broken images in the style of those at Baidyanath, especially fragments of the quadrangular obelisks. One stone is rather remarkable, containing three female figures with ruffs, like those used in the reign of Elizabeth, and probably the dress at the court of the Siviras. The largest image, and which, probably, was that originally worshipped, represents Mahavira, the warlike monkey. West from the great mass, and north from the village of Srirampur, is another considerable elevation of stones, brick, and earth, like that called the Shoe-makers Quarter, but having no appropriate name. South from Srirampur is a circular mound, pretty high, and called Baghban, or place of refreshment, probably because the people of the village go there in the evening and sit under a tree on some stones, which they have collected from the ruins. It was probably a temple. Three of the tanks drawn in the plan, although they have Hindu names, were probably dug by the Muhammedans, as their greatest length is from east to west, and as the tomb of Saiud Aly, lately mentioned, is on the side of the most considerable. About a mile south from Nindaur, at the bottom of a small hill, is a village called Pateswar, perhaps from having been the residence of the Rajas spiritual guide. Under a tree at this place there have been collected many fragments of carved stones, such as are usual in the works attributed to the Suir; and lately, in cleansing a tank, there was found a large image of Mahavira, which, after having been disgraced, has again come into favour, and is well anointed with oil and red lead; but it is half hid in a terrace of clay, on which it has been placed. As the Mahavira or Hanuman of the Suir differs a good deal from the manner in which he is now usually represented, having no resemblance to a monkey, except in being provided with a long tail, I have given a drawing, PI. 9, No. 2,

> taken from the ruins at Bhuyili, in the Merzapur district, where the image is entire; and, so far as I could judge from the parts remaining or visible here, quite the same with those at Nindaur and Pateswar. (Martin 1838, volume 1, pp. 466ff)

It is clear from Buchanan's description that Nindaur represented a large and high mound with a number of sculptures and sculptural fragments in the general area.

P. Singh, Rakesh Tewari and R.N. Singh (1999-2000) re-discovered the mound in 1999-2000. According to them, it measures 750 m square and possesses a height of 20 m. At the northwestern corner of the mound they noted in an exposed section the traces of a 5 m wide burnt-brick fortification wall of the early centuries AD. The explored pottery consists of black-slipped ware (BSW), BRW, NBP and general red and grey wares. A terracotta ring-well of the early historic period has also been noted along with terracottas of the early centuries AD and fragments of later Brahmanical and Jaina sculptures. According to our estimate, the mound may not be more than 30 acres in extent with about 10 m height. Singh, Tewari and Singh (1999-2000) write that "the fortified town of Nindaur should have served as an administrative and trading centre of early historical periods" (Singh, Tewari and Singh 1999-2000: 144).

The find of the city-site of Nindaur between Bhabua and Chakia once again highlights the significance of this route through the Kaimurs. It also appears probable that this was the centre of an ancient *Janapada,* supporting the tradition of *Karusha Janapada* in this region (Anand 1995).

From Nindaur, the Chakia road comes straight to the Karamnasa river, which is crossed at Mongraur. Here, the modern village stands on a 5/6 acre-mound with BRW and pottery of the early centuries AD.

I.2. Ghurhupur/Basaha

However, before the Karamnasa is reached, and apparently even before Nindaur is reached, there has been a discovery of MRE at Ghurhupur/Basaha. It was formally reported on 15 January 2009 and forms the subject of a monograph by K.K. Thaplyal, who is a noted scholar of ancient Indian history and epigraphy from Lucknow (Thaplyal 2009). It has further been reported in *Sanatan,* an electronic archaeology journal issued from Delhi (Sharma 2009). There is some controversy about this find, but there is no reason to call it a fake. The find-spot is about 60 km from Varanasi via Chakia. The Ghurhupur village can be approached from Chakia via Saidupur. There are rock-shelters in vicinity of the village, and some of these rock-shelters are also found to contain paintings. One such rock-shelter contains the inscription. This particular rock-shelter falls in the jurisdiction of the neighbouring village Ghurhupur or Ratanpurwa.

> These caves appear to have been occupied as early as prehistoric times is suggested by the primitive rock paintings on the walls of some of the caves... These continued to be occupied by the Buddhists for centuries as the evidence of paintings and images of Buddha, stylistically datable to Gupta and post-Gupta period, indicate (Thaplyal 2009)

The inscription contains nine lines in Asokan Brahmi. The first line occurs at the height of 2.95 m from the floor of the rock-shelter and the last line at the height of 2.39 m. The floor is about 4.27 m wide and possibly a few metres more in length. The projecting rock cover of the shelter is at the height of 7 m. The lines are engraved over a smooth chiselled surface of 100 cm x 46 cm. The language is Magadhan Prakrit, and it has been claimed by Thaplyal that the inscription itself is virtually identical with the Sasaram version of MRE I and that some of its letters throw light on the letters which were found damaged in the Sasaram version.

The content of the inscription says it has been two and a half years since Emperor Asoka became a Buddhist worshipper. More than a year has passed since his association with the *Samgha* (congregation of Buddhist monks). It further states that the people of Asoka's empire mingled with god as he made his people virtuous. He said that leading a virtuous life leads to heaven and not only men of high rank can attain it but even those of low ranks can achieve the same. This can be achieved by adopting *Dhamma*, as Asoka has achieved. He added that this message should reach to everyone (to low- as well as high-ranked persons) and even to those who are outside the territory. He further added that the effect of his zealous effort will increase and last long. He notifies that the declaration was made by him during his tour where 256 days have already been passed. He instructs that the inscription should be engraved on rocks and on pillars (the summary of the content according to A. Sharma in *Sanatan* 20).

The above-quoted observations were issued on behalf of an Indological research institute called *Jnanapravah* in Banaras. The veracity of their findings has been questioned by some scholars of the Department of Ancient Indian History, Culture and Archaeology of Banaras Hindu University (Tripathi, Upadhyay and Kumar 2009).

> A close look at the inscription clearly shows that the colour of the rock on which the inscription is carved is quite different from its adjacent surface colour, which suggests, it was recently engraved. In fact, the inscribed

> surface itself is relatively new than the adjacent surface of the hill. It is a wonder that there is no patination or weathering of rocks in the inscribed area even after a lapse of several centuries. The Asokan Edict is inscribed on the rock-surface on the eastern end of the hill outside a cave. It is widely open to sun, rain and wind action. Considering the weathering rate and softness of the sandstone, it is very difficult to explain how it is so preserved during these 23 centuries. This Minor Rock Edict is very similar in content with the one found at Sasaram, approximately 70 km east of this place. Ahraura Rock Edict of Asoka is only 25 km west of this hill. Many letters of both the inscriptions are undecipherable because of rock weathering, whereas inscribed on the same kind of rock; Basaha inscription is fresh and intact. The nature of inscription, especially the freshness of letters, makes one think twice about the genuineness of the inscription. A deeper examination of this inscription is required before accepting this as a genuine Asokan inscription (Tripathi, Upadhyay and Kumar 2009).

The electronic journal *Sanatan*, from the 20th issue of which the above report and comments are taken, has also published the photographs of the edict. As far as one can judge, the probability of its being a genuine discovery is much more than the chance of its being a fake, something which was engraved by a modern Buddhist monk before the celebration of the birth of the Buddha in that area. What is further interesting is the profusion of painted rock-shelters in this sector. It has been reported that one of these paintings shows a Buddhist stupa.

We must, however, dispute Thaplyal's contention that this edict was located in a 'remote place'. Those who are aware that a major route from Pataliputra passed precisely through this region will not consider that this edict-bearing site was a 'remote place' in the third century BC. Secondly, there is no reason to agree with Thaplyal's belief that this and other Asokan inscriptions were "meant primarily for the Buddhists, and not for people in general". Thirdly, there is no substance in his argument that "the Minor Rock Edict I at Ratanpurwa, as also other copies of Minor Rock Edict I, were recorded within the precincts of Buddhist monasteries". Regarding the location of Ratanpurwa MRE site, he states that "this is the first site where we find a natural rock floor in front of the inscription capable of accommodating about twenty persons. According to him, this "gives us a clear idea that the inscription was meant to be read to the lay Buddhist worshippers who sat on the floor". My own field-observation is that there is only one MRE site which can be said to have been associated with a Buddhist monastery (cf. the location of the Panguraria MRE in the immediate area of the 'Upunitha vihra'). There can be no general rule that the Asokan edicts were associated with the Buddhist monasteries or that they were meant to be read out to people.

The main goal in this sector was to reach Ahraura, but there was a knot of routes here. First, there was a feeder route to the Robertsganj plateau through the Karamnasa and the Chandraprabha valleys, which could offer anybody coming from Rajgir/Patna and going to central India or the Deccan an alternative and direct passage to the upper reaches of the Son valley. By taking this route, one could avoid going to Chakia and move straight to the Son crossing by reaching the Sonbhadra plateau or the Robertsganj plateau. The archaeological wealth of this plateau has been highlighted in a number of publications (cf. Singh, Tewari and Singh 1999-2000, Tewari, Srivastava, Saraswat and Singh 1999-2000, Tewari 1999-2000; for earlier work, Singh, Tewari and Singh 1999-2000: 138-139), which draw attention to the microlithic, painted rock-shelter, megalithic, BRW, black-slipped ware (BSW), NBP and later historical sites of the area. A major BRW site – Raja-Nal-ka-Tila – has been excavated in the Sonbhadra plateau (cf. Tewari and Srivastava 1997, 1998). Sites like Naugarh and Latif Shah mark important communication points in this sector.

Sites of different types have been reported, including microlithic, painted rock-shelter, megalithic, BRW, black-slipped, NBP and later historical sites. To underline the links between this area and the Robertsganj area of the Sonabhadra plateau, we would emphasise the location of iron-using BRW sites and NBP sites both here and in the Sonabhadra plateau where a major BRW and later site called Raja-Nal-Ka-Tila (Tewari and Srivastava 1997, Tewari and Srivastava 1998) has been excavated. As I wrote earlier (Chakrabarti 2005):

> The ancient site of Naugarh was levelled during the construction of a late mediaeval fort on its top, but evidence of early occupation is still visible. Another important site is Latif Shah, which is not far from Chakia. This site (approximately 5 acres), located on the bank of the Karamnasa, has BRW and later pottery and may even mark a place, in addition to Mangraur, where the Karamnasa can be crossed, at least in dry months when the large flat stone slabs spread across the river bed are exposed. The present road to the Robertsganj area through the Karamnasa and Chandraprabha Valleys skirts the forested high edge of the valley. Parts of the valley bottom are now flooded because of the construction of dams both across the Karamnasa and Chandraprabha, but one can easily make out that the valleys here formed an easy corridor of movement.

Chakia is only at a short distance from the Karamnasa crossing at Mongraur or Latif Shah. From Chakia, one can go straight to Ahraura, but before going to Ahraura one should know how Varanasi, with which Ahraura is directly connected, can be reached from here. The Ahraura-Varanasi route goes through Bhuili, which can also be approached straight from Chakia via Sherwan.

Tewari *et al.* (1998-99: 196) reported painted rock-shelters, BRW, BSW, Brahmanical sculptures of the 10th-12th centuries AD, Muslim monuments, etc. at Sherwan. The area between Sherwan and Bhuili is dominated by Kaimur ridges which harbour many modern stone quarries. In a rock-shelter of Bhatwara Khurd village in this area, Tewari and Singh (2000-01: 104, note no. 9) reported two small painted inscriptions dated to the second-first century BC. There is a low hill with painted rock-shelters and historical inscriptions at Bhuili. The NBP has been reported from the Bhuili mound which lies by the side of the Bhuili-Sherwan road. There are also reports of early mediaeval Brahmanical and Jaina sculptures in the modern habitation area of Bhuili (Tewari *et al.* 1998-99: 186). The historical details of Bhuili were earlier noted by Cunningham (1880: 130-132, 1885: 130). I have further argued that "the present Bhuili-Narayanpur-Ramnagar alignment marks an old alignment to Varanasi from the direction of Bhuili" (Chakrabarti 2005).

In addition to the MRE on the top of a hill to the left of the road which comes from Varanasi, Ahraura also possesses a small but fortified mound with traces of a moat around it. The pottery found at the mound includes the NBP and BSW. I have earlier judged the place to be "an administrative and military centre of the Mauryan period". More importantly, Ahraura was a nodal point of communication. The road coming from Bhabua through Chakia could go straight to the area around Mirzapur where it was joined by a route coming from Sravasti via Jaunpur. On the other hand, the route coming from Varanasi could proceed, via Likhania which has paintings on the rock wall by the side of its waterfalls, to the top of the Sonbhadra plateau. Through this plateau, one could reach, via the Panchmukhi hill in the outskirts of modern Robertsganj, to the Agori crossing of the Son. Beyond the Son, there was a route to Chhattisgarh and the Deccan through the Surguja plain. Interestingly, as the road climbs towards Sukrit, the first major stop on the top of the Sonabhadra plateau, there are Gupta period remains associated with an artificially dug reservoir in a neighbouring hill (personal information from Dr. R.N. Singh and Professor P.N. Singh).

To come back to our main point that the MREs of Sasaram, Ratanpurwa (or Basaha/Ghurhupur) and Ahraura were in a sense parts of a chain, I believe I have cited enough data to argue that these inscriptions came up at some (possibly) crucial segments of the route which began at Rajagriha or Pataliputra and proceeded in the direction of central India and the Deccan via the Varanasi sector. The Kaimurs had to be traversed, and it is indeed worth reflecting that these three MREs fall in a sense in the Kaimur zone which seems to possess a profusion of rock-shelters and the ruins of an ancient city.

I.3. Ahraura

The hill-top location of the MRE is shared by the local Bhandari devi temple. Narain (1993) argues that in the Ahraura version of the MRE, '256' is written both in figures and words and that it should denote 'years' and not 'nights', as is generally believed. Sircar's reading of the last paragraph of the inscription is as follows:

> This declaration (has been made by me while I am) on a tour (of pilgrimage) for 256 nights (i.e. days) since the relics of the Buddha ascended (i.e. were caused to be installed by me on) the platform (for worship) (Sircar 2000: 82).

Sircar (2000: 79) further adds that:

> The Ahraura version of the edict is the only Asokan record which states that the pilgrimage was undertaken immediately after the installation of the relics of the Buddha on a platform no doubt for worship in the capital city of Pataliputra.

It appears that there is some serious discrepancy between Sircar's and Narain's readings of the Ahraura MRE but the way Sircar tries to explain his final paragraph by invoking Asoka's hypothetical "installation of the relics of the Buddha on a platform" in Pataliputra regretfully carries no conviction. Narain's argument that the king Asoka could not simply afford to be away from his capital continuously for 256 days makes sense.

It was D.C. Sircar who edited the Ahraura epigraph in *Epigraphia Indica,* which is the traditional source of definitive epigraphic material in India. It is not clear why Asoka in this edict should make a reference to the installation of the Buddha's relics on a platform, especially in the light of the fact that he had such relics installed in the stupas built during his reign at many places. There is also no justification in mentioning 'platforms' when the mention of 'stupas' would have been more appropriate in the context of the Buddha relics.

Another point needs attention in this context. RE-VIII categorically mentions that Asoka instituted 'tours of morality' after he had visited

Bodh Gaya ten years after his coronation. Now, in Sircar's translation of the Ahraura version of MRE-I, we find a reference to a pilgrimage which lasted for 256 nights (days). Were the royal tours of morality separate from his 'pilgrimage' which covered more than 8 months at a stretch?

II. RUPNATH

We have noted that a route from Ahraura goes to Mirzapur where it is joined by a route coming from Ayodhya and Sravasti via Jaunpur, in the outskirts of which there is a fortified ancient city. From Mirzapur, the route goes in the direction of modern Rewa which has in its vicinity the early historic mound of Itaha, possibly the ancient *Sottivati Nagari*. The Vindhyan scarp is climbed in this section at Lalganj and Halia. From Rewa one goes to Amarpatan and from there to Bharhut, and beyond Bharhut, to Rupnath. It is an open corridor between the two ranges of the Vindhyas, going in the direction of ancient Tripuri near Jabbalpur. At this point, it is important to remember that this stretch is also accessed from the area north of Mirzapur in the Ganga plain, especially Prayag and Kausambi. The routes from these two places converge upon the modern Sankargarh-Mau section on the west bank of the Yamuna, and from here the route climbs the Vindhyan scarp at Sohagi Ghat with the prominent Buddhist stupa-complex of Deur Kothar at this point. Once on the top of the Vindhyan plateau, this route goes to Rewa via Keoti, and in the Rewa area it merges with the route coming straight from Mirzapur, becoming a part of the route going in the direction of Bharhut and Rupnath. At Amarpatan on the way to Bharhut, the road from Rewa bifurcates, one going to Bandhogarh and Chhattisgarh and the second to Bharhut.

There is another bifurcation of route beyond Bharhut. The route branches off at Katni and goes straight in the direction of Bandhogarh and then Shadol-Amarkantak area and Chhattisgarh. When we think of the routes from the Gangetic plain to the Deccan, we have to think not in terms of a single linear movement but in terms of a network of routes.

Rupnath, which lies at the edge of the range forming the northern edge of the east-west corridor from Satna and Bharhut, has a cluster of pools. This apparently sacred spot is near the city-site of Kakrehta which has about a kilometre long mound and possesses NBP and earlier pottery (including BRW). One would think that this city-site was a part of the east-west movement through this area, and the sacred spot of Rupnath got its MRE not merely because of its position on a prominent route but also because of its proximity to a major city-site of the area.

The location of the Rupnath MRE has been described well by Cunningham (1877: 21-22):

> The Rupnath rock is a single flinty block of dark red sandstone lying at the foot of the Kaimur range of hills, just below the fertile plateau of Bahuriband. Here a small stream breaks the crest of the Kaimur range, and after three low falls, forms a deep secluded pool at the foot of the scarp. Each of these pools is considered holy, the uppermost being named after Rama, the next after Lakshman, and the lowest after Sita. The spot, however, is best known by the name of Rupnath, from a lingam of Siva which is placed in a narrow cleft of the rocks on the right. There are similar falls and pools at Ram Tal, a few miles to the southwest, where the Kair river pours over the crest of the Kaimur range from the plateau of Saleya. This spot is also esteemed holy. An annual fair was formerly held at Rupnath on the *Sivaratri* in honour of Siva, but this has been discontinued since 1857. The lowermost pool, however, or Sitakund, which never dries up, still attracts a few pilgrims. The edict of Asoka is inscribed on the upper surface of the rock, which has been worn quite smooth by people sitting upon it for hundreds of years at the annual fairs. It is now of a very dark dirty-red colour, and the inscription might easily escape observation.

Hultzsch's version of the Rupnath text adds something new: "(line K) And (wherever) there are stone pillars here, it must be caused to be engraved on stone pillars. (L)According to the letter of this (proclamation) (you) must dispatch (an officer) everywhere as far as your district" (Hultzsch 1925: 167). The term used for 'stone pillars' is *Salathave* (or *Silathambhani*). The problem is that the Rupnath MRE is engraved on a piece of rock and not on a stone pillar.

III. PANGURARIA

Panguraria does not lie on a straight alignment from Rupnath, although from Rupnath it is approachable via the fortified ancient city of Tripuri on the north bank of the Narmada near Jabbalpur. Although this route is not easy, one can follow the northern bank of the Narmada up to the area south of modern Bhopal, where there is a fortified city-site called Nadner in the Betwa Valley. Panguraria falls between this section south of Bhopal and the mound of Ninnore on the northern bank of the Narmada, which marked an old crossing point of the river.

However, Panguraria falls easily in a communication line coming from the Ganga-Yamuna plain along the Betwa valley. This route comes all the way from the modern Lucknow area and beyond. It crosses the Ganga at Kanpur which has on its outskirts the large mound of Jajmau.

From Jajmau the route leads straight to the Yamuna, on the left bank of which lies the site of Musanagar with two early stupas in its neighbourhood. The Yamuna is crossed at Musanagar and in this area the Betwa joins the Yamuna. The alignment of the Betwa leads, from near Musanagar, to the Vidisa area through the major ancient sites of Ehrich and Tumain. From Vidisa, the valley leads straight to the area of Nadner south of Bhopal and from there to Panguraria and Ninnore.

In and around Panguraria, there is a large complex of rock-shelters called the Panguraria-Bayan complex of rock-shelters. The main rock-shelter is locally called *Saru-Maru* cave. For Panguraria, I may depend on my earlier notes on the site.

> First, one can easily see a number of platforms with rubble revetments at different levels on the slope of the hill. Each of these platforms contains a stupa made of dressed stones. The diameters of these stupas, of which about a dozen have been traced, vary between 2 m and 16 m. Above these platforms is the main rock-shelter *Saru-Maru*. The platform in front of the rock-shelter, which also has an Asokan Minor Rock Edict engraved on its face, is fairly large and seems to contain occupational deposits. The inscription is currently much abraded. Above the level of *Saru-Maru,* there are 21 similar stone-built Satdhara-type stupas, some on platforms. Moreover, in their vicinity, there a few monastic cells and a water trough within rubble enclosures. At the ground level of the slope is the largest, similarly stone-built, stupa of this area, which is 76 m in diameter and has a *Pradakshinapatha* around it.
>
> On the slopes of another hill to the west, there are more stupa complexes within stone enclosures, and somewhere in this sector is the rock-shelter locally known as *Bawan Paga* which measures 76.20 m by 10.60 m and has a frontage covered with a rubble-made wall. In the valley below, an earthen dam was constructed across the flow of the Babar Nala to create a water reservoir which is also supposed to possess a spill-channel.
>
> In the valley below the *Saru-Maru* complex, we noticed some occupational debris, but more importantly, there were scatters of microliths.
>
> More stupas have been reported from near Budhni (a brick-built stupa) and Talpura. There are two stone-built stupas at Talpura, also near Budhni. The diameters these stupas, located near two rock-shelters, are 21 m and 10 m. They lie within two separate but adjoining enclosures. There is a 1 m wide and 1.50 m high terrace around the stupas, to which a stone-paved pathway led from the ground level.
>
> We found an inscribed long shaft of an umbrella and the umbrella itself, both bearing Mauryan polish, in the house of the local Archaeological

Survey of India *Chowkidar*. The *Indian Archaeology – A Review* report of 1976-77 mentions these finds but does not make it clear if they are from the main stupa at the ground level below *Saru-Maru* or if they come from one of the Talpura stupas.

The Panguraria version of the Asokan Minor Rock Edict I was engraved in three segments of the rock-façade and, as edited by D.C. Sircar (1979), is represented as addressed by Asoka to the local governor who was *Kumara Samva'* (*Kumara* is interpreted by Sircar as 'a scion of his family and probably not a son of his'). The monastic complex itself is called in the edict *Upunitha-Vihara* or *Opunitha-Vihara,* and the area of its location is called *Manema-Desa*. One does not seem to be familiar with this particular geographical term in any other ancient context (Chakrabarti 2005)

Thus, Panguraria marks the area of a major archaeological complex: many rock-shelters, stupas, a Mauryan period umbrella and its decorated umbrella shaft, two city-sites (Nadner/Nadnur and Ninnore), one each at the northern and the southern limits of the area, and finally, the MRE itself. The area was important enough to be considered fit for the governorship of a person of royal lineage, and it is probable that *Kumara Samva* mentioned in this MRE was stationed at Nadner, apparently the capital of the *Manema* country or *Desa*.

Across the Narmada at Ninnore, the route led, on the one hand, by modern Hosangabad and Betul to the modern Vidarbha area near Nagpur and on the other to the Tapti crossing at Burhanpur via Khandwa and Asirgarh.

The actual state of the Panguraria edict has been described by Sircar thus (2000, pp. 95-96):

The Panguraria text of Minor Rock Edict I is damaged and fragmentary. Since the inscription has been written here in three sections, it appears that the surface of the rock was found unsuitable for engraving the record in continuous lines of writing of a uniform size in a particular area. Of the three sections, the smallest one at the top consists of only five lines, each having about five or six *aksaras* of a fairly big size. This part, as we shall see below, forms a kind of preface to the edict proper just as an address is to a letter. The edict proper is engraved below in the other two sections in smaller characters.

The problem lies with the interpretation of this 'preface' part. Falk considers it completely separate from the main edict, i.e., MRE I and gives it the status of a 'separate edict' on the model of such edicts at Dhauli, Jaugada and Sannati. Falk's text of the Panguraria edict is completely different from Sircar's version and does not fit in the general range of inscriptions of the period.

> The king, who (now after consecration) is called Piyadassi, (once) came to this place on a pleasure tour while he was still a ruling prince, living together with his (unwedded) consort.

Sircar (2000: 94-103) writes:

> The king named Priyadarsin (speaks) to Kumara Samva from his march (of pilgrimage) to the Upunitha-vihara (or Opunitha-vihara) in Manema-desa. (This) declaration (was issued by me when I was) on a tour (of pilgrimage and had stayed away from the capital for) 256 (nights, i.e. days).

He (1960, p.98) offers a lengthy interpretation of how he arrived at his translation.

> The earlier part of this section shows that it was an address of the king, whose name was *Priyadarsin* (i.e., King Asoka), to the *Kumara* (i.e., a member of the royal family, if not actually the king's son), named *Samva*, who must have been stationed at a city that was situated in the vicinity of the inscribed rock at Panguraria. The latter part of the section refers to one's *yatra* or pilgrimage to a monastery called *Upunitha-vihara* (or *Opunitha-vihara*) situated in a territory, the name of which looks like *Manema-desa*. Asoka seems to have sent the copy of the edict engraved below to the *Kumara* who was the viceroy of the region when the king was proceeding to the monastery in question in the course of his pilgrimage sometime after the promulgation of the edict.... It should better not be regarded as an order of the king asking the viceroy to visit the monastery in question. It is clear that the entire period of pilgrimage was not passed by Asoka at one monastery or hilly place.

Sircar assumes that the premise of Asoka being on tour for 256 days at a stretch is a fact and that his supposed visit to this monastery was a part of that pilgrimage. However, on the basis of Sircar's translation, it is also possible to assume that the king was asking the royal governor to visit the monastery in anticipation of the promulgation of the MRE-I at this place. The question which also remains unanswered is why the record of a royal or viceregal visit to this particular monastery had to be put in the relevant inscription. The Narmada flows a little to the south of Panguraria with the major but unfortified settlement of Ninnore on its northern bank. Across the Narmada, the roads go to Vidarbha and also the crossing of the Tapti at Burhanpur. Northwards, the area falls to the south of Vidisa. The fortified city-site of Nadner is the major site here and probably housed the royal governor *Samva*. Sircar (2000) points out, on the basis of the occurrence of the terms *Daraka* (interpreted as 'one's own son') and *Devikumaras* (interpreted as 'other queeens' sons') in Pillar Edict VII (Delhi-Topra version), that the term *Kumara* probably did not signify the same sort of relationship with the king as the term *Aryaputra* of the southern edicts signified. The latter term denoted the king's own sons.

IV. GUJARRA

Another MRE site is linked to the Betwa alignment to central India from the Ganga-Yamuna plain. The Gujarra MRE, which was discovered in 1953 (Sircar 2000: 86-93), is located to the north of the village of Gujarra and at the foot of a low bouldery hill called *Siddham ki todiya* or 'the hill of those who have obtained bliss'. After the Maski MRE, this is the first MRE to include the royal name *Asoka* (*Asokarâjasa*). Falk (2006: 75-77) offers his own reading: '*asake rajâ*, is taken for *Asoke rajâ*'.

Although there is no large settlement site in the immediate vicinity of Gujarra near Datia, the general early historic importance of the area is beyond dispute, as 30-odd early historic sites have been reported from this belt. Datia itself lies on a route which leads from Agra and the ancient site of Bateshwar to Jhansi at the doorstep of the Betwa valley via Bhind-Morena. More importantly, Datia or Gujarra can easily be approached from the major early historic site of Chakranagar in the Yamuna badlands near Etahwa. This large site has a pre-NBP antiquity and is set in the ravines on the right bank of the Yamuna. The ravines have been a late feature because the city-site itself has been cut into ravines. The point is that Gujarra is easily approachable from this area, and through Jhansi, the ancient city-site of Ehrich on the southern bank of the Betwa, is also easily approachable.

The MREs which we have been discussing so long, i.e., the edicts found at Sasaram, Ghurhupur/Basaha, Ahraura, Rupnath, Panguraria and Gujarra, are linked in various ways to the network of routes which linked the Gangetic plain with the Deccan. The two other northern MREs – the ones found at Bahapur/Srinivaspuri, Delhi, and Bairat – are also connected in some way with one of the routes which led from the direction of Delhi to central India through Rajasthan.

V. BAHAPUR/SRINIVASPURI, DELHI

The location of the outcrop on which the edict is engraved lies below the Kalkaji hill in Delhi (Sircar 1969-70). The Delhi ridge is a prehistoric area in the sense that prehistoric artefacts from the palaeolithic to the microlithic have been found extensively over it. Microlithic flakes have been picked up in the valley below the Kalkaji hill, *Kalkaji* being the most important mother-goddess shrine of Delhi. Whether the antiquity of this shrine – or strictly speaking, the antiquity of the sacredness of the spot – reaches back to the pre-Asokan phase of Delhi is impossible to determine, but the location of the edict-bearing place not far from the Kalkaji shrine is worth pointing out. Delhi of the Asokan period was the site of modern Purana Qila or old Indraprastha, which lies well below 10 km to the north of the Bahapur site. These three places – Purana Qila, Bahapur, Kalkaji – all lie in a north-south orientation which is in accordance with the general Delhi-Mathura alignment. In a sense, the Bahapur MRE is located both for the possible visitors to the Kalkaji shrine and the travellers approaching Delhi from the direction of Mathura.

VI. BAIRAT

The Bairat MRE is located just where the road coming from Sariska and eventually from Delhi approaches the fortified early historic site of Bairat. Another edict, known as the Bhabru edict, was reputedly found in the same area, but the Bhabru edict does not fall under the category of the MREs. That Bairat falls on a major route coming from the direction of Delhi need not be questioned. The Mehrauli area of Delhi yielded the figure of a Sunga period *Yakshini*, and in the Gurgaon-Alwar sector, the Sunga period remains have been pointed out at two places – Bhadas and Hathin. Further, it may be noted that the present Ballabhgarh-Rohtak-Jind-Hissar-Abohar alignment, which, as I have elsewhere argued (Chakrabarti 2009), was a major alignment both in the Indus and the historic times, was directly linked to Delhi on the one hand and Mathura on the other. Bairat falls on the modern Delhi-Gurgaon-Alwar road via Sariska, but that the route continued in ancient times beyond Bairat is shown by the occurrence of Sunga period stupa railings in a late period *Chhatri* or burial structure at Lalsot (Agrawal 1962). Our general inference is that this route led, possibly both to the Sarai Madhopur section of Rajasthjan and to the Kota area. Malwa can easily be reached through both these areas.

Considering that Bairat fell on a route emanating from Delhi, the Delhi MRE at Bahapur and the MRE of Bairat can be grouped together. The Bairat edict, known since 1870-71 when A.C.L. Carlleyle (1878) reported it, overlay four cinerary urns covered by two large stones, but the inscription was in no way connected with them. Falk (2006: 63) believes that the location of the edict was due to its proximity to the *Bhimsen Gupha*, a 6 m x 6 m cave containing the evidence of mother-goddess worship.

The northern MREs, i.e., those at Sasaram, Basaha/Ratanpurwa/Ghurhupur, Ahraura, Rupnath, Panguraria, Gujarra and Delhi, admit of some variations in the reading of their texts. We have repeatedly noted this. One of the crucial questions, as we have already noticed, is the interpretation of '256' in the widely varying senses of 'nights' and 'years'. The difference in the readings of the Panguraria text by Sircar and Falk, and the way Sircar finds mention of the installation of the Buddha relics on a platform in Pataliputra in the Ahraura version of the MRE seem to be indicative of the fact that there is as yet no unanimity regarding the very text of the Asokan edicts and the interpretations of many of the terms mentioned by them. The way a scholar of the stature of Buhler tried to date the death of the Buddha on the basis of the Sasaram, Rupnath and Bairat versions of the MRE and the way his idea has been given up must be considered a matter of serious surprise. Buhler was not *interpreting* anything; he simply read a few words in the concerned edicts, but the later scholars apparently set no score by his *reading*. As far as we can judge, the impressions of the concerned inscriptions available to Buhler were as good as those available to the later scholars.

Here we are concerned only with the issue of historical geography but, nonetheless, it is important to note that differences still persist among Asokan scholars even over such a basic issue as determining a unanimously accurate version of the text.

VII. THE SOUTHERN MINOR ROCK EDICTS

With the exception of the MREs at Yerragudi and Rajula Mandagiri, which lie in the Kurnul district of Andhra, the southern MREs all lie in the Raichur, Bellary-Kopbal and Chitradurga districts of Karnataka. Maski in Raichur is the northernmost one, and the three MREs of Chitradurga – Brahmagiri, Siddapur and Jatinga Ramesvar – are the southernmost. The four MREs of Bellary-Kopbal – Nittur, Udegolam, Gavimath and Palkigundu – occupy a more or less central position. The Gooty-Patikonda section of Kurnul, which has the Yerragudi and Rajula Mandagiri MREs, lie roughly to the east of Nittur and Udegolam. With Bellary as the central point, all these MREs should lie within a radius of 150 km. The concentration of the MREs in a comparatively limited area is no doubt noteworthy, and to understand their locations, one has to look at them site by site.

VII.1. Nittur, Udegolam, Maski

They lie roughly to the northwest of Bellary-Sirguppa road via Tekkalakota. The location of both of them is a few km southwest of Tekkalakota, Udegolam being about 5 km southwest of Nittur. The exact find-spots of the inscriptions in both the cases are outcrops of rocks in the cultivated fields of the area. Namita Sugandhi's survey (Sugandhi 2008) found some potsherds at Nittur whereas at Udegolam, she found nothing. What is interesting is that Tekkalakota possessed, in addition to the hill-top Neolithic remains, evidence of Iron Age, early historical and later historic occupations in the general area. Four Mauryan period occupational areas were identified, two of them with a "high density of Iron Age and early historic pottery, lithic tools and iron slag on the surface" on the opposite sides of the Tekkalakota hili. She also identifies the former existence of several reservoirs, one of which was apparently large with signs of early historic and Vijayanagara period retaining walls. Another evidence of early historic presence in the area is a silver punch-marked coin.

Falk (2006: 101-103) did not find anything sacred on the folk-level at Udegolam but draws attention to a what he calls 'a donation panel' in his photograph of the general area of the site. At Nittur, he (Falk 2006: 83-85) refers to the probable existence of an old settlement in an island in the Tungabhadra near the site, but gives more importance to "the painted rock of Cukkudadappa right behind the edict rocks", which is "worshipped before marriages and on all major festivals".

Nittur seems to suggest that MRE-I and MRE-II were, indeed, meant to be separate edicts. Here they are engraved on separate rocks. In both cases, 'king Asoka' is mentioned. Udegolam has only MRE-II.

The Bellary-Sirguppa road leads to Sindhnur and from Sindhnur to Maski, another MRE site. So, in a sense there is some kind of alignment linking Maski, Nittur and Udegolam. Maski itself seems to be oriented through Lingsugur with the Bagalkot-Bijapur-Solapur alignment, and if the premise is true, this will mean that Maski, Nittur and Udegolam were connected with a major line of communication which reaches the southern Deccan from the Pune area of Maharashtra via Solapur.

The occupational remains of Maski are well-known: Period I – Neolithic-Chalcolithic; Period II – 'Megalithic' or Iron Age; Period III – Early Historical, and Period IV – Mediaeval. The long continuity of occupation is noteworthy, and the area has the advantage of being linked to a wide area of Karnataka, Maharashtra and Andhra. It may be remembered that the final battle between the army of the Muslim Deccanese kings and that of Vijayanagara was fought at Talikota in 1565. Talikota on the bank of the Dhoni River is about 80 km to the southeast of Bijapur, and the thrust of the Muslim invading force was by Lingsugur, Mudgal and Maski. It may further be pointed out that the ancient inscriptional name of Maski was Mosangi, which "suggests its identity with the battlefield of Musangi, where, according to Tamil records, the Chalukyan king Jayasimha II was defeated by Rajendra Chola I" (Hultzsch 1925: xxvi). The Tamil record in question is the Tirumalai rock inscription (c. AD 1025) of Rajendra Chola I: "Jayasimha, who, out of fear and full of vengeance, turned his back at Musangi and hid himself" (Hultzsch 1907-08: 233). He was the Western Chalukyan king Jayasimha II with his base at Badami.

Maski was discovered in 1915 by C. Beadon, a gold-mining engineer, and H. Krishna Sastri (1915) offers a description of the find-spot of the inscription inscribed on an irregularly shaped boulder at the southern entrance to a cavern. The Maski MRE mentions 'priyadarsi' by his name Asoka. Sastri takes care to emphasize that the country around Maski "shows clear traces of its having been once, in very remote times, the most important gold-working centre; for at Hatti which is not very far, the shaft of the old workings, as Mr. J.D. Hay, the Manager of the Hutti Gold Mines, kindly informs me, is the deepest in the world, known so far".

Koppal/Kopbal is now a district town of Karnataka. The Koppal district was formed out of the former district of Raichur. The hill on the west of the settlement is Palkigundu which contains on the top an Asokan MRE. The hill-spur on the east of the settlement is Gavimath which is much lower than the Palkigundu hill. An annual fair takes place here. Currently, Gavimath is a centre of Lingayet monks. Some dolmens have been reported from the Koppal area, but it is noted these days mainly for its fort which covers a large area and belongs primarily to the 18th century. The fort may have an earlier antecedence and shows the geopolitical significance of the Kopbal area which is also highlighted by its proximity to Hospet and Hampi, the centre of Vijayanagara power. During the Vijayanagara period (1336-1646), the area received routes from various parts of the Deccan and the coast, principally from Belgaum-Dharwar, north and south Kanara, and the areas lying both to the north and the south. Whether the same is true of the much earlier Asokan period is doubtful but there is no denying the fact that Kopbal occupied an important geo-political position in the map of the Deccan, just as Hospet-Hampi did in the much later Deccanese history.

VII.2. Brahmagiri, Siddapur, Jatinga Ramesvar

All these three edicts lie within the maximum distance of about 5 km from each other, and the place from where one can easily approach them is Hanagal/Hangal on the Chitradurga-Bellary road. Roughly to the south of Bellary, the area is linked primarily with the Mysore-Bangalore-Tumkur-Chitadurg section of Karnataka. The Tumkur-Chitradurg segment controls the line of different movements in Karnataka including those coming from the coast and Belgaum-Dharwar. From Tumkur, the Kolar-Bangalore belt is also not far off. For reasons discussed in detail elsewhere in the volume, we consider *Isila* of the Brahmagiri MRE to be the large (730 m square) ancient settlement of Chandravalli at the foot of the Chitradurg hill.

One is not sure if these three MREs can be considered a separate category and listed as MRE-II. The Brahmagiri version begins by saying that the *Aryaputra* or the prince and the *Mahamatras* (a class of officers) stationed at Suvarnagiri will address the Mahamatras stationed at Isila and tell them of the following command of 'Devanampriya'. Here follows the standard text of MRE which we have been considering so far, but when this version ends, there is a line (in Hultzsch's translation Line M): "moreover, Devanampriya speaks thus". From Line N onwards, the Brahmagiri text reads the following:

(N) Obedience must be rendered to mother and father, likewise to elders, firmness (of compassion) must be shown towards animals; the truth must be spoken; these same moral virtues must be practised.

(O) In the same way the pupil must show reverence to the master, and one must behave in a sensible manner towards relatives.

(P) This is an ancient rule, and this conduces to long life.

(Q) Thus one must act.

(R) Written by Chapada.

The scribe Chapada wrote his name in Kharosthi, clearly showing that a scribe from the northwestern frontier was employed to engrave the edict. Siddapur, although considerably damaged, bears the same text. Jatinga Ramesvar is badly damaged but seems to bear the same text nonetheless.

The justifiability of relegating the southern MREs to a separate category of MREs called MRE-II can be called to question. The southern examples simply bring in the additional elements of showing obedience to mother, father, elders and teachers. A similar kind of obedience has also been invoked in RE-III and RE-XI, and one wonders if this justifies the postulate of a separate category of MREs, not unless we are willing to put all southern MREs under this separate category. As the major rock edicts of the south at Yerragudi and Sannati do not display any such regional feature, it will possibly be better if we avoid any geography-based classification in the case of the MREs as well.

Falk (2006: 66) points out that the Brahmagiri hill contains a cave with a water reservoir which can be approached by an underground passage. Because of the clean and drinkable water from this reservoir, this could be considered a sacred spot where people gathered on one or more occasions of the year. This could also lead to the local reputation of the Brahmagiri rock possessing medicinal quality.

Siddapur lies some way up a hill about a mile to the west of Brahmagiri. Jatinga Ramesvar is about 3 miles or more north by west of Brahmagiri, and the floor where the inscription is cut here is immediately in front of the stairs leading up to the Jatinga Ramesvar temple.

VII.3. Yerragudi and Rajula Mandagiri

Yerragudi/Erragudi lies by the side of the road which leads from Gooty to Adoni, and Rajula Mandagiri can be approached from Pattikonda. What is interesting is that through Adoni one can trace a direct alignment towards Raichur and Yadgir, the latter near the Asokan edict-bearing site of Sannati on the bank of the Bhima. South of Gooty, the alignment goes southeast to Cuddapah and south to Anantapur. The Cuddapah alignment eventually leads to Tirupati and Chittoor at the entrance to Tamil Nadu near Arkonam and Vellore, whereas the Anantapur alignment leads to the Kolar-Bangalore sector and eventually to the Dharmapuri sector of Tamil Nadu. From the Gooty area one could also go to Nandiyal and from Nandyal to the Krishna valley across the Nandikanama pass. *Suvarnagiri* of the Yerragudi edicts has been argued by us to be not Kanakagiri or Jonnagiri near this site, which does not have any trace of occupation at all in the vicinity, but with Sannati which is the only regional city-site large and important enough to be the centre of Mauryan administration on the level of Ujjayini and Takshasila where, as at Suvarnagiri, the governors were *Kumaras* or sons of the king.

The Asokan inscription at Rajula Mandagiri lies on the top of a low hill which also contains a few late period temples. The MRE is engraved on a rock in front of what appears to be a well. Sircar (2000: 104) points out that the first eye-copy of the Rajula Mandagiri MRE was prepared early in the nineteenth century for the collection of Colin Mackenzie. Although many of the letters of this edict are found damaged, they can be reconstructed with the help of the letters surviving on the Erragudi counterpart of the edict, as both the edicts are more or less undifferentiated except for minor variations.

As an edict-bearing site, Erragudi amply brings out the difficulties of reading an Asokan edict and preparing a definitive text. Here, the edicts are inscribed on six boulders on the top and slopes of a hill which one can easily observe on the left side of the Gooty-Pattikonda road. The first major publication on this complex was published by D.R. Sahni in *Annual Report of the Archaeological Survey of India 1928-29* (Sahni 1928-29). The boulder no. A lies on the top of the hills; the others (nos. B to F) lie on its slope. The inscribed surface is rough, which means that with the exception of the inscriptions incised on the north face of the boulder A, and those on the boulders B and F, they are only partially decipherable and that too "with the greatest difficulty". Edicts I, II, III and VI do not have blank spaces or dividing lines between them, and "as the surface has peeled off considerably, it was only with great difficulty that it was possible to determine where they began and where they ended". The Erragudi MRE is, as Sahni (1928-29) puts it, "a confused mass of writing": ... as many as eight of the twenty-three lines were inscribed from right to left. And if we eliminate from consideration lines 8 and 14 of the inscription, the first fifteen lines are at once found to be in boustrophedon style ... The inscription under consideration leaves no doubt that the boustrophedon style of Brahmi epigraphs was not unknown in the time of Asoka". In Sahni's version of the text, all the lines of the edict have been given serial numbers 1 to 23, whereas in Sircar's edition, the edict is listed separately as MRE-I and II, with the portion from the line 13 onwards representing MRE-II. The upper portion represents MRE-I. Equally interestingly, there is some serious difference between their translations. The line 11 of Sircar's version of MRE-II reads the following: "In this way you should pass orders on the elephant-riders, the scribes and charioteers and (the teachers of) the Brahmana (community)". Sahni's translation of the same section is the following: "Thus should you command the Karunakas riding on elephants and the Brahmanas driving in vehicles." R.K. Mookerji (1955: 260) finds in the same section references to 'elephant corps', scribes or judges, charioteers and Brahmanas. It is such uncertainties which call for close readings of the texts of the edicts and their in-depth grammatical analysis (cf. Andersen 1990), although it is highly unlikely that the uncertainties will all be removed.

VII.4. Observations on the Locations of the Southern MREs

Maski near Mudgal and Lingsugur in the central Raichur doab, Palkigundu and Gavimath around Kopbal, Nittur and Udegolam near Tekkalakota (itself near Bellary), Yerragudi and Rajula Mandagiri between Gooty and Pattikonda, and finally, Brahmagiri, Siddapur and Jatinga Rameshwar between Chitaldoorg and Bellary – all of them lie in a sense in the approaches to the Mysore plateau (including the south Kanara coast) and Tamil Nadu through the southern Deccan and the Rayalseema section of Andhra. It is not always appreciated that this is one of the most geo-politically sensitive regions of the subcontinent. The early Chalukyan power centre of Badami lies in the western part of the Raichur doab, with the mediaeval power centre of Bijapur lying only a little to the north. In the Gulbarga-Bidar section, which lies broadly to the north of Raichur, there is the major Mauryan metropolis of Sannati, and a little further up, there are the Rashtrakuta power centres of Manyakhet and the later Chalukyan power centre of Kalyani. The point to note is that all these power centres were trying to expand their base to the south and also to the Andhra coast. Similarly, the major southern powers of the Pallavas, the Cholas and the Pandyas were equally keen to make thrusts toward the southern Deccan and the Andhra coast.

As I put it elsewhere:

> The political powers of the Chalukyas and Rashtrakutas with their base in southern Deccan were always pushing up to the Konkan coast, Gujarat, Malwa and the central part of the Ganga plain, besides moving up the Andhra coast up to Vengi and trying to take over the southern domain up to the Kaveri.... It would also not be correct to imagine that the southern dynasties lay confined only to the southern domain. The Pallavas always targeted southern Deccan and the Andhra coast, and the Cholas and the Pandyas, whenever they had the chance, came up along these lines (Chakrabarti, 2010).

There is some justification to argue that the distribution area of the southern MREs was the cockpit of the Deccanese and also partly of the Andhra history. I have already drawn attention to the fact that Maski or Mosangi was the battle-place where Rajendra Chola I defeated Jayasimha II of the Western Chalukyas. From the 12th century onwards, the regional political situation has been summed up by J. Gommans (1998), who contrasts the high rainfall zone of the Konkan coast with the high aridity of the Deccan interior, the *desh*. This arid belt continues southeastward to Kurnool and Cuddapah. "This became a hotly contested border region between the prevalent powers in the Deccan to the north and Karnataka to the south." According to Gommans, "during the seventeenth and eighteenth centuries, Afghan traders and warriors succeeded in establishing a string of principalities along the dry east-west belt of Rayalseema by playing on the rivalry between the Vijayanagar successor states and the various Muslim Sultanates of the Deccan. From their strategic centres in Savanur, Kurnool and Cuddapah, they not only controlled the supply lines of horses and mercenaries from the north, but also the important pilgrimage route from the Deccan to Tirupati."

Whether the close spread of the southern MREs is related to the geo-political importance of the region cannot be confidently asserted, but the fact that the area was geo-politically important has to be pointed out.

The area also happens to be rich in gold. The case of the Hatti gold-mines near Maski is well known but, interestingly, a report by the Mineral Exploration Corporation Limited in 2003 located gold in the "Dona East Block, Jonnagiri schist belt, Kurnool District", 4 km NE of the Jonnagiri village. It was estimated that the total geological in situ reserves of the rich ore-shoots of gold in the Yerragudi area amounted to "3.356 million tonnes of 3660 g/t Au". Some evidence of old workings of gold were found in this area, and the Hatti gold mines are known to have a pre-Christian antiquity.

The question of historical geography surfaces repeatedly. A mineral-rich zone lying on the path of the powers contending for supremacy both to the north and the south, this enjoyed one added advantage for the Mauryan power. Their presence in the Bellary-Kurnool area ensured that there was no difficulty in their movement via the Nandiyal valley and the Nandikanama pass to the Krishna valley, where at Amaravati they left behind an edict. Besides, any power controlling the Bellary-Kurnool sector can also control the Anantapur-Cuddapah-Chittoor entry to Tamil Nadu. The Brahmagiri/Siddapur/Jatinga Ramesvar cluster ensures the extension of their orbit both to the Mysore plateau and north Kanara.

VIII. MANEMA DESA, SUVARNAGIRI AND ISILA

The major problem of place-name identifications in the MREs centres around *Manema desa* of the Panguraria MRE and Suvarnagiri Isila mentioned in the Brahmagiri and Siddapur versions. Going by Sircar's reading, *Manema desa* is basically the area south of Bhopal up to the Narmada. The problem lies in the fact that it is geographically a limited area and although there are two city sites – Nadner and Ninnore – in this sector along with a number of stupas, one wonders if the area deserved the presence of a royal prince – *Kumara* – there. The *Kumara* is mentioned by name – *Samva* – although this name does not figure in any other source of the period. The same is true of the term *Manema* territory. On the other hand, Falk's version of this edict is so much out of the main drift of the Asokan inscriptions that it fails to make any historical sense.

The Brahmagiri and Siddapur versions of MRE record the following:

"From Suvarnagiri, at the word of the prince (*aryaputra*) and of the Mahamatras at Isila must be wished good health and be told this" (Hultzsch 1925, p. 177).

Hultzsch added the following note:

> This place (Suvarnagiri) seems to have been the capital of the province administered by the *Aryaputras* and his *Mahamatras*. Buhler compared the second separate edict at Dhauli, according to which, a *Kumara* and his *Mahamatras* resided at Tosali. The separate edicts of Dhauli and Jaugada were addressed by the king to the local authorities themselves, while in the Mysore edicts the king commands the authorities of the Suvarnagiri province to communicate his orders to their subordinates at Isila. In Fleet's opinion the Mysore edicts were issued from Suvarnagiri by Asoka himself; and he identified the place with one of the hills, still known as Sonagiri, near Rajagriha in Bihar. H. Krishna Sastri connects Suvarnagiri, i.e. the gold mountain, with the country around Maski, which abounds in gold-workings. Perhaps it may be identified with the synonym Kanakagiri, south of Maski and north of the ruins of Vijayanagara (Hultzsch 1925, p. 177, note 5).

In 1894-95, G. Buhler suggested that the extent of Asoka's possessions certainly 'included more than the northern extremity of Mysore' and that Suvarnagiri should be considered 'the headquarters of the viceroy of the Dekhan'. "If it still exists, it will now go by a name like Songir or Songadh, Sondurg, Suvarnadurg, or the like" (Buhler 1894-95, p. 137).

J.F. Fleet, who identified (Fleet 1909) Suvarnagiri with Sonagiri of Rajagriha, thought that "Isila was evidently an ancient town situated somewhere in the locality where the records are, and it was, no doubt, a subdivisional town of the Vanavasi kingdom: its name has apparently now disappeared".

The opinion that the occupational site represented by the level ground near the site of Brahmagiri inscribed boulder was ancient Isila gained ground after Mortimer Wheeler's excavation of the site in 1947 (Wheeler 1948, p. 185). N.P. Chakravarti (1948) wrote that "Isila must be identified with the site of the ancient town at the foot of Brahmagiri near Siddapur" and that Suvarnagiri, although unidentified, was the headquarters of the southernmost province of Asoka's empire. Regarding Isila, we here draw attention to two points. An Amaravati inscription (inscription 1248 of Luders' list) of the time of the Satavahana king Vasishthiputra Pulumavi refers to a householder called Isila (Sanskrit Rishila). Thus, Isila can both be a personal name and a place-name. More importantly, our observation is that the level field available near the edict-carrying boulder at Brahmagiri was too constricted to be considered a city-site, which Asoka's Isila apparently was. In fact, the other site explored by Wheeler along with Brahmagiri, i.e. Chandravali, has a much better claim to be considered a city-site: "the main body of the ancient town was some 800 yards long in that direction, and the configuration of the valley suggests that it may have had an approximately similar width" (Wheeler 1948, p.270). Chandravalli lay much nearer modern Chitaldurg than Brahmagiri. Location-wise, Chitaldurg has an easier access to Bellary, Dharwar, Shimoga and Hassan than the Siddapur area, although the latter is in the modern Chitaldurg district. We would say that if Isila was an important enough place to have Mauryan *Mahamatras* or judicial officers in this part of Karnataka, its likely jurisdiction possibly included a chunk of the Bellary-Dharwar-Shimoga-Hassan sector of Karnataka. From this point of view, Chandravalli enjoys the advantage of a better location. We would place Mauryan Isila at the site of Chandravalli.

If Suvarnagiri was the centre of the Mauryan administration of the south and important enough to have a prince as the governor, there can be only one contemporary site which displays that level of significance. The site is Sannati, a large fortified site with the remains of two stupas outside its fortification. One of these stupas is represented by the excavated remains of Kanganahalli, which have yielded exquisite sculptures of the Amaravati style. In the local Chandralamba temple, inscribed stone slabs containing Rock Edicts XII and XIV and the two separate edicts of Dhauli and Jaugada were found, and I.K. Sarma and J.V. Rao (1993) have listed a total of about 83 inscriptions from this indisputably large and fortified city-site, including those of the Satavahana rulers. Although the modern place-name 'Jonnagiri' near the site of the Erragudi edicts sounds like Suvarnagiri, there is nothing except this similarity to justify its identification as Suvarnagiri of the edicts. There are no visible occupational debris in the sweep of the cultivated fields below the Erragudi hill, and although only a thorough exploration of the area can settle the issue, the pre-eminence of Sannati as a site is so visible and its location is so suitable to control the southern possessions of the Mauryas that we have no hesitation in identifying Sannati as Suvarnagiri.

3

The Fourteen Major Rock Edicts and the Two Separate Edicts

The major edicts occur as a set of fourteen rock edicts, but have not survived everywhere as a full set. Only fragments of three rock edicts (REs VIII, IX and XI) have been found at Sopara. Although the full set occurs at Shahbazgarhi, Manserah, Kalsi, Girnar and Erragudi, the quality of their survival has depended to some extent on the degree of erosion the parent rock has suffered since the edicts were inscribed. Dhauli and Jaugada, both in Orissa, have the first ten edicts and the edict XIV. The XI, XII and XIII edicts are missing at these two places and their places have been taken up by the two 'separate edicts'. Edicts XII and XIV occur at Sannati along with the two 'Separate Edicts' found at Dhauli and Jaugada which, interestingly, do not possess Edict XII.

The texts of the individual edicts have been obtained on the basis of close comparisons between the surviving texts in all the relevant places. If a particular letter is not fully legible at a particular place, it may be so elsewhere. As a result, there is no major doubt about the basic text of any of the fourteen rock edicts, although different scholars tend to translate them differently, seldom violating the sense of the original.

I. THE CONTENTS OF THE FOURTEEN EDICTS

RE-I uses the term *Dhammalipi* to denote this and other edicts. Although the term literally means "writing on morality", Hultzsch prefers to translate it as "rescript on morality", whereas Buhler prefers "religious edicts". RE-I has mainly two points. First, no living being must be killed and

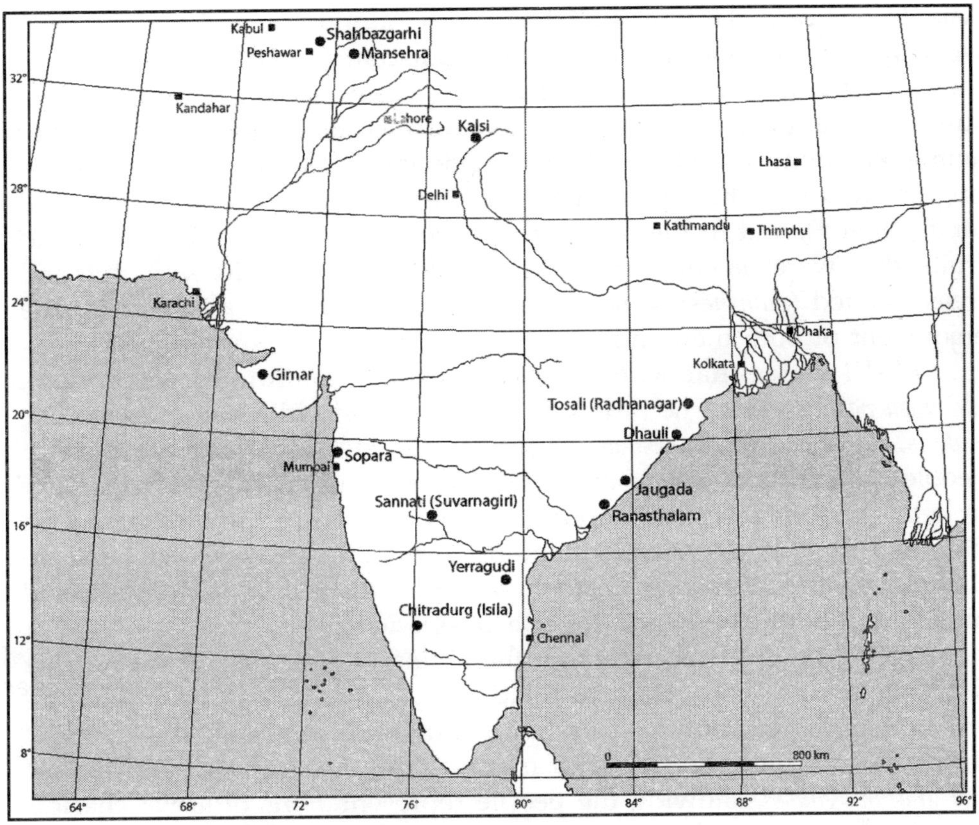

Map 2. Major sites mentioned in Chapter 3.

sacrificed, and although "many hundred thousands of animals" (*bahuni-prana-sahasrani*) were once killed for food in the royal household, the number had come down to only three (two peacocks and one deer) when this edict was being engraved. Even these three animals were being killed only irregularly, and the royal assurance was that the practice would stop altogether in future. Secondly, RE-I issues an injunction against the practice of holding *samajas* or 'festival meetings'. The reason was that the king saw 'much evil in festival meetings'.

RE-II is important on two counts. It refers to the south Indian states of the Cholas, Pandyas, Satiyaputra, Keralaputra, and even Tamraparni or Sri Lanka as Asoka's 'borderers' and to the *Yona*-king *Amtiyako* and the kings who were near this *Amtiyoka*. The latter were, apparently, his contemporaries in west Asia. These references came up in the context of his organizing health care for men and animals not merely in his own kingdom but also in the contemporary states of south India and west

Asia. In one case, the limit stretched up to Tamraparni and in another, it went up to Syria, and to the territories adjacent to Syria on the west. In the case of animal care, the term used is *Pasu-chikichha,* and one is not sure if this applied only to cattle, as Hultzsch has suggested, or to the animal kingdom as a whole. The latter possibility seems to be closer to the original meaning. The suitable medicinal herbs were, if necessary, imported (and planted), and in the areas where there were no suitable roots and fruits, they were also imported and planted. Further, wells were dug and trees planted (*pamthesu kupa cha khanapita, vrachha cha ropapita*) for the enjoyment of both men and animals (*paribhogaya pasu-manusanam*).

RE-III states that when Asoka had been anointed twelve years (*dvadasa-vasabhisitena*), he ordered that everywhere in his dominions, the *Yuktas, Rajukas* and *Pradesikas* would set out every five years to instruct people in morality as well as for other business. This instruction in morality upheld the following behavioural norms as meritorious: obedience to parents, liberality to friends, acquaintances and relatives and also to Brahmanas and Sramanas, abstentation from the killing of animals, and moderation both in expenditure and possessions.

According to RE-IV, although the killing of animals and the hurting of living beings, discourtesy to relatives and discourtesy to Brahmanas and Sramanas had continued for 'many hundreds of years', 'the sound of drums has become the sound of morality' (*dhammacharanena bherighoso aho dhammaghosa),* showing the people representations of aerial chariots and representations of elephants, masses of fire and other divine figures. This was also the result of the 'practice of morality' on the part of the king. This practice meant abstentation from killing animals and hurting living beings, propagation of courtesy to relatives, Brahmanas and Sramanas, and suggestion of obedience to parents and elders. It was hoped that this tradition would continue under the sons, grandsons and great-grandsons of the king "until the aeon of destruction of the world", because 'instruction in morality' was the best possible work. Further, the practice of morality was not possible for a person devoid of good conduct. RE-IV was caused to be written by the king after he had been anointed twelve years.

RE-V was issued after the king had been anointed thirteen years. It begins by saying that it is difficult to perform virtuous deeds and those who perform virtuous deeds perform something difficult. Many virtuous deeds have been performed by the king and he hopes that his sons and grandsons will continue to perform this duty. He who will neglect even a portion of this duty will perform evil deeds, because "sin is easily committed". This edict also refers to the institution of *Dharma-mahamatras* established for the specific purpose of persuading "all sects in establishing morality" including his "western borderers" of the *Yonas, Kambojas, Gandharas, Rishtikas, Petenikas* and others. The office of the *Dharma-mahamatras* was instituted after the king had been anointed thirteen years. Occupied with various groups of people including servants and masters, money-less prisoners, children, the incurably ill and the aged, the *Dharma-mahamatras* could be found everywhere, both in Pataliputra and the outlying territories.

RE-VI puts emphasis on Asoka's concern with the well being of his subjects and his readiness to be in constant touch with the affairs of the state, without any consideration of time and place. The *Pativedakas* or 'reporters', who were posted everywhere, would report to the king the affairs of the people "at any time", wherever he was. The same urgency applied in reporting to him the disputes and amendments in ministerial council meetings and how his verbal commands were taken care of by the *Mahamatras*. The king gave such orders because no duty was more important to him than promoting "the welfare of all men" and because he might make them happy in this world and fit for heaven in the next. It was finally hoped that this rescript on morality would last long and that his sons, grandsons and great-grandsons might conform to this for the welfare of all men, although it was difficult to accomplish this without great zeal.

RE-VII expressed the royal desire that all sects might reside wherever they wished to reside. Great emphasis was also laid on "both self-control and purity of mind". Even a greatly liberal person was to be considered mean in the absence of "self-control, purity of mind, gratitude, and firm devotion".

RE-VIII records that when he had been anointed ten years, the king went to *Sambodhi*. Previously the kings used to go on pleasure tours which involved hunting and other amusements. However, Asoka instituted the system of going on 'tours of morality', in the course of which the Brahmanas and the Sramanas were visited and gifts were given to them. Visits were made to the elderly too, and support of 'gold' was made available to them. Contacts were also made with the ordinary subjects – 'the people of the country' – who received instructions in morality and were questioned about morality. Such tours of morality which replaced the previous tours of pleasure and were instituted after the royal visit to *Sambodhi* afforded the king greater pleasure.

RE-IX begins by pointing out the custom of performing various ceremonies by people on occasions like illness, marriage of a son or a daughter, birth of a son, going out on a journey, etc. The king further points out that on such occasions, women indulged in "various vulgar and useless ceremonies". According to the king, the ceremonies should certainly be practised but be replaced at the same time by the practice of morality which means "proper courtesy to slaves and servants, reverence to elders, gentleness to animals (and) liberality to Brahmanas and Sramanas". There is also no gift more meritorious than "the gift of morality or the benefit of morality". It was the royal wish that people should discuss among themselves what was meritorious and what would lead to heaven because nothing was more desirable than the attainment of heaven.

RE-X suggests that no glory or fame is more important to the king than his effort to spread the message of obedience to morality and conforming to the duties of morality. This is for the sake of gaining merit in the other world and avoiding the danger of demerit. Both for the high and the lowly, the task is difficult to accomplish without great zeal and without setting aside every other aim. Among these two categories of humans, the highly placed ones will find it more difficult to accomplish the task.

RE-XI also harps on morality. No gift can be as valued as the gift of morality, acquaintance through morality, distribution of morality, and kinship through morality. Morality is defined as proper courtesy to slaves and servants, obedience to parents, liberality to friends, acquaintances, relatives, Brahmanas and Sramanas, and abstentation from killing animals. All persons – "a father, or a son, or a brother, or a friend, an acquaintance, or a relative, (or) even (mere) neighbours" – should insist that only meritorious things are done. By this 'gift of morality', the attainment of happiness is secured in this world and endless merit is produced in the other one.

RE-XII states in the opening sentence that all sects comprising both householders and ascetics are honoured by the king by the bestowal of both gifts and honours. To none of these gifts and honours he attaches more value than the "promotion of the essentials of all sects". This promotion can be achieved by guarding one's speech, refraining from praising one's own sect and blaming other sects and by being "moderate in every case". By following these rules and by duly honouring other sects, one is promoting one's own sect and benefiting other sects. By acting otherwise, one hurts the cause of one's own sect as well as the cause of other sects. The king adds that "concord alone is meritorious and the different sects "should both hear and obey each other's morals". It was the king's desire that "all sects should be full of learning and should be pure in doctrine".

RE-XIII deals unequivocally with the king's conquest of Kalinga after he was anointed eight years and its consequence: one hundred and fifty thousand deported, one hundred thousand killed, and many more dead from other causes. The king confesses to being deeply pained by the killing, dying and deportation, and he admits that he is more pained by the fact that those who observe the practice of morality in the conquered areas are injured, killed and separated from their loved ones. Even those who are not directly affected find their friends, acquaintances and relatives affected. He clearly mentions that this suffering caused by the conquest of Kalinga turned his mind towards the principles of *Dhamma*. The king points out that in all countries except the ones of the *Yonas*, the Brahmanas and Sramanas are found, and there is no country where people do not practice a religion. Therefore, the killing, dying and deportation of a hundredth or even a thousandth part of the number of the dead in Kalinga is now painful to the king. Now he believes that even wrong-doing may be forgiven where forgiveness is possible. Even the forest-dwellers in the royal domain are entreated and persuaded with reason to act properly. They must realize that the king, despite being affected by remorse, has the power to punish them, if necessary. The royal ideal now is non-injury, restraint and impartiality to all living beings, even where wrongs have been committed. The conquest of *Dhamma* is the true conquest, and this has been achieved on the king's borders and in the realm of Antiochus, which is 600 *Yojanas* away from the royal borders, and also in the realms of four kings beyond Antiochus' realm – the realms of Ptolemy, Antigonos, Magas and Alexander. The same has been achieved in the royal domain among the *Yonas*, Kambojas, Nabhakas, Nabhapamktis, Bhojas, Pitinikas, Andhras and Palidas. Even where the royal messengers of *Dhamma* have not reached, people follow the principles of *Dhamma*, and the king considers this fruit of his endeavour more important in the next world. Finally, he states that he had these *Dhamma-lipis* engraved so that his sons and grandsons may not like to make further conquests, and if necessary, pursue the conquest of *Dhamma* alone.

RE-XIV states that the king had his *Dhamma-lipis* written in brief, medium length and extended forms. His kingdom was vast, and not all of them occurred everywhere. Some themes occur repeatedly in them, and that is because of their sweetness and the king's desire that people may act in accordance with them. If anything written is incomplete, that is because of the locality, nature of the object and the fault of the scribe.

II. THE FINDSPOTS OF THE MAJOR ROCK EDICTS AND THE SIGNIFICANCE OF THEIR LOCATIONS

II.1. Shahbazgarhi

Shahbazgarhi is situated in what used to be known, at least till the end of the nineteenth century, as the Yusufzai territory, i.e., the territory occupied by the Yusufzai Afghans between Chitral and Yasin to the north and the Kabul river to the south on the one hand and between Bajaur and the Swat river to the west and the Indus river to the east. Swat and Buner fell in this area, and so did the Peshawar plain which used to be known then as the British Yusufzai. Regarding the Peshawar plain, Cunningham's observation is that it corresponded with the district of Peucolaitis of the Classical sources and Pushkalavati of the ancient Indian literature. Although the plain was thinly peopled in the late nineteenth century, "the numerous mounds of ruined cities and villages which still stud the Yusufzai plain in all directions" indicated that it was "once much more thickly populated". This was also the opinion of H.W. Bellew who first published the results of his archaeological and other surveys of the Yusufzai plain in his *A General Report on the Yusufzais* in 1864 (Bellew 1864). The general wealth of its archaeological relics is described by Cunningham (1872-73, p. 6) in the following terms:

> The ancient remains found on these mounds consist of sculptures, pieces of pottery, beads of all sizes, and bones, both of men and animals. The sculptures are chiefly Buddhist, but a few rare pieces are Brahmanical. The coins are very numerous; and from their evidence alone I can state that many of these mounds are the ruins of villages which were occupied from a period preceding the invasion of Alexander down to the time of Mahmud of Ghazni.

The site of Shahbazgarhi lies in the Sudam valley created by the Makam river whose channel was not too deep to permit the withdrawl of water from it by the Persian Wheel system of irrigation. Cunningham adds that on both its banks, the signs of ancient irrigation are abundant. The river, he infers, had temporary embankments along it, and its water was distributed over a wide area by numerous channels. These embankments were all temporary ones which were made of boulders. Cunningham, and Bellew before him, inferred that the number of ruined mounds in the Yusufzai plain was greater than that of the settlements they observed in their time.

The first report on the Asokan edicts at Shahbazgarhi came from M. Court (1836) of Ranjit Singh's army. He called the script 'Bactro-Pali', published a few letters and described the place being located about 2 miles from Kapurdigarhi, a major village of the area. Captain Alexander Burnes tried to get a good copy of the inscriptions in 1838 (cf. Masson 1846) but it was not satisfactory. This prompted Charles Masson, then stationed in Peshawar, to undertake a journey to the site himself in order to make a satisfactory copy of the inscription.

"As we passed along the plain, ... we observed to our right and left many circular mounds, and we found that similar objects are interspersed not only throughout its extent but generally over the Yusufzai country: they are invariably strewed with fragments of pottery, and many of them have a well, as all of them probably once had, attached to them" (Masson 1846, p. 295).

Interestingly, near Hoti, a village near Mardan, Masson encountered 'a multifarious assemblage of men and animals'. A caravan or *kafila,* they were coming from Swat with grain laden on bullocks.

On the basis of the copy made by Masson, E. Norris (1846) published the edict in the same volume of the *JRAS* where Masson published his report. This particular copy of the *JRAS* carried, after the article by Norris, "a note by the Director" of the Royal Asiatic Society, who was then H.H. Wilson (1846). Norris could read *Devanampiyasa* in the text of the edict which he compared in detail with the Girnar and Dhauli inscriptions, confirming their similarity. Wilson attempted a detailed comparison with Girnar (also, Wilson 1850).

Cunningham (1872-73) mentioned a much earlier visit by the first Mughal king Babur to Shahbazgarhi. Babur went there on 15 February, 1519 (Thackston translation, 1996, p. 269). Although he liked the Shahbazgarhi hill commanding 'superb vistas', he was not happy with the tomb of Shabaz Qalandar located on it. From his point of view, Shahbaz Qalandar was 'a heretic wandering Dervish' and he ordered his followers to pull down the tomb. However, "since it was an agreeable place and the air was so good", he smoked some narcotics and sat there for a while. In any case, the name of the village, Shahbazgarhi, is derived from the name of Shahbaz Qalandar, and this village is much closer to the edict site than Court's Kapurdigiri.

Cunningham found the remains of an ancient city-site at Shahbazgarhi: the Pukai mound on the north, the Khere and Butsahri mounds on the east, and the Hinduan mound on the south. The rock edict lies half way up the hill overlooking the Hinduian mound. He found many smaller mounds within the city limits. Several extensive mounds were also noticed at Chanak-ka-dheri, about a mile to the north, and in the Karamar hill to the northeast, there was a large cave with two chambers. On the basis of the bearings given by Xuanzang to *Po-lu-sha* in the 7th century and by another Chinese pilgrim Sung-Yun (early 6th century) to *Fo-sha-fu*, Cunningham felt that they could be referring to the 'city of Sudatta' of the *Vissantara jataka* where the king Sudatta displayed extraordinary charity.

A recent scholar (E. Errington, cf. Falk 2006) is said to have disputed this identification and located the city of Sudatta at Sahri Ballol. Cunningham (1872-73, pp. 36-46) also took note of Sahri Ballol where the main mound was 1200 feet long, 600 feet broad and 90 feet high, and the city was surrounded by a number of both small and large mounds. Sahri-Ballol is situated in the open plain below the range which houses the Takh-i-Bahi monastery. One of the surrounding mounds at Sahri-Ballol was a large stupa "standing in a quadrangle of chapels, about 250 feet square, with a 200 feet square monastery attached to its east side". Cunningham identified this monastic complex with the stupa built, according to Xuangzang and Sung-Yun, to commemorate the Buddha's donation of his eyes in charity. Cunningham also thinks that the city that he found at Shahbazgarhi was Bazaria which was mentioned by Arrian in his account of the invasion of Alexander.

In Cunningham's words (Cunningham 1877, p. 9), the exact location and features of the Shahbazgarhi Asokan major rock edict are the following:

> The great inscription of Asoka is engraved on a shapeless mass of trap rock, lying about 80 feet up the slope of the hill, with its western face looking downwards towards the village of Shahbazgarhi. The greater portion of the inscription is on the eastern face of the rock looking up the hill, but all the latter part, which contains the names of the five Greek kings, is on the western face. The mass of rock is 24 feet long and about 10 feet in height, with a general thickness of about ten feet.

A smaller rock containing the 12th edict was discovered by Captain Deane, Assistant Commissioner of Mardan (no date, cf. ARASI 1922-23, pp. 17-18).

II.2. Mansehra

The 17th volume of the *Imperial Gazetteer of India* (p. 203) has a description of the Mansehra village: headquarter of the Mansehra *tehsil* of the North Western Frontier Province and located on the right bank of an affluent of the Siran River – north of Abbotabad on the main road to the Kashmir border – centre of trading in grain and other country produce – two inscribed rocks near the village. The Mansehra *tehsil,* a cone-shaped area of 1845 square miles, has mountain ranges on either side of a glen or valley called Kagan.

R.K. Mookerji (1955, p. xi) points out that the Mansehra inscription was discovered in parts by Captain Leigh and by an Indian employee of the Panjab Archaeological Survey in 1889. This does not conform to Hultzsch's observation (Hultzsch 1925, pp. xii-xiii) that the two first inscribed stones were discovered by Cunningham and the third by the Indian employee of the Panjab Archaeological Survey in 1889.

Regarding the estampages taken of the Shahbazgarhi and Manserah edicts, Buhler (1894) points out that James Burgess took good quality estampages of these edicts in 1886-87, whereas in 1922 H. Hargreaves took their estampages again for Hultzsch's study (ARASI 1922-23, p. 101). Mansehra required 72 large sheets of estampages and Shahbazgarhi 92 such sheets.

The Mansehra rock edict site is found to the north of the Mansehra village and has edicts engraved on three boulders, the edicts 1 to 8 on one boulder, the edicts 9 to 11 on the north face and edict 12 on the south face of the second boulder, and the edicts 13 and 14 on the third boulder.

According to Buhler (1894, p. 447), it is "perfectly certain that the Mansehra version is most closely related in its wording to that of Kalsi".

II.3. The Historical-Geographical Significance of the Locations of Shahbazgarhi and Mansehra Rock Edict Sites

Shahbazgarhi lies about 9 miles to the north-northeast of Mardan, almost in the centre of the Peshawar plain which covers about 6415 square kilometres and has the areas of Peshawar, Charsadda, Mardan, Nowshera and Swabi as its major components. The distribution and significance of the Mauryan sites in the Peshawar plain have been highlighted by Ihsan Ali's settlement survey (2003). Historically, the Mauryan phase in this plain (32 sites) was preceded by the Achaemenid phase (12 sites, all of which continued to be occupied in the Mauryan period). The major centres of the Achaemenid period were the Bala Hissar mound of Charsadda and the Nisatta graveyard which is located to the southeast of Charsadda on a major ferry crossing of the Kabul River. Six out of the twelve Achaemenid sites are aligned to the Charsadda-Peshawar-Mohmand Agency-Afghanistan route. Nisatta lies at the junction of two major routes, one to the east across the Indus and the other aligned with Peshawar-Malakand-Swat. This latter alignment marks the beginning of the

Karakoram route. According to Ali (2003, p. 87), only three Mauryan sites are unrelated to any route and the Mauryan route network in the Peshawar valley is more or less widely spread. Regarding the location of Shahbazgarhi, Ali (2003, p. 87) writes:

> This location is oriented to the Karakoram route, and thus the Mauryans like the Achaemenids understood the significance of this route in maintaining links with central Asia and perhaps China.

Sixteen Mauryan sites are associated with the Panjab-Swat-Karakoram alignment and five Mauryan sites are associated with the Charsadda – Mohmand Agency alignment to Afghanistan. It appears from Ali's map (map-V) that Shahbazgarhi is conveniently located for a number of trade routes: through Jamalgarhi, north of Mardan, to Buner, Swat and Malakand Agency; through Takhti-Bahi to Malakand Agency; through Rustam to Buner; through Swabi and Topi to Panjab; through Mardan and Nowshera to Panjab; through Lahor and Hund to Panjab; and finally, its position on the arterial Peshawar-Charsadda-Mardan-Swabi-Topi-Panjab alignment and also on its shortened version via Lahore and Hund.

Mansehra lies near Abbottabad to the east of the Peshawar plain. H. Falk (2006, p. 129) adequately explains its location:

> The place obviously was chosen because it marks the diversion from the main valley to the upper regions leading to Kashmir and to Gilgit via Balakot over the Babusar Pass along the Kundar. The southern road led to Taxila ... there was also the possibility to turn west at modern Haripur and to proceed via Shahbazgarhi towards Pushkalavati.

One may add that at Shahbazgarhi one can join a vast network of routes. It is likely that the determining factor of Mansehra's location was the route to Kashmir which went from Taxila via Abbottabad. Of all the routes to Kashmir from the plains, the Abbottabad route was considered the easiest in the pre-1947 period.

Falk (2006) points to the existence of a well associated with the Mansehra edict site. It measures 4 m x 1.2 m at the mouth, is about 1 m deep and cut artificially into the rock. Falk infers that this well was dug at the same time when the site was prepared for the edict.

One of the objections raised against the *Arthasastra* being dated in the Mauryan period is that it mentions Chinese silk which, according to some scholars, was not possible because there is no evidence of Mauryan contact with central Asia and China. After taking into consideration the significance of the locations of Shahbazgarhi and Mansehra Asokan edicts, the argument does not seem to be at all convincing.

II.4. Girnar

It is possible that the first mention of the site of Girnar edict is in the first edition of James Tod's *Annals and Antiquities of Rajasthan* (Crooke 1920, p. 4) where he refers to the inscriptions on the "rocks of Junagadh". Regarding the ancient city, "at the foot of, and guarding, the sacred mount Girnar", he adds that he has "little doubt that it is the Asaldurg or Asalgadh, of the Guhilot annals".

Girnar or Junagadh near which this range of hills lies occupies a central position in the north-south alignment of the western section of the Kathiawar peninsula. Its position in the old route network of Gujarat is not clear. The eighth volume of the *Gazetteer of the Bombay Presidency*, which deals with Kathiawar speaks of a road joining Valabhi with Junagadh and Vanthil. If this road dates back to the late 5th century AD when the Maitraka dynasty of Valabhi (about 40 km northwest of Bhavnagar) comes into focus, an early link of the Girnar area with the east coast of Kathiawar can be postulated. However, the main trade routes of the Kathiawar peninsula followed the coastline. The interior routes were not of great significance, and even then Girnar/Junagadh does not figure prominently in the network of these routes. V.K. Jain's map of the land routes of early mediaeval Gujarat (Jain 1990) attaches no special significance to Girnar or Junagadh. As the *Gazetteer of the Bombay Presidency* (Volume 8, 1884, p. 219) explicitly states, "in old times, the chief trade route in the province followed the coast from Gogha, southwest to Somnath and thence northwest to Dwarka. The chief land routes were those joining the Peninsula with the mainland."

The political power based in Junagadh is likely to have had close links with the coast since the beginning of such power there. According to the *Gazetteer* (p. 230), the principality of Junagadh in the 1880s had 87 vessels, 70 at Veraval and 17 at Mangrol. The details of the sailing vessels built at Veraval (near Somnath) may be interesting. These 30 to 50 feet long boats varied in tonnage between 20 and 125, and had two masts (a main mast in the middle and a mizzen-mast towards the stern or the rear of the boat) and three sails (two to the main mast and one to the mizzen-mast). They used to sail to Mumbai, Goa, the Malabar coast and Cochin on one side and to Karachi, Muscat and Aden on the other side. The voyage to Mumbai took about a week, to Cochin a month and a half, and to Aden, 3 to 4 months. These ships used to sail between November and May. Interestingly, among all the ports on the Kathiawar coast in the 1880s, Porbandar, which was a separate princely state, had the most wide sailing coverage including not merely the stretch between Karachi and

Malabar but also Muscat, Basrah, Aden, Lambu, Zanzibar (the last two places on the east African coast), Calcutta, Colombo and Malacca. The voyage to Basrah took about 2 months, with onward voyage in July-August, and return voyage in October-November. The voyage to Zanzibar used to take place after January-February and took about 4 months.

Porbandar is not far from the Junagadh area, and we assume that during the Mauryan period, when the whole of the Kathiawar peninsula was under the Mauryas, the sailing coverage of the entire region could look to the vast arc of the Indian Ocean coast between Zanzibar and the Strait of Malacca. This is likely to have given an added importance to the Mauryan occupation of Kathiawar where Girnar apparently occupied a special place.

The *Gazetteeer* (p. 65) specifies that of all the ports on the Kathiawar coast, only Bet in the northeast corner of Okhamandal had a good harbour where the boats could lie through the southwest monsoon. There was no lack of ports on the Kathiawar coast in the 1880s: Vavania, Jodiya, Beri and Salaya on the Gulf of Cutch; Dholera, Bhavnagar and Gogha in the Gulf of Cambay; and Mahuva, Jafarabad, Diu, Veraval, Mangrol, Navibandar and Porbandar directly on the Indian Ocean. It has further been said that of these Vavania, Jodiya, Beri, Salaya, Navibandar, Mahuva, Bhavnagar and Dholera are on creeks and communication with them depended on the tide, while Gogha, Veraval, Mangrol and Porbandar were "little better than roadsteads". Regarding Veraval, the *Gazetteeer* (p. 66) cites an opinion which says that there could not be many places with 'fewer natural advantages for a harbour.' It was open to the Indian Ocean and the bottom of the harbour being bare rock was a bad holding ground. On the other hand, it was the only good port of Junagadh.

Our main point is that the location of Girnar has to be envisaged not merely in terms of its immediate territory but also in terms of the traditional and vast maritime network of the region.

The hill ranges of Girnar harboured many sacred spots and temples. Of the five main peaks of the area (Amba Mata, Gorakhnath, Oghad Shikhar, Guru Datatriya and Kalka's peak), the Amba Mata carries on its top the temple of that goddess and Kalka's Peak is supposed to be the resort of *Aghoris* or the followers of a particular type of Tantric sect. The other peaks are not known to possess direct religious associations, but they have, in and around them, many temples and sacred spots. For instance, Girnar is sacred to the twenty-second Jaina *Tirthankara*, Neminatha, and has many Jaina temples. Three famous *Kundas* or reservoirs – Gau Mukhi, Hanuman Dhara and Kamandal Kund – have all sacred associations, as their very names suggest. An impressive piece of rock, called *Bhairav Jap*, has some notoriety because mendicants desirous of being freed from the cycle of birth, re-birth and death used to jump into the void from it. At the immediate base of the Girnar hill lies *Balisthan* or modern Bilkha and a little away from it lies *Vamansthali*, the old capital of an uncertain age. The ancient name of the Girnar hill is supposed to be *Ujjayanta* or *Girivar*. The source is the famous Junagadh rock inscription of Rudradaman (Kielhorn 1905-06) which mentions the city as *Girinagara* and the mountain as *Urjayat*. The inscription also mentions *Suvarnasikata* and *Palasini* streams, both of which are known by these names today.

The exact location of the rock bearing the Asokan inscription is between the Vagheshvari gate which gives entrance to the Girnar hill and the Vagheshvari Mata temple. "The boulder lies a few yards to the right of the road, and a few hundred yards from the Vagheshvari gate" (for a description of the whole Girnar complex, the *Gazetteer*, pp. 441-444). Portions of the edicts V and XIII were blasted by gunpowder by workmen building a causeway from Junagadh to Girnar, and its pieces were found in the associated debris by Lieutenant Postans in 1838 and later on published by Emile Senart in 1900 in *JRAS*. A number of estampages were prepared till 1875 when James Burgess had got a definitive copy made. The estampage on the basis of which James Prinsep deciphered the script was taken in 1835 by Captain Lang. An interesting part of the Girnar edict is a portion below the 13th RE, right side: "white elephant bringing indeed happiness to the whole world" (Hultzsch 1925, pp. 26-27). In addition to the Asokan edicts which the Girnar inscribed boulder carries, it carries the inscription of the second century AD Saka king Rudradaman and the fifth century AD inscription of Chakrapalita, son of Parnadatta, during the reign of the Gupta king Skandagupta (Chhabra and Gai 1981, pp. 296-305). The lake Sudarsan carried, in fact, an inscriptional history of about 800 years from its construction in the 4th century BC to the 5th century AD, with the inscriptions of Rudradaman and Chakrapalita keeping its memory alive. We do not know how long it continued, but apparently it was not in use in the 19th century.

What is also important in this context is the existence of eight separate groups of Buddhist caves at Junagadh and its vicinity: Khapra Kodia, Uparkot (inside the fort), Baba Piyara's Math, Bakota, Shakriya Timbo, Pancheshvar, Matri and Hothal Padmini near Padaria. The Uparkot or the citadel of the Junagadh fort contains many Buddhist caves. It has been said that "the whole of the ditch and neighbourhood is honeycombed with caves or their remains" (the *Gazetteer*, p. 487). The Ihaprakotia caves, possibly two or three storeys in height, were possibly monasteries but have been severely damaged by quarrying activities.

The *Gazetteer* (p. 442) points out the location of the famous Sudarsan lake of Girnar:

> It was in the enclosure of the hills to the north of the Girnar mountain. Here the hills enclose like a circle a large basin, the only exit being the Suvarnarekha river. A bund 300 yards long and fifty feet high here would enclose a four-sided figure each side of which would be about one mile long. It would amply repay the Junagad Darbar to build up this pass into the hills, and again restore the lake, if only for irrigating the neighbouring country.

The Damodar reservoir on the bank of the Suvarnarekha stream is the site of an annual fair in February.

Shubhra Pramanik's field-research in the area of Sudarsan lake (Pramanik 2004-05) has led to interesting results: regular early historic settlements in what has been called "four cardinal valleys – Hasnapur in the north (Jogania hill), Ramnath in the south (Gadhesing Dongar), Suraj Kund in the east (Datar hill) and Khapra Kodia caves in the west.

> The dam located at the northwestern side of Uparkot fort is almost touching the Khapra Kodia cave, on the confluence of Sonrekha and Palasini stream. The remnant of the dam is about 130 m in length and 22 m in height. It is 95 m wide at the base and 11.35 m at the top. The dam was constructed on the natural sand; stone was used for the foundation to prevent shifting of mud at the back. It is having an excellent workmanship with chisel marks on the stones. Stone was also used in the earthwork, probably for bonding of the mud.

This part of the dam belongs to the 1st-2nd centuries AD, i.e., the period of Rudradaman. However, excavations at the neighbouring site of Sone-nu-Nadi yielded courses of parallel brick structures set at a gap of 1.5 m. This suggests a canal and dates from the Maurya period, with its bricks measuring 48x30x8 cm. Further traces of an embankment and a well, and as many as 36 early historic sites have been found, thus testifying to the general significance of the Sudarsan lake area.

From whichever way we look at it, Girnar was an important area. It has an impregnable religious association with the Hindus (Amba Mata and various other cult spots), Buddhists (the profusion of rock-cut caves) and Jainas (Neminatha). It is the area of the Sudarsan lake, the largest lake of its kind in ancient India and immortalised by the Girnar inscriptions of Rudradaman of the second century AD and Skandagupta of the fifth century AD. Its antecedence goes back to Chandragupta Maurya of the late 4th century BC, during whose reign it was constructed by the provincial governor Vaishya Pushyagupta. During the rule of Asoka, conduits were added to it by the *Yavana* king Tusaspha who was the provincial governor of Asoka. These facts suggest that it was likely to be the centre of Mauryan administration in Kathiawar. Finally, Girnar was closely allied to the vast mercantile network of the Indian Ocean trade from Zanzibar and Aden to the Strait of Malacca. Whether the sailing vessels were reaching Zanzibar from Verawal in the Mauryan period is not the main point, but the fact that Girnar was tied to the Indian Ocean trade is an important point to consider.

II.5. Kalsi

H.G. Walton's *Gazetteer* of the Dehradun district (Walton 1911) contains a clear description of the location of the Kalsi edict:

> From the Jumna up to Kalsi the land on the western bank of the river is formed in two successive ledges or steps, each about one hundred feet high. Near the foot of the upper ledge is the celebrated Kalsi stone ... The Kalsi stone is a huge quartz boulder some ten feet high, ten feet long and eight feet broad at the base, the breadth diminishing towards the top. The southeastern face has been partly smoothed and bears the greater part of the inscription, but a portion of the record has been inscribed on the left hand side of the rock, the prepared surface having been evidently found insufficient for the whole. On the right hand side an elephant is traced in outline with the word *Gajatame* between the legs. The natives call it *Chitrasila*, the inscribed or picture stone ... When first discovered by Mr. Forrest, early in 1860, the letters of the inscription were badly visible, the whole surface being incrusted with the moss of ages, but on removing the black film the surface became nearly as white as marble.

Because of its location near the popular town of Dehradun at the foot of the Himalayas, Kalsi could be easily approached in the nineteenth century, and getting estampages of its edict was not a problem (Cunningham 1877). The historical significance of the location, however, cannot be easily settled. Basically, it lies where the Yamuna comes out of the Siwaliks and fans herself out with a lot of boulders. There is no reason to believe that the Kalsi inscribed boulder is not in its original place. It is possible that the Yamuna valley used to be followed by pilgrims to reach the sacred areas of Gangotri and Yamunotri, the glaciers which give birth to the Ganga and the Yamuna respectively. The fact that a road to the inner hills via Chakrata goes by Kalsi also makes this idea both possible and interesting.

Archaeologically, Kalsi dies not lie in a vacant zone (Chakrabarti 2007). From the plain side, the low, broken landscape around Kalsi is only the edge of a plain which is full of protohistoric and later sites. The adjoining district of Saharanpur has, in fact, a good number of sites of the Harappan and OCP traditions. The Jagatgram area in the immediate vicinity of Kalsi contains the inscribed brick remains of what was possibly a series of sacrificial altars of about the third century AD. The inscriptions are generally associated with a king called Silavarman, about whom little is so far known except that his capital was at *Yugasaila,* possibly in the same area. These Jagatgram brick inscriptions have been palaeolographically dated between AD 250 and 300. This archaeological fact at least drives home the premise that the Kalsi area in the early centuries AD was part of a political nucleus.

If one takes a somewhat wider view, one becomes aware of the significance of Lakha Mandal in the Jaunsar-Bawar area which lies in the north of the Dehradun district. Among other things, one of its temples yielded an inscription, dated by Buhler (1892) between c.600 and c.800 AD, giving the genealogy of eleven kings belonging to the kingdom of Singhapura. Interestingly, this kingdom figures in Xuanzang's account of his travels in India in approximately the same area. The inscription was a panegyric, a *prasasti* composed by Bhatta Vasudeva and incised in stone by Isvaranaga of Rohitaka. It deals with the dedication of a Siva temple by the princess *Isvara* (of the royal family of Singhapura) in the memory of her deceased husband, Sri Chandragupta, the son of a king of Jalandhara. The names of all the kings mentioned in this inscription end with *Varman,* and taken together, there is a possibility that this dynasty was certainly ruling in this area in the 7th century in Xuangzang's time and that it could have its origins going back a couple or more centuries earlier. The names of eleven kings have been mentioned here: Senavarman, Aryavarman, Dattavarman, Pradiptavarman, Isvaravarman, Vriddhi-varman, Simghavarman, Jalavarman, Yajnavarman, Achalavarman and Divakaravarman. What is important is that the name of the king who performed the Asvamedha sacrifice at Jagatgram near Kalsi was Silavarman. It is probable that this king belonged to the Varman dynasty which finds mention in the Lakhamandal *Prasasti.* The point is that in the 7th century AD at least – and possibly as early as the third century AD, provided Silavarman was an earlier king of the same dynasty – there was a political formation covering a part of the plains and the Dehradun sector of the hills. Assuming that such a political reality prevailed in this sector as early as the Mauryan times when eventually it was annexed within the

Mauryan dominions, the location of an Asokan edict site at Kalsi will possibly be a little more revealing both historically and geographically. What, however, is crystal clear is the significance of the Himalayas in this segment in the Mauryan scheme of things.

II.6. Sopara

Fragments of REs VIII, IX and XI found at the site link Sopara, one of the most important early historic ports on the west coast of India, directly to the world of the Mauryas. Archaeologically, very little is known coherently of this site beyond B.L. Indraji's discovery of the fragments of the REs VIII and IX and excavations at the site of a Buddhist stupa (Indraji 1881-82), although some recent publications (cf. Howell and Sinha 1994, Tripati and Gaur 1997), including B. Arunachalam's article in *Indian Cartographer* in 2002 and Savita Ghate's study in *Man and Environment* (Ghate 2007), are helpful. The location of Sopara is north of Mumbai, between Agashi in the north and Bassein in the south. Ghate has drawn attention to the occurrence of microliths in the area, but the basic archaeological sequence is clear from the study by J. Howell and A. Sinha (1994):

> Provisional study suggests that the earliest deposits contain Black and Red Ware, but not the Red Polished Ware (RPW) associated with the Indo-Roman period. There is also a tiny fragment of Northern Black Polished Ware (NBPW) from this phase, which may put the earliest occupation of the site in the third or second centuries BC (Howell and Sinha 1994: 192).

As far as we can judge, the co-occurrence of Black and Red Ware and NBP in the earliest phase makes it very likely that this phase is much earlier than what is thought by Howell and Sinha. One may unhesitatingly put it in the 6th century BC, if not earlier. We feel that the spread of the NBP to the Sopara area could not be much later than the date of its beginning in the Ganga plain. At the other chronological end, Sopara as a major port of the 10th-12th centuries AD was mentioned by Al Masudi, Al Biruni and Al Idrisi (cf. Elliot and Dowson 1867: 66, 85). Arunachalam (2002) provides the clear topographical details of the ancient site.

> The early archaeological finds in the area center around Nirmal, where in a low mound called the Burud Rajache Kot, a Buddhist stupa was excavated by Bhagwanlal Indraji in April 1882, containing within it a coffer within a brickbuilt chamber, holding images of Maitreyi Buddha set in eight cardinal directions. The stupa itself is dated to the third century BC but the metal images appear to have been placed in it around

> 9th century AD. A silver coin of Gautamiputra Satakarni of 2nd century BC was also found in the mound. Close by in the Brahma hill of Vakal, circular burials of unhewn boulders, dating to 2nd century BC have been noted. A second area of findings is around Sopara and Gas to its south. In the N.W. of Sopara around the shallow Chakreshwar lake and temple are noted relics of a Hindu temple and memorial stones, while south of Sopara, near Ram Kund, and an old Muslim grave-yard were found fragments of Asokan edicts VIII and IX. In 1956, fragments of Asokan edict XI were also found in the coastal village, Bhui (Bhuigao). Apart from the above findings, old built-up areal and structural lineaments have been noted in the central depression between Nirmal and Sopara-Gas areas, beneath rice fields, and two smaller Buddha stupas south of the Nirmal. In a more recent excavation of 1993, a number of features have been noted – a ring-well, fragments of Roman amphorae red polished ware, glass all dating to the beginning of the Christian era, a Portuguese period landing place east of Gas, and a stone-paved crossing called Dagdibandh between Gas and Achole. Pali and Prakrit inscriptions in Brahmi have been found in Brahma Hill, Sopara, Gas and Bolinj. Mediaeval Hindu and Jain temple relics are plenty. These archaeological and historical findings fall within two N-S linear belts: Vagholi-Nirrmal-Bhui (Bhuigao) on the west side and Sopara-Gas on the east. All the findings in Sopara and Gas are to the east of the line of lakes and the settlements, in or near a low terrace sloping east towards a former creek.

Arunachalam's remote-sensing study of the area led him to the following conclusions:

> In the area under study though the Vagholi-Nirmal-Bhui (Bhuigao) area on the west directly faced the sea, and had small creeks parallel to the sea-face, they do not appear to have attracted a port site. The sheltered inland sea behind the Sopara and Vasi islands approached through either of the estuarine openings was far more ideal for safe sailing and anchoring. The deepest part of the sea-depression lies in the middle, to the north of Manikpur-Chulne and south and east of Gas, where the tidal flows converge from three directions. The most probable port site thus appears to have been to the south and east of Gas, with an adjoining deep water pool for safe anchorage for a few vessels. The largest archaeological findings of the Roman Era lying east of Gas in a low terrace are an indicator in this direction. The findings of the mediaeval stone pavement (Dagdibandh) leading from Gas across the terrace towards Achole, a probable landing site on the mainland face is also suggestive. The sites of ship building and a Bandar of the Portuguese times are also suggestive. A 17th century Kutchi sea manual talks of a regular cargo trade route through the Bolinj-Sopara creek from Gujarat to Mumbai and Thane. As this creek silted up, the cargo vessel traffic slowed down and receded seaward on

> both ends of the creek. Thus, the Sopara Bandar near Nile-more, the Ranpada Bandar and the Agashi Bandar indicate three successive stages of this recession in the 19th and 20th centuries. Agashi was a ship-building centre of 17th century where the Marathas as well as Portuguese built vessels up to 500 tonnes size. The loss of port function of Sopara by the 17th century is the outcome of the islands getting fused with the mainland.

Thus, Sopara appears to be not merely an important port of the early historic and later periods but also a part of the changing pattern of the coastal trade of the area till the 17th century.

As far as its ancient history is concerned, B.L. Indraji (1881-82) offers a remarkably thorough investigation of its antiquity, first identifying the modern place with the ancient port of Surparaka/Sopara on the basis of the available textual and inscriptional sources. According to him, it was the capital of Aparanta, the coastal geographical unit south of Navsari in Gujarat. The traces of ancient occupations were found spread over a mile from east to west over modern Sopara and its adjoining villages and comprised sculptured and dressed stones, pieces of broken images and large old bricks, seven large tanks or lakes, three small ponds or *Kundas* and several old wells. A low mound about 50 yards to the east of the Bhatela lake (near which the REs were found) could mark the site of the old landing place. According to Indraji, the edicts were engraved on the large blocks of basalt which are common in the neighbourhood of Sopara. These blocks were set together like a wall or a face of rock. Subsequently, they got separated and were broken into fragments by people. There is a basalt hillock about a mile to the southwest of Gas village under the name of Vakala or Brahmatekdi. Four inscribed basalt blocks were noted in a basalt hillock (Vakala or Brahmatekdi) about a mile to the southwest of the Gas village, containing 5 inscriptions which were written in characters "much resembling those used in the fragment of the Asoka edict" (Indraji 1881-82: 289). The inscriptions, all personal names, are in all probability donors' names and suggest the location of an Asokan period stupa on the top of the hill.

The stupa which was excavated by Indraji (*Buruda Rajacha Kota*) showed a round plinth (18 feet high and 268 feet in circumference). There was an eighteen feet broad terrace at its centre, and from it rose a 15 to 18 feet (or even 30 feet) high dome which was possibly crowned by a 7 feet high tee crowned with flags and umbrellas. There was a rectangular enclosure of 4 feet thick brick wall with towers at the corners around the stupa. A circular stone box (17.5 inch high and 2 feet in diameter) made of a smoothed yellow trachytic trap was found in the centre of the stupa.

The outer surface of the box was varnished with a special glaze with which the old Jaina and Brahmanical images are darkened and smoothed. The box contained an egg-shaped copper casket which was surrounded by a circle of eight small seated copper images of different manifestations of the Buddha. The copper casket contained in turn four caskets, one enclosed within the other and made successively of silver, stone, crystal and gold. Between the original copper and the silver caskets enclosed inside that, there were gold flowers of seven varieties which had in their midst a Buddha image made of a thin plate of gold and 13 stones. The same context also revealed 31 stone beads, 2 button-shaped gold drops, 2 round gold drops, 3 gold tubes and a silver coin of Yajna Satakarni (dated by Indraji at AD 160). In the space between the silver and stone caskets, there were more gold flowers. This stone casket, as has been noted, revealed a crystal casket which led in turn to a gold casket. More gold flowers were placed in the gold casket which also showed "thirteen tiny pieces of earthenware".

> The objects of worship in whose honour the *stupa* was raised are beyond doubt the tiny pieces of earthenware. That so large a structure should have been raised to preserve so tiny and so few fragments of clay seems to prove that the builders of the relic mound believed them to be pieces of the begging bowl of the world-honoured Gautama Buddha (Indraji 1881-82: 309-310).

On the basis of Yajnasri Satakarni's coin, Indraji dated the stupa to the second century AD, with the possibility of its being opened for repairs in the 7th or 8th century AD.

The rain-swept marshy areas in and around Sopara are not ideal places for undertaking extensive archaeological investigations, and as we have seen, not much substantial information has emerged out of Sopara. However, Sopara is the basic forerunner of Bassein which under the Portuguese dominated the maritime trade of this particular section of the coast till the advent and dominance of Mumbai under the English. On the basis of the references in the *Jatakas* which, we believe, can be dated as a body of texts to c.500 BC, it can be assumed that trade through Sopara could be a full-fledged affair long before Asoka decided to put up his major rock edicts there in the third century BC.

II.7. Sannati

Although noted as a Buddhist site as early as 1954 (for the history of research on Sannati, Sarma and Rao 1993, the preface and Part I) Sannati on the right bank of the Bhima near Chitapur (c. 50 km northwest of Chitapur) has its primary regional reputation because of its temple dedicated to the goddess Chandralamba, which possibly has been in existence since c.8th-9th century AD. The fragment of the granitic slab, which contains REs XII and XIV and two Separate Edicts (found previously at Dhauli and Jaugada) and was identified in January 1889, was discovered during a process of temple renovation. The slab served as the pedestal of the image of the goddess and was found to contain the above-mentioned Asokan edicts on both sides. The obverse had 8 lines of the edict 12 and 4 lines of the edict 14. The reverse carried 17 lines of the 'Separate 'edict of Dhauli and ...... lines of the 'Separate' edict of Jaugada.

The original context of the inscribed slab has been visualized in the following fashion by I.K. Sarma and J.V. Rao (1993, p. 7):

> Since both the broad faces of the stone contained the inscribed records, there is no doubt that this huge slab measuring 2.33 x 1.2 metres and 30 cm thick, might have originally been a stele placed vertically in position within a structural set-up....
>
> From the tenor of the lines, it appears that the inscriptions were engraved after installation of the stele in vertical position. This is apparent from the irregular spacing between the letters, varying sizes of the letters, lack of horizontality in each line, particularly in the upper part and irregular space left at the lower region on both faces of the stele.

It is clear that the original context of the slabs bearing the Asokan edicts, which were possibly multiple in number has been uncovered. Only one of these slabs seems to have been shifted to the Chandralamba temple in the early medieval period. Sarma and Rao's hypothesis that the inscribed slabs were put up in vertical positions for easy viewing by the public cannot be disputed. However, whether Sannati had the full complement of 14 edicts with the addition of two 'separate' edicts, as they argue, is a moot point. There is also no reason to accept M.C. Joshi's opinion ('foreword' to Sarma and Rao 1993), apparently on the basis of the inclusion of two 'separate edicts', that "the area of Sannati was included in the Mauryan *vijita* almost around the same time when he conquered the Kalingas, perhaps after defeating rulers of Sannati as well". The opinion has also been echoed by Sarma and Rao in the main body of their text.

The archaeological topography of Sannati has been well described by J.R. Howell (1995). The outer fortification of the site encloses an area of 86 hectares. The brick fortification wall survives to a height of about 4 m and has several breaches along its length, suggesting the positions of gateways. Brick structures are visible through the eroded tops of the wall.

At regular intervals along its length, the wall gets thicker and shows both inward and outward right-angled 'returns'. These are, in all probability, square watch-towers or bastions. The bricks used in this construction are said to be typical bricks of the Satavahana period.

The inner citadel, locally known as *Ranamandala*, enclosed 25 hectares. At least one silver punch-marked coin and many lead die-struck coins of the Satavahana kings have been found in this section, along with terracotta figurines, etc. A massively constructed structure with small rooms and corridors has been found to survive to a height of 4 m at the edge of this sector, overlooking the river. It might have been a part of the river-front fortifications.

The lower city covers about 60 hectares between the inner citadel and the outer fortification. The occupational sequence of the site shows a Mesolithic phase which terminates in a sterile gap between this and a phase of non-Megalithic black-and-red ware. Period IIIA is supposed to be pre-Satavahana (pre-1st century BC, by the short chronology of the Satavahanas; pre-2nd century BC by the long Satavahana chronology). Period IIIB contains Rouletted Ware, russet-coated red ware, etc.

Many Satavahana and later sculptural pieces and many Satavahana period inscriptions have been sporadically removed from Sannati which has, outside the fortifications, at least three stupas. Howell's Stupa 1 and the associated monastic complex (the site San 4) lies about 1.5 km downstream from the city-site. Its traces suggest a solid dome of about 25 diameter, which was encircled by an elevated circumambulatory path. The site also yielded many sculptured panels and showed traces of a monastery immediately to its south. About 2 km to the east of the modern village and well outside the fortification is the Stupa 2 site, which, after excavations by Howell, showed a stupa of about 70 m diameter, an elevated circumambulatory path and peripheral brick structures. There is a 'tile-manufacturing site' of the early period to the east of the Chandralamba temple, which itself stands on an occupational mound. Howell notes the traces of two ancient bathing *ghats* as well, one near Stupa 1 and the other opposite the inner citadel.

Howell's Stupa 3 turned out to be a significant early Buddhist stupa site with rich architectural and sculptural relics. A sculptured panel found here shows a royal figure with his queen. Of the accompanying maids, one carries a parasol and the other a fly-whisk. The panel bears the inscription 'king Asoka', leaving no doubt about the identity of the royal figure. The basic shape of this Kanganahalli stupa has been described in *Indian Archaeology – A Review* of 1993-94 (pp. 65-66).

> This circular burnt-brick (51 x 27 x 7.5 cm) stupa belongs to a single occupational phase and stands on a limestone nodule foundation. Rectangular *ayaka* platforms (1 x 1.6 x 1 m) abutted the drum of the stupa in the cardinal directions, with small limestone slabs found on them suggesting the former existence of *ayaka* pillars. A roughly rectangular limestone coping stone found near the western entrance indicates that the *ayaka* pillars carried copings. There is a circumambulatory path paved with limestone slabs, and the trace of a railing around the stupa is indicated by the finds of uprights with mortices and cross-bars, both decorated with lotus medallions. Rectangular panels with decorated borders, which show elephants and other animals including running antelopes, seem to have decorated the exterior of the stupa.

Some more details are available from *Indian Archaeology 1994-95* (pp. 37-39). The stupa proved to be 19 m in diameter and its drum portion was made of limestone slabs. The lower portion of the drum carried panels (1.20 x 1.10 x 0.15 m) decorated with various episodes from the life of the Buddha. Between the main body of the stupa and the decorated panels, there are two rows of bricks set in lime. The lower portion of the drum (about 1.55 m high) was topped by a cornice and a fluted top containing numerous Brahmi donative and other inscriptions. The upper drum (extant height: 2 m) was enclosed, as in the lower section, by rectangular limestone blocks with fine joints of dry masonry. The decorated panels (3 x 1.16 x 0.16 m) depicted various Buddhist themes in three registers, also with inscriptions. The hemispherical dome above the drum carries the traces of a stone umbrella on top.

Interestingly, the foundation pit of the Kanganahalli stupa yielded a piece of the NBP. Palaeographically, the inscriptions have been bracketed between the first century BC and the third century AD, and this chronological bracket is suggested by the sculptures as well.

The archaeological complex of Sannati is, thus, a massive complex. I find the discovery of a piece of NBP in the foundation trench of the Kanganahalli stupa exciting, indicative of the probability that the stupa site has a pre-Satavahana, possibly Mauryan, ancestry as well, although the stupa was embellished in the Satavahana period.

It may be appropriate to record here that the post-excavation care of the Kanganahalli stupa and its sculptural finds is reminiscent of the care which the Amaravati stupa finds once received and possibly still receive in certain quarters. In 2004 (about 10 years after the excavations) when I visited the site, I found its architectural and sculptural remains lying in the open in mud. Any attempt to photograph them in their muddy location was discouraged with personal threats by the ground staff employed by the Archaeological Survey of India. I was told that a museum would be built to house the antiquities and the architectural remains would be preserved. However, the fact that sculptures of the quality of Amaravati sculptures could be allowed to lie in the open in mud for about ten years after excavations offers insight into how 'heritage' is looked after in modern India. In 2005 I saw some sculptural finds from Amaravati in the Madras government museum. They were vandalised by the incision, with some sharply pointed metallic implements, of personal names of the visitors. That the visitors can undertake vandalism of this type in a government museum with many gallery 'guards' in attendance was indicative of the level of administration of the museum concerned. As I type this in November 2009, I am not sure if more than a few pages have been published in print on the Kanganahalli sculptures by the site's excavator.

Regarding the location of Sannati, I have elsewhere pointed out the following:

> Sannati is linked on the northwest to Ter, and on the northeast to Kondapur. In the south, this seems to be aligned towards the Adoni-Pattikonda sector of Kurnul, and from this sector the Bellary-Kopbal segment is easily approachable. From Sannati it was also possible to move in the direction of Alampur on the Tungabhadra, cross the river in that section and proceed towards the Nandiyal valley from where there is a straight route through the Nandikanama pass to the Andhra coast. From the Nandiyal valley, again, one could move in the direction of Cuddapah and Chittoor from where a route led to the modern Tamil Nadu sector. It thus appears that Sannati, or as we have argued, ancient Suvarnagiri occupied a nodal position in the network of communication between the Deccan and the south (Chakrabarti 2010, p. 204).

II.8. Yerragudi / Erragudi

This site has been discussed in the context of the MREs. In fact, this is the only site where the complete set of fourteen rock edicts occurs alongside the Minor Rock Edicts including both the northern and more usual MRE 1 and the southern addition to it. In the same MRE context, we have pointed out the significance of the location of Yerragudi giving access to Anantapur, Cuddapah and Chittoor, all on the way to Tamil Nadu on the one hand and the more southern sections of Karnataka on the other.

II.9. Dhauli

The site near modern Bhuvaneshwar and on the bank of the Daya River appears to have noted first by Markham Kittoe in *JASB 7* and later figured prominently in Beglar's report on the area (Beglar 1882, pp. 95-98). Regarding the Mauryan figure of an elephant coming out of the rock, he referred to his 'personal' knowledge that the elephant was held in 'great veneration in the whole neighbourhood, and even so far as Khurda'. His further impression was that *Dhavaleswari Mata* was the tutelary goddess of this spot, which might lead to its name being Dhauli. It also appeared to him that the flat terrace of the hill near the elephant and also the one facing it on the opposite side contained the remains of stupas. A few rock-cut caves, both natural and artificial, can still be noted in the vicinity.

II.10. Jaugada

Markham Kittoe appears to have been also aware of the existence of the inscriptions at Jaugada which lies on the bank of the Rushikulya River. Although later reported by others, the authentic description of the archaeological site occurred in Beglar's report of 1882 (p. 112):

> ... an old quadrangular earthen fort, nearly square, with two entrances in each face, or eight entrances in all. The fort was originally surrounded by a wide and deep moat, whence no doubt, the earth was dug up to form the ramparts. The moat was not continuous, unexcavated slips being left at the various entrances for ingress and egress. The walls had towers, also of earth, at each of the four corners, and also on each flank of each of the eight entrances. All these still exist, though of course the rain of centuries has reduced them now to high, shapeless mounds in continuation of, but slightly elevated above, the line of ramparts. The moat has got greatly filled in, but so great was its depth and extent that to this day they are more than 7 feet deep towards the middle ... they form respectable lotus-covered marshes, in which wild duck and waterfowl swim secure from danger, for although they may be shot readily enough, the lotus-covered marsh is too dangerous to send swimmers out to secure them. The walls are exclusively of earth...

Two tanks were noted inside the fortification and the larger group of rocks there contained the inscriptions.

II.11. The Identification of Tosali

The first epigraphic occurrence of this term in the sense of a city is the first and second separate edicts of Dhauli. In the first of these edicts, the context is *Tosaliyam ma(ha)mata (naga)la(v)i(yo)halak(a)* – 'the Mahamatras at Tosali, who are the judicial officers of the city' (Hultzsch 1925, p. 95). The second of these edicts writes *Tosaliyam kumale mahamata cha* – 'the prince (governor) and the mahamatras of Tosali' (*ibid.*, p. 99).

The earliest textual reference to Tosali is that of Ptolemy in the 2nd century AD: Tosalei, a metropolis (Majumdar-Sastri 1924, pp. 230-231).

The earliest inscription after the Dhauli edicts is a 3rd century AD Ikshvaku inscription from Nagarjunakonda (Vogel 1929-1930, p. 23) which lists the areas where Buddhism was preached by the monks of Tamraparni or Sri Lanka: China, Chilata (Kirata), *Tosali*, Avaranta (Aparanta), Vanga, Vanavasi, Yavana, Damila, Palura and the isle of Tamraparni.

It is thus clear that Tosali was both the name of a region and a city.

In the later inscriptions of Orissa, a distinction was made between North and South Tosali.

North Tosali or 'Uttara Tosali' is mentioned in the Soro copper-plates edited by N.G. Majumdar (1935-1936) who puts them in the 6th century AD. Plate A clearly mentions 'Uttara-Tosalyam'/'in UttaraTosali' while Plate B mentions *Odra-Vishaye Uttara-Tosalyam Sarephahara-Vishaye* or a village called Adyara in the 'Sareph-ahara-vishaya in North Tosali', which again formed part of Odra-vishaya. The term 'Uttara-Tosalyam' also occurs in the Neulpur grant of Subhakara of the 8th century AD (Banerji 1919-1920). The donated villages were all identified in the Balasore area as were the donated villages in the Soro grant, Soro standing for the ancient Sareph. It appears that the Balasore area was the centre of North Tosali.

Dakshina Tosali or South Tosali figures in the Patiakella grant of Maharaja Sivaraja of the 7th century AD (Banerji 1907-08). The Patiakella zamindari was in the Cuttack district. According to N.G. Majumdar (*ibid.*, p. 200), South Tosali "included Kangoda-mandala which according to some scholars was to the southeast of Puri and might have extended as far as the border of the Ganjam district".

Going by this definition, 'Tosali' connotes in a sense the whole of the Orissan coast from the Suvarnarekha mouth to the Rushikulya river. Further details are available in Snigdha Tripathi's *Inscriptions of Orissa*, vol. 1 (Tripathi 1997): the Kanas plate of Lokavigraha, year 280 (c. 6th century AD) and Asanpat Nataraja image inscription of Satrubhanja, also of the 6th century AD (*ibid.*, pp. 184-185, 171-172). Lokavigraha was ruling in Tosali comprising 18 forest states (*Tosalyam sashtadasattavirajyam)* and Satrubhanja was ruling in both the Tosalis. Tripathi (*ibid.*, p. 172, note 7) adds that 'Ubhaya Tosali' is evidently Uttara Tosali and Dakshina Tosali of the later Orissan epigraphs, comprising the region from Balasore district up to the northern part of Ganjam district. The boundary extended up to Chilka lake, with the Mahanadi dividing the two Tosalis. In the second volume of her work (Tripathi 2000, p. 3, note 1), she offers full explanation:

> The south-western part of Midnapore district in West Bengal and the Orissan districts of Balsore, Mayurbhanj, Dhenkanal, Cuttack and

> probably Keonjhar were included in the division of Uttara Kosali. Dakshina Tosali comprised the Orissan districts of Puri and the northern part of Ganjam, situated to the south of the river Mahanadi. Parts of Puri and Ganjam districts formed the kingdom of Kangodamandala of the Sailodbhavas during the 7th and early part of 8th century AD which came again under the division of Dakshina Tosali during the rule of the Bhauma-Karas.

Utkala, which denoted Balasore and parts of Mayurbhanj in the 7th century AD, was included in Uttara Tosali of the Bhauma-Kara kings, which included the the coastal districts of Balasore and Puri and the non-coastal districts of Mayurbhanj, Keonjhar and Dhenkanal. The same coastal districts also came to be known as Odra-vishaya.

In his Sisupalgarh excavation report, B.B. Lal (1949, p.66) wrote the following:

> The possibility of Sisupalgarh being identical with either Tosali of theAsokan edicts or Kalinganagara of Kharavela's inscription or both may, however, be considered. But it must be stated at once that no inscription or other authentic evidence has so far been obtained to settle the proposition either way.

The Sisupalgarh mud rampart (phase 1, 25 feet high and 110 feet wide at the base) was built in the earliest stage of black-and-red ware at the site. This stage was put by him at c. 200 BC on the ground that between the presence of the rouletted ware in the Sisupalgarh sequence around 50 AD, according to his calculation, and the earliest stage of black-and-red ware, there was a cultural deposit of 10 feet, for which he assigned only 2 to 3 centuries. The rouletted ware, which is a common enough pottery at many excavated sites between the Ganga and Kaveri-Vaigai deltas, may be placed at least around 100 BC, and for 10 feet of cultural debris to be deposited at a non-deltaic site like Sisupalgarh, it should take at least 4-5 centuries. Thus, on the whole, the date of the first phase of Sisupalgarh fortifications is unlikely to be later than c. 500 BC. Interestingly, between the lowest black-and-red ware deposit and the natural soil, there was a 4 feet thick cultural deposit, thus taking the general antiquity of the site to c. 700 BC or thereabouts.

Apart from the Sisupalgarh mound and the ruins of Udayagiri and Khandagiri, the Bhuvanesvar area itself seems to be devoid of correspondingly early remains. The fragmentary Asokan pillar of the Bhaskaresvara temple and the rather roughly executed bell of a pillar, which are reported from modern Bhuvanesvar, cannot be positively claimed to have come from Bhuvanesvar itself and might even be fake (Falk 2006).

On plan, the Radhanagar mound on the right bank of the Kimiria, a tributary of the Baitarani, seems to correspond greatly to the Sisupalgarh mound: square plan with each arm of its mud rampart – 4-5 m high, 40 m wide – measuring 1250 m on each side. There are three projections on each side (two at the corners and one in the centre) and two gateways, north and south, both located near the central projections.

However, when one looks at the relics scattered around it, this site seems to acquire a high degree of significance. First, at a low hill called Kaima, situated to the south of the site, there is a monolithic free-standing elephant set in a prepared surface with 4 monolithic stone pillars set at its four corners. The pillars also bear traces of medallions. Although Jitu Mishra (2000) dates the elephant and pillars at 2nd-1st century BC, we would consider them unreservedly Mauryan. This hillock also has a few plain rock-cut caves with grooves and possibly cisterns located on their floors. There are traces of a brick stupa at the hill-top.

The remains of early historic Langudi, Duburi and Vajragiri stupas are in 'the close vicinity' of Radhanagar. At Langudi, there are 34 rock-cut stupas in the Amaravati style along with a large central rock-cut stupa. Langudi has also yielded Sunga period terracottas, lotus medallion in rock and 43 rock-cut panels of miniature stupas. Forty early rock-cut stupas are said to exist in the surrounding hill ranges. A fragment of an inscription in Brahmi of the 1st century AD identifies the Langudi site as *Pushpa-sabhara giriya* (a hill loaded with flowers) or Pushpagiri monastery mentioned by Hsuan-Tsang.

It is useful to remember that most of the early major Buddhist monastic sites of Orissa are in the Jajpur area or the Baitarani valley. For instance, the antiquity of Lalitagiri has been pushed back to the 2nd-1st century BC on the basis of the finds of the base of a railing pillar with half-lotus medallions on the model of Bodhgaya (Das and Mohanty 2000, p. 446). A hoard of silver punch-marked coins ranging in date from the imperial Nandas to Mauryas has also been found in the Radhanagar area. On the whole, on the basis of whatever has been reported from the unexcavated site of Radhanagar in the Jajpur sector, it may be claimed that this is as important an early historic city site of Orissa as Sisupalgarh. In fact, considering the major Buddhist monastic relics from the same area, we would venture the conclusion that Radhanagar was likely to have been more important in early historic Orissa than Sisupalgarh. Viewed from this angle, Radhanagar has a better claim to be considered Tosali than Sisupalgarh. The fact that the term Tosali is found in the two edicts outside Sisupalgarh does not necessarily make it ancient Tosali. It may be noted that Tosali was also the abode of a Mauryan prince, and only Taxila, Ujjain and Suvarnagiri were the Mauryan cities where a prince was stationed. Sisupalgarh does not look as significant as Taxila or Ujjain. Suvarnagiri, to which we shall turn in the next section, is still unidentified. We think that Radhanagar was more likely to represent ancient Tosali than Sisupalgarh.

II.12. The Significance of the Locations of Dhauli and Jaugada

On a general level, the three sites of Radhanagar, Sisupalgarh and Jaugada dot the coastal belt of Orissa and mark in a sense an important line of movement from the eastern edge of the Ganga plain to the south. When one looks at the positions of Dhauli and Jaugada in detail, one realizes that the reality may be more complex. Bhuvaneshwar is the capital of modern Orissa, and long before the excavations at Sisupalgarh, it had been known as a focal centre of ancient Orissan temples. That the ancient Jainas had a preference for the site is clear from the ruins of the Udayagiri-Khandagiri hills in its outskirts. Cuttack, the centre of British Orissa, is only across the Mahanadi from Bhuvaneshwar which does not lie in the delta but at its head. This position must always have endowed Bhuvaneshwar with great geographical significance in the history of Orissa. Apparently, a less known fact is that the Khurda sub-division of the Puri district of British India adjoins the southeastern fringe of the Chhotanagpur plateau.

> Khurda was the last portion of territory held by the independent Hindu dynasty of Orissa. The Maratha cavalry were unable to over-run this jungle-covered and hilly tract; and the ancient royal house retained much of its independence till 1804, when the Raja rebelled against the British government and his territory was confiscated (the IGI, vol. 15, 295-296).

By virtue of its control of the Bhuvaneshwar area, the Asokan power in Orissa appears to have included both the coastal belt and the hilly but wide valleys to its north.

The Ganjam district of British India, of which Jaugada is a part, was the northernmost district of the Madras Presidency and fell in ancient Kalinga. It was the second major ancient city site of Kalinga, the most important one being the ancient Dantapura or modern Dantavruk. The Jaugada sector also appears to be well linked with the Jeypore section of modern Orissa, covering the whole hilly, rocky and forested stretch from Bastar to Vizianagram. This northern part of Ganjam was also interspersed with valleys and fertile plains. The early reputation of Ganjam in British India was not good:

> ... most of the numerous zamindars in this area (who had 34 forts and 32000 irregular troops) were contumacious, frequently annexing government villages, quarrelling with one another or over disputed successions, and declining to pay any tribute until compelled by force.
>
> In 1816, 4000 or 5000 Pindaris entered the District from Jeypore and swept through the whole of it, plundering and burning (the IGI, vol. 12, p. 146).

One would not be surprised if in the Asokan time, Jaugada was meant to control this rather difficult territory lying almost athwart the line of movement from Bengal to the south. It was also probable that Jaugada was an easy point to reach in Kalinga provided one came through South Kosala.

III. THE SEPARATE EDICTS

These edicts have been known for a long time at Dhauli and Jaugada but their occurrence at Sannati has opened up the question of their general distribution. The original position of the inscribed slab (233 x 121 x 30 cm) at Sannati was probably vertical. Its front side carries parts of Sep. Edicts whereas the backside contains parts of REs XII and XIV.

Separate Edict I begins with what is obviously an order of *Devanampriya* to the *Mahamatras* or *Nagalaviyohalakas* or *Nagara-vyavaharakas* (judicial officers) of Tosali. Declaring that *Save munise paja mama* ('all men are my children/subjects'), the judicial officers of Tosali were urged to deal with all of them impartially, putting aside the elements of envy, hurry, want of practice, laziness and fatigue. They were ordered to ensure that 'neither undeserved fettering' nor 'undeserved harsh treatment' was meted out to men. To check if this order to the civic officials was being observed, the king would send a *Mahamatra* on an inspection tour every five years. The royal princes in charge of Ujjayini and Takshasila would send such *Mahamatras* every three years.

It was further noted that this edict "must be listened to (by all) on (every day of) the constellation Tishya". This could also be listened to by a single individual on "frequent (other) occasions between (the days of) Tishya".

Separate Edict II includes also the royal prince in charge of Tosali in the scope of Asoka's order to its civic judicial officials. Here the focus is on the 'unconquered borderers' – *Amtanam avijitanam*, the people living at his borders but not directly conquered or subjugated. The prince and the civic officials of Tosali were ordered "to inspire confidence to those (borderers) and (to secure their) welfare and happiness in this world and in the other world". Further, "this rescript must be listened to (by all) every four months on (the day of) the consellation Tishya" but could be listened to even by a single person, if he so desires, "also on frequent (other) occasions between (the days of) Tishya".

It may be noted that apart from mentioning Tosali, the two Separate Edicts have noting specifically regional about them, and now that Sannati has to be included as a relevant find-spot, the Separate Edicts must be considered as having as much universal appeal as most of his other edicts.

Interestingly, Sircar (2000, p. 97) does not believe in the validity of a separate category of Asokan rock edicts as 'Separate Edicts'. He calls them Rock Edicts XV and XVI.

IV. THE RELATED HISTORICAL AND GEOGRAPHICAL ISSUES

It is apparent that much of the text of the fourteen rock edicts is concerned with the enunciation of the significance and the features of what, according to Asoka, constituted *Dhamma*. Its interpretation and comparison with the philosophical and religious tradition of India both before and after Asoka have no doubt been a major theme of scholarly research. The text *per se* of these edicts, and the analysis of their grammar and dialects remain throughout a constant focus of scholarly research, and this is true of all other categories of Asokan edicts. However, in the case of the fourteen major rock edicts, royal attention is given primarily to different aspects of *Dhamma* and the methods accepted for its propagation.

A number of administrative officers – the *Mahamatras, Yuktas, Rajukas, Pradesikas* and *Prativedakas* – are mentioned in this context, and although they do not shed any specific light on the historical geography of Asoka's dominions, they do suggest how these dominions were knitted together. More directly relevant to the issue of historical geography is the listing of various groups of people. Some of them are mentioned as the king's "western borderers" (RE-5) while a few others are mentioned as belonging simply to the royal domain (RE-13). The mention of the contemporary kings to the west, beginning with that of Antiochus of Syria whose territory abutted the Mauryan frontier in Afghanistan, is equally important from the point of historical geography because the mention of the kings – Ptolemy, Antigonos, Magas and Alexander – beyond Antiochus' territory, the other end of which was Syria, is significant not merely because these references to the contemporary kings define independently Asokan chronology but also throw light on the historical geographical context of the Asokan dominions. They exemplify how the Mauryan state may also be visualized as a part of a chain of ancient states running from beyond

Egypt and the Mediterranean to Tamraparni or Sri Lanka. Finally, two geographical terms are important in the context of the major rock edicts – *Kalinga* and *Sambodhi*. Their connotations have to be examined in detail. *Sambodhi* stands for Bodh Gaya where the Buddha obtained *nirvana* or *bodhi*. According to Hsuang Tsang, he donated a stone throne to the place. This oblong stone throne with honey-suckle motifs and geese on each of its four sides and a pattern of intersecting circles on its top still survives at the site, although vandalised by a coat of gold all over it by the local Buddhist monks.

The issue of Kalinga remains far more problematic.

V. WHERE DID THE BATTLE OF KALINGA TAKE PLACE?

V.1. The Epigraphic Context

The reference to the battle of Kalinga occurs in the Rock Edict XIII of Asoka. The reference has survived well in the Kalsi, Girnar, Shahbazgarhi, Manserah, Erragudi and Kandahar versions of the edict. Its relevant portion is quoted below from E. Hultzsch's translation of the Kalsi version.

"(A) When king Devanampriya Priyadarsin had been anointed eight years, (the country of) the Kalingyas (our note: the original term *Kaligyani*) was conquered by him.

(B) One hundred and fifty thousand in number were the men who were deported thence, one hundred thousand in number were those who were slain there, and many times as many those who died.

(C) After that, now that (the country of) the Kalingyas had been taken, Devanampriya (is devoted) to a zealous study of morality, to the love of morality, and to the instruction (of people) in morality.

(D) This is the repentance of Devanampriya on account of his conquest of (the country of) the Kalingyas" (Hultzsch 1925, p. 47).

The term *Kaligya* occurs in the following contexts in the Kalsi version: *Kaligya Vijita* ('the Kaligyas conquered'); *Kaligyeshu* ('in the Kaligyas'), and *Kaligyani* (the plural of *Kaligya*). However, the more usual term *Kalinga* is also mentioned in the Kalsi version (*Kalingeshu* – 'in the Kalingas'). The Kalsi version thus uses *Kaligya* and *Kalinga* interchangeably. The Girnar version uses *Kalinga* ('the Kalingas'; 'in the Kalingas'). The Shahbazgarhi and Manserah versions use the term *Kaliga*: 'the Kaligas'(Shahbazgarhi), 'in Kaliga' (Shahbazgarhi), and 'in the Kaligas' (Shahbazgarhi and Manserah). The Erragudi version uses the term *Kaliga* ('the Kaligas', 'in the Kaligas' – cf. Sircar 1979, p. 33). The Greek version of this edict, as obtained from Kandahar (Sircar 1979, p. 49), offers its condensed version. It is not a complete version of the edict which is obtained from other relevant places..

The Asokan scholars do not appear to have given any thought to the place where the battle of Kalinga was likely to have been fought. For instance, Romila Thapar ignores this issue in her discussion on the Kalinga war (Thapar 2002, p. 36). Much earlier, Vincent Smith (1924, p. 172) made no comment on it except stating that "the eastern territories, including the conquered Kalinga, was governed by a viceroy stationed at Tosali, the exact position of which has not been ascertained". Similarly, R.K. Mookerji (1955) is silent on the issue. Among the recent scholars, H. Falk (2006) does not raise the problem even in the context of Dhauli.

It was only after Sisupalgarh excavations in 1950 that B.B. Lal (1949) suggested that the Sisupalgarh ruins could represent Asokan Tosali. There was nothing positive in favour of this idea except the fact that there was an ancient city-site near the Dhauli edict which mentioned Tosali. The idea which we hear bandied about by the tourist guides of modern Bhuvaneshwar that the Kalinga war was fought near Dhauli has also nothing specific in its favour.

V.2. The Location of Kalinga

Kalinga is a well-known territorial unit in the ancient history of India. The substantive body of textual and epigraphic evidence on the location of Kalinga and its capital city Dantapura or Kalinganagara has been generally discussed by B.C. Law (1954, pp. 149, 156-159; 1943, pp. 158-163; 1937, pp. 49-50, 142, 157) and P. Gupta (1973). As in the modern context Kalinga has a strong association with Orissa, its location has also to be separated from those of the two other territorial units which denote Orissa – Odra and Utkala.

Two textual references set up Kalinga as one of the first recognizable territorial units of the subcontinent. It is mentioned in Panini's grammar (4.1.168) and the Buddhist *Jatakas* (cf.Law 1943, p. 159). However, these references do not make clear its position on the map, and for that, the evidence furnished by Hsuan-Tsang (Watters 1905, pp. 193-198) is unequivocal. He travelled 700 li to the south-west of Karnasuvarna in the Murshidabad area of West Bengal to reach Wu-tu or Ota (Odra) which had many Buddhist places including the monastery of Pu-sie-po-ki-li or Puspagiri. Its capital city was Che-li-ta-lo "which was a thoroughfare and resting-place for sea-going traders and strangers from distant lands". Although Alexander Cunningham (Majundar-Sastri 1924) identified this city with Puri, Watters pointed out that the older channels of the Mahanadi below Cuttack were called Chitratola (reminiscent of Hiuen Tsang's Che-li-ta-lo) channels and that the villagers pointed out the site of an old port on what is now a vast expanse of sand in the river-bank. From Ota, Hiuen Tsang went to the area of Kung-yu-jo. This term has been translated as Kongudha or Kanyodha, and the area has been placed near the Chilka lake of Ganjam (Majumdar-Sastri 1924). The administrative unit of *Kangoda-mandala,* which is mentioned in the two grants of Dandi-mahadevi, is placed there in South Kosala. These grants are not considered earlier than the 13th century AD (Kielhorn 1900-1901). In a sense South Kosala, basically Chhattisgarh, Bastar and parts of north Orissa, continues up to Ganjam, and from that point of view the assumed position of Hsuan Tsang's 'Kangudha' in the Chilka lake-Ganjam area is acceptable.

Kalinga or Ka-leng-ka came next in Hsuan Tsang's itinerary and thus has to be further south along the coast from the Chilka lake. More specific clues to its location are obtained from inscriptions. The Aihole eulogy of Pulakesin II (Sircar 1983, p. 444) states that he conquered Kalinga, mentioning the forts of Pishtapura (modern Pithapuram in the East Godavari district of Andhra) and Kollair lake (West Godavari district of Andhra) in that context. A grant of the Eastern Chalukyan king Vishnuvardhana Bhima I, found in the Kasimkota village of the Ankapalle taluk of the Visakhapatnam area, records the grant of a village in "Elamancha Kalingadesa and Devatrashtra Vishaya" (Rangacharya 1919, vol. 3, p. 1665). Elamancha or modern Elamanchili is near Ankapalle. The Visakhapatnam inscription (c. AD 1118) of Anantavarman Choda-ganga of the Eastern Gangas mentions the possession of Kalinga by the kings of that dynasty (Sircar 1983, pp. 84-85).

An important epigraphic mention of Dantapura in the sense of the capital of Kalinga is provided by the inscription of Indravarman, in the Ganga year 149 (Ramadas 1917-1918). It was Indravarman IV, 'son of Danarnava', whose date falls in the first half of the 7th century AD. The inscription records the grant of the village Bhukkukura in the *Kuraka rashtra* to a Brahmin who was an inhabitant of *tirilinga.* The king introduced himself as *Sakalakalingadhipati,* 'the lord of the whole of Kalinga', and the grant was issued 'from his victorious residence at (the city of) Dantapura'. What Ramadas, the editor of the edict in *Epigraphia Indica,* wrote about the location of Dantapura is worth quoting:

Dantapura is mentioned in the *Daladavamsa.* It is said that the left canine tooth of the lower jaw of Buddha was brought by one of his disciples to Kalinga and a large stupa was built over it. In course of time, a large city rose round the stupa and it was called Dantapura. The Buddhists all lived in a village close by. The people of Ceylon, attracted by the miracle worked by the tooth, established a colony not far from Dantapura. Ultimately, when the stupa was destroyed by the malice of the Brahmans, the tooth was taken away to Ceylon. On the way from Chicacole to Siddhantam (Siddharthaka grama, a Buddhist village) and close to the latter place, a large tract of land is shown as the site of the fort of Dantavaktra. Valuable jewels, images of all kinds, coins and other articles formerly used to be found there by the cultivators. Even now, the people believe that there was once immense wealth there. About twelve miles north of Siddhantam and on the same side as Nagavali is the village Hiramandalam, which name is only a corruption of Iramandala (the Tamil Ilamandalam), the ancient name of Ceylon. Siddhantapura must have been the village where the Buddhists lived. These facts prove that Dantapura stood on the place which is now shown as the site of the fort of Dantavaktra (Ramadas 1917-1918, p. 361).

Kuraka rashtra denotes, according to Ramadas, the modern Palagonda taluk.

This identification nullifies Cunningham's earlier identification that Dantapura was to be located either at Rajahmundri or Coringa in the Godavari delta (Majumdar-Sastri 1924).

At least two other inscriptions – the Visakhapatnam plates of Anantavarman Chodaganga (Bhandarkar 1929-1930, p. 148) and the Nadagam plates of the king Vajrahastadeva of the same dynasty (*ibid.*, p. 147) – were issued from the capital of Kalinga, which was also known as Kalinganagara. In both these inscriptions, the kings call themselves 'lord of trikalinga' or the 'lord of three Kalingas'. Cunningham (Majumdar-Sastri 1924, pp. 592-594) drew attention to the three-fold classification of Kalinga by Pliny of the 1st century AD, who refers to Maco-Calingae and Gangarides-Calingae as separate peoples from the Calingae. According to Cunningham, these three Kalingas stood for Kalinga proper, the Amaravati area in the Krishna valley, and Warangal in the Andhra interior. As there is no positive clue to the identification of Pliny's Kalingas, all such theories are entirely speculative.

The earliest epigraphic evidence of Kalinga and its capital Kalinganagara occurs in the Hatigumpha inscription of King Kharavela who has been placed by the *Epigraphia Indica* editors of his inscription, K.P. Jayaswal and R.D. Banerji in the first half of the second century BC (Jayaswal and Banerji 1929-1930). This dating is not accepted by all (cf.

Sircar 1965, for its dating in the 1st century BC on palaeographic ground), but if Kharavela is placed in the 1st century BC, one has to contend with a political vacuum in this part in the post-Mauryan context. There are also debates about the reading of the inscription's text. For instance, Sircar (1965) reads *Musikanagari*, as read by Jayaswal and Banerji, as *Asikanagari*. Musikanagari cannot be identified, but for Asikanagari, Adam which has shown the term *Asika* on a terracotta sealing (Nath 1995) can be claimed to be Asikanagari, although the evidence is by no means conclusive.

Kharavela called himself *Kalingadhipati* and the name of his capital was *Kalinganagari*. According to Jayaswal and Banerji, Kalinganagari, the capital of the Kalinga country, was represented by Kalingapatnam near the mouth of the Vamsadhara river. They cite a local tradition according to which the ancient capital of Kalinga was 'swallowed up by the sea'. Interestingly, they mention that "fragments of bas-reliefs of the Maurya period with the well-known protuberance of the head-dress" were discovered by Banerji in the temples of Mukhalingesvara and Kurmesvara of the locality. However, such bas-reliefs are no longer traceable at Kalingapatnam, and the archaeological evidence, as both G. Ramadas (1917-1918) and B. Subrahmanyam (1999, pp. 30-31) pointed out earlier and as we feel on the basis of our observations at the site, points clearly to the modern Dantavaktrunikonda in the Srikakulam area as the site of the capital of ancient Kalinga. It is difficult to give any credence to the identification of Paloura in the Ganjam district as Dantapura or Kalinganagara. The fact that Paloura is mentioned by Ptolemy does not necessary establish its credentials as Dantapura.

It is seldom possible to draw the boundaries of the ancient Indian geographical terms with any precision, but in the case of Kalinga, S.N. Majumdar-Sastri's comment (Majumdar-Sastri 1924, p. 735) that it "comprised modern Orissa to the south of the Vaitarani, and the sea-coast southward as far as Vizagapatam" is clearly acceptable. However, from time to time its western boundary could also extend further west up to the fringe of the Godavari delta. An equally important point about Kalinga is that its antiquity, on the basis of the evidence of Panini and the Jatakas alone, can be stretched back to c.500 BC, and if so, it has to be included in the list of the Mahajanapadas or Janapadas during the time of the Buddha.

Two more geographical terms remain to be noted in this context: Odra and Utkala. Both the terms have a respectable antiquity (Law 1943, pp. 333-336). As *Ukkala*, Utkala had two merchants (Tapussa and Bhallaka) who were among the direct disciples of the Buddha. Odra or Ota, as we have seen, was mentioned by Hiuen Tsang, and earlier, it figures in the *Mahabharata*. *Oddavishaya* or the administrative division of Odra was conquered by Rajendra Chola (Law 1954, p. 178). There are also several epigraphic references to the administrative division of Utkala or *Utkalavishaya* (Law 1954, p. 197). According to Law (*ibid.*), the limits of Utkala stretched from the Rishikulya river in the west to the Kasai valley in modern West Bengal. Although these are separate terms, it is possible that their connotations varied in time and were also used interchangeably. As we understand it, the Suvarnarekha delta, including the adjacent parts of West Bengal, could denote the Odra territory and the Mahanadi delta proper including the area up to the Rishikulya might mean Utkala.

Although this is nothing more than mere supposition, this makes sense in view of the fact that here two geographical units – the Suvarnarekha and the Mahanadi deltas – are involved. This geographical division might have been reflected in their separate ancient names. There is also no reason why in these areas Buddhism could not be as old as the period of the Buddha himself.

However, the problem of the location of Kalinga does not yet seem to be over. No less an epigraphist than D.C. Sircar (2000, p. 53) defines Tosali as "modern Dhauli, the ancient capital of Kalinga". In view of the epigraphical data that we have cited above to discuss the location of Kalinga, this opinion from such a scholar is a matter of serious surprise. Upinder Singh (1994, p. 40, note 55) identifies Tosali with Dhauli and thinks that it is the name of a city in Kalinga. Similarly, H. Prusty, P. Mohanty and J. Mishra (2000) prefer to put 'Dantapura, the capital of ancient Kalinga' at Radhanagar near Jajpur in the Baitarini valley of northern Orissa. To reinforce the normal source-based point of view which we here have put forward regarding the location of Kalinga, we turn once again to Cunningham's *Ancient Geography of India* (Majumdar-Sastri 1924). Calculating on the basis of Hsuan Tsang's testimony that the Kalinga territory was about 800 miles in circuit, he points out that "the principal feature in this large tract of the country is the Mahendra range of mountains ... this range is mentioned also in the Vishnu-Purana, as the source of the Rishikulya river, and as this is the well-known name of the river of Ganjam, the Mahendra mountains can at once be identified with the Mahendra Male range, which divides Ganjam from the valley of the Mahanadi (*ibid.*, p. 591)".

This line of unimpeachable argument has also been put forward by H.C. Raychaudhuri in his *Studies in Indian Antiquities* (Raychaudhuri 1932). He accepts the intimate association of the Mahendra range with Kalinga and further points out that "Pargiter identifies the Mahendra range with the portion of the Eastern Ghats between the Godavari and the Mahanadi rivers, part of which near Ganjam, as pointed out by Wilson, is still called Mahendra Malei or hills of Mahindra" (*ibid.*, p. 107).

The only conceivable reason to call Dhauli or Radhanagar the ancient capital of Kalinga is that Kharavela called himself 'the lord of Kalinga' and that he got this engraved in Hatigumpha in the outskirts of modern Bhuvanesvar. In his expedition to Rajagriha and Gorathagiri, both in Magadha, Kharavela must have come to this area, either to take the more usual route through southwest West Bengal to reach Gaya from where Rajagriha and Gorathagiri are easily accessible or to follow the far more difficult but still possible route from Cuttack / Bhuvanesvar to Keonjhargarh and from there to Chaibasa, Hazaribagh, Nawada and Rajgir-Gaya. He had no problem in leaving behind an edict in a territory he reached as a victorious king. He also no doubt controlled this part of modern Orissa but as *Kalingadhipati*, the lord of a territory which lay far to the southwest of this zone.

When one thinks of the Hatigumpha inscription of Kharavela, one generally tends to forget that there are at least three more related inscriptions in the same place: inscriptions 1346, 1347 and 1351 of H. Luders' list of Brahmi inscriptions up to AD 400 (Luders 1912). Inscription 1346 is from Svargapuragumpha and records the "establishment of a cave for the *Kaliga* (Kalinga) monks (*samana*) in honour of the *arahamtas* (arhats) by the chief queen (agamahishi) of (siri-khara)vela, emperor (?chakavati?) of Kaliga and daughter of *rajan* Lalaka, great grandson of Hathisimha" (Luders 1912, p. 161).

Inscription 1347 from Manchapurigumpha shows the following: "the cave of the noble (*aira*) maharaja, the lord of Kalinga Mahameghavahana Vakadepa-siri (sri-Vakradeva)" (*ibid.*). Inscription 1351 from Baghgumpha was "the cave of the town-judge Bhuti". Thus, one of these three inscriptions clearly belongs to the chief queen of Kharavela, and the second one seems to belong to a member of the same dynasty as Kharavela. Kalinga is mentioned in both cases. The impression one gets is that the Mahameghavahana dynasty, to which the kings Kharavela and Sri-Vakradeva belonged, had the area, where this cave-complex is located, under their control. It appears that the cave-complex was sacred to the Jainas, and apparently it was for this reason that the two Mahameghavahana kings and the chief queen of one of them donated caves there. However, it does not necessarily follow that the area concerned has to be viewed as belonging to the specific geographical area called

Kalinga. The Satavahanas and the Western Kshatrapas left behind their inscriptions at Nasik but this fact did not make Nasik the Satavahana capital. Neither did it suggest that Nasik fell in the home territory of the Satavahanas whose primary Puranic identity was as *Andhra* kings. Similarly, the fact that the Udayagiri-Khandigiri caves fell in the territory annexed to the Kalinga kingdom by the kings with their home base in Kalinga does not make these caves or their area ancient Kalinga.

Another example of the inscriptions of the Mahameghavagana dynasty emerged at Guntupalle as a pillar inscription occurring on each of the four pillars of a *mandapa* associated with a stupa at the site. Its text, according to I.K. Sarma's reading (Sarma 1988, p. 68) is the following: "gift of mandapa by Maharaja Sri Sata or Sada, lord of the Kalinga-Mahishaka countries and belonging to Mahameghavahana dynasty. The scribe of the record is Kshudra Goma, i.e. Goma, the younger". Palaeographically, Sarma puts this in the 2nd-1st century BC, and *Mahishaka* country has been interpreted by him as the Krishna delta. From their core Kalinga base, i.e., Ganjam-Srikakulam base, it was easy for the Mahameghavahana kings to take possession of the Krishna delta, at least for some time.

One also recalls that the term for this area in the two separate edicts of Dhauli is *Tosali* which, as we shall see below, was by no means a rare term in the history of inscriptions from this region. However, in this section, our problem has been to pinpoint the location of Kalinga and suggest on that basis an area where the battle of Kalinga is likely to have taken place.

V.3. Possible Place of the Kalinga Battle

If one thinks of an ancient invasion from modern Patna (Pataliputra) to the modern Ganjam-Srikakulam zone (ancient Kalinga), which the Asokan invasion of Kalinga undoubtedly was, one has an exact later parallel in the invasion of the area by Samudragupta. About 600 years later than Asoka, Samudragupta's ambition was not limited only to the Ganjam-Srikakulam tract. He proceeded along the coast, possibly right up to Nellore, and took a cross-country march from there to invade Kanchipuram. To move with an army along a thousand kilometre long coast-line, far from the home-base, was a great feat of arms, and Vincent Smith's appellation of Samudragupta as an Indian Napoleon (Smith 1924) is no doubt an example of a very apt analogy.

Among the Dakshinapatha kings whom Samudragupta first defeated and then showed the favour of releasing, King Mahendra of Kosala is mentioned first, thus showing that the Gupta king came via modern Chhattisgarh or ancient 'South Kosala'. In the 8th century, its capital was Sirpur, but in the 4th century, its capital is likely to have been Malhar whose antiquity, as I have elsewhere argued, presumably goes back to the Mahajanapada period. The next in the line of his royal adversaries was Vyaghraraja of Mahakantara (literally, a very large forest tract) which denotes, at least partly, the forest kingdom of Bastar. This forest area falls on the way from the Raipur section of Chhattisgarh to Vizianagram of Andhra. The details of the areas, which were subsequently mentioned in Samudragupta's Allahabad inscription, are not necessary here, but on the whole, his coastal march from the Ganjam-Srikakulam section, where he arrived from Chhattisgarh and Bastar, to the area south of the Krishna and Kanchipuram through the modern East and West Godavari districts is clear (for details, Chhabra and Gai 1981, pp. 12-20).

It is no more than a hypothesis that Asoka 's army came from Pataliputra to the Ganjam-Srikakulam section or ancient Kalinga by a route which was used much later by Samudragupta. It is, nonetheless, an acceptable hypothesis, because both these monarchs came from Pataliputra and both had Kalinga in their purview. If one travels from Chhattisgarh to the Andhra coast today, one first reaches the modern Vizianagram area of Andhra. For the Ganjam-Srikakulam area, one has to turn east along the coastal belt. There is no other option. This is true now and must have been true in the Mauryan context as well.

Here one has to think of another acceptable hypothesis. The battle for Delhi used to take place not in Delhi but at Panipat which lies on the way to Delhi but is still separated from it by some distance. One presumes that the battle for the Mauryan possession of Kalinga took place in an area between Vizianagram and the ancient Dantapuri which lies to the east of the modern town of Srikakulam. The Mauryan army was most likely to have been confronted by the force of Kalinga in this stretch. For what it is worth, it has to be noted that there is a place called *Ranasthalam* ('the place of battle') between Srikakulam and Vizianagram, which lies on the highway between these two places. Ranasthalam (18-12-13 N/83-41-26 E) is the centre of a modern 'mandal taluk'. Whether this was the place where Asoka's battle for Kalinga was fought or not cannot, of course, be satisfactorily determined, but there is, as we have seen, an acceptable logic to argue that this battle could take place only between Vizianagram and Dantapuri or modern Dantavrukanagara. If so, the term *Ranasthalam* makes sense as the actual place of battle. On the other hand, there is no geographical justification to think that the battle for Kalinga took place in the outskirts of Bhuvanesvar.

4

The Edicts from Vidarbha, Bairat (Calcutta-Bairat or Bhabru Edict), Afghanistan and the Northwest, and the Barabar Hills

I. VIDARBHA

Two relevant inscriptions have been reported from Vidarbha, one in 1878 and the other in 1987-88.

I.1. The Inscription from Deotek in the Chandrapur District

This example, first noticed by Beglar (1878, pp. 123-125), comes from a ruined Siva temple of c.4th century AD at Deotek, about 22 miles or about 35 km southeast of Pauni in the Wainganga valley. The inscribed piece of rock which contains two inscriptions is 9 feet long and 3 feet 6 inch to 2 feet 10 inch wide. The first inscription, which consists of four lines, occupies 'the middle half' of the stone and possess characters 'of the kind known as those of the Asoka edicts'. The second inscription, later analysed by V.V. Mirashi (1960: 109-117), belonged to the Vakataka king Rudrasena I of the 4th century AD and recorded the construction of a religious place or temple (*dharmasthanam*) at Chikambari. A part of the first inscription was chiselled off to make room for the second.

Mirashi was inclined to refer the first inscription to the age of Asoka. The characters are early Brahmi, "resembling in many cases those of the Girnar edicts of Asoka". The language is early Prakrit, "the same dialect being used as in the Girnar edicts. Most of the words are either identical

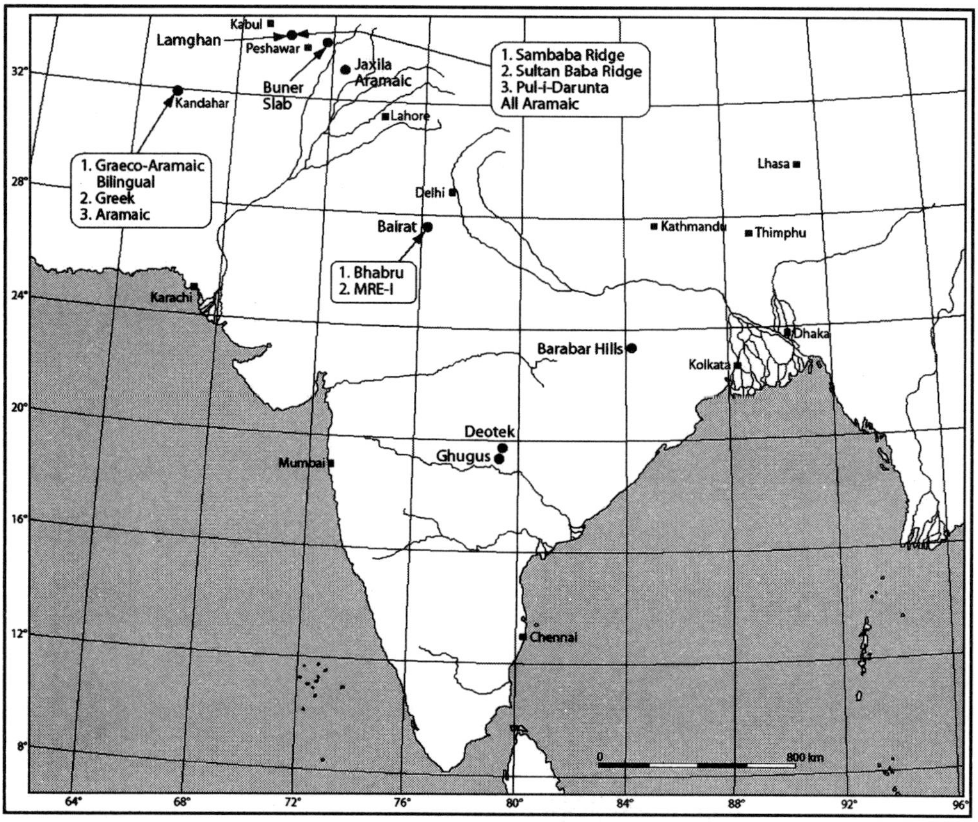

Map 3. Major sites mentioned in Chapter 4.

with those used in the latter or similarly formed". Mirashi has published his reading of the four available lines of this inscription, and his final comments are the following:

> Owing to the loss of nearly a half of this record, it is not possible to give a detailed account of the contents. However, there remains fortunately sufficient portion of it to indicate that its object was to record the command of some lord (*Sami*) (who is called 'king' in l.4), prohibiting the capture and slaughter (evidently of some animals in certain seasons as in Asoka's fifth pillar edict, or, may be, throughout the year) and declaring some punishment for such as dared disobey it. The third line mentions executive officers whose duty may have been to enforce these orders. The last line contains the date, 14, denoting possibly the regnal year in which the record was incised.

The inscription does not mention, directly or indirectly, Asoka but the facts that it prohibits slaughter of animals and calls it a punishable offence and that both palaeographically and linguistically, it fits in the category of Asokan inscriptions, may suggest that the edict was issued, at the royal behest, by a local or regional 'lord' or *Svami* during Asoka's reign.

I.2. The Untraceable Edict, Possibly from Ghugus, in the Chandrapur District

The xerox copy of a few lines engraved on a stone slab, reputedly found by an unidentified individual at Ghugus, reached Ajay Mitra Shastri in Nagpur. He published it in *Puratattva* 28 (1997-98), pp. 55-58, pointing out that "its contents and even the wording are those of the well-known Bairat stone-slab or Calcutta-Bairat inscription".

> The xerox contains only eight lines of writing in Asokan Brahmi with its characters sharing all the characteristics noted in Asokan Brahmi edicts.... The language is Magadhi Prakrit as in most other known Asokan edicts in India.... The record commences with the mention of the emperor Asoka as *Priyadarsi* the king of Magadha. He salutes the Buddhist order and enquires about its well-being. He next expresses his high esteem for the Buddha, *Dhamma* and *Sangha*, the well-known Buddhist trinity in the prescribed order. After that it is impossible to make out anything from the xerox though there is absolutely no doubt that many more lines must have followed.
>
> That it is definitely an inscription of Asoka is apparent from not only its palaeography but also from the phrase *Piyadasi laja* referring to Asoka at its beginning. Looking for comparable Asokan edicts, we find that its contents and even the wording are those of the well-known Bairat stone-slab or Calcutta-Bairat inscription. Like the latter, it commences with the expression *Piyadasi laja magadhe*. In fact, the preserved matter of the inscription is almost exactly identical with the first two lines of the latter (Mitra Shastri 1987-88, p. 56).

Regrettably, the relevant issue of *Puratattva* did not publish Shastri's xerox copy of the inscription, but there is no reason to doubt the veracity of his reporting and his reading and interpretation of the text.

I.3. Comments on the Vidarbha Finds

On the basis of Vasudev Vishnu Mirashi's and Ajay Mitra Shastri's opinions, the finds of two Asokan inscriptions in the Chandrapur district of Vidarbha cannot be doubted. At least they clearly proclaim the former existence of two such edicts in the Chandrapur section of Vidarbha. From the point of view of historical geography, the point to note is that Chandrapur lies on the route from Vidarbha to Andhra via the Wainganga valley. Its position on the route network is the following.

First, Chandrapur is linked to the route which goes from the Ganga plain to the Andhra part of the Deccan through Balaghat. In Vidarbha this route follows the Wainganga valley and crosses this river on the way to the Karimnagar section of Andhra at Pauni. Primarily, this route goes to Tripuri or the Jabbalpur area first and moves from there, through Seoni, to Balaghat or this route may also move to Balaghat through the Chhindwara area. Another route may come straight from the Hoshangabad section of the Narmada valley and move, through Betul, to the Saoner section north of Nagpur. For people keen on reaching the Andhra coast, this route also will take them to Chandrapur in the first instance. The route which also eventually originates in the Ganga plain but first touches the Chhattisgarh plain on the way to the Maharashtra section of the Deccan goes through the modern Raipur and Bhandara areas before proceeding further west to western Maharashtra. For the Andhra coast, this route bifurcates towards Karimnagar in Andhra in the Bhandara area. This route is the Wainganga valley route going through Pauni and with Chandrapur on the way.

The routes to Andhra through Chandrapur need not have only Karimnagar in sight. Nizamabad in Andhra, which contains the major early historic site of Bodhan, can also be approached from the north through Chandrapur. The former occurrence of Asokan inscriptions at Deotek and Ghugus (a small town to the west of Chandrapur) need not, in fact, come as a surprise.

II. CALCUTTA-BAIRAT

Cunningham (1877) described it as "second Bairat rock" which was found by Captain Burt in 1837 from below a canon-shaped rock on the top of a low hill by the side of an ancient road passing through Bairat. This rock forms an overhang and thus a rock-shelter. The edict is also known as 'Bhabru edict', Bhabru being the name of a village at some distance to the west of Bairat.

Hultzsch's version of its text is as follows:

(A) The Magadha king Priyadarsin, having saluted the Samgha hopes they are both well and comfortable.

(B) It is known to you, Sirs, how great is my reverence and faith in the Buddha, the Dharma (and) the Samgha.

(C) Whatsoever, Sirs, has been spoken by the blessed Buddha, all that is quite well spoken.

(D) But, Sirs, what would indeed appear to me (to be referred to by the words of the scripture): thus the true *Dharma* will be of long duration, that I feel bound to declare.

(E) The following expositions of the *Dharma*, Sirs, (viz.) (1) the *Vinaya-samukasa*, (2) the *Aliya-vasas*, (3) the *Anagata-bhayas*, (4) the *Muni-gathas*, (5) the *Moneya-suta*, (6) the *patisa-pasina*, and (7) the *Laghulovada* which was spoken by the blessed Buddha concerning falsehood, – I desire, Sirs, that many groups of monks and (many) nuns may repeatedly listen to these expositions of the *Dharma* and may reflect (on them).

(F) In the same way both laymen and laywomen (should act).

(G) For the following (purpose), Sirs, am I causing this to be written, (viz.) in order that they may know my intention.

Even in Cunningham's time, the hill was locally called 'Inscription Hill' or '*Bijak Pahar*'. He found the ruins on the top of this c.200 feet high hill in the form of two "contiguous level platforms, each 160 feet square, which are covered with broken bricks and the remains of brick walls". The upper platform is 30 feet higher than the lower one. The approach to this platform was on the south side where Cunningham found traces of a large entrance with a flight of stone steps.

D.R. Sahni's excavations at the site in 1935-36 revealed in the upper terrace two or three ranges of cells on each side of a central quadrangle, none of the excavated objects in this section being later than the second century AD. However, the more important part of the work was done in the lower terrace where Sahni investigated the remains of a circular Buddhist temple which was 27 feet in diameter and possessed a wall made alternatively of wood and brick and enclosed in turn by a circumambulatory passage. The entrance to the temple was from the eastern side.

> ... As this temple was undoubtedly the work of Asoka, the stupa may have contained a body relic of the Buddha. One or two bits of brick-work from the back of the stupa in question have survived in situ and I was also fortunate enough to find, both in and around this temple, fragments of a large stone umbrella of Asokan workmanship and a few fragments, which fit together, of a large bowl of the same material and similar technique (Sahni 1935-36, p. 85).

Equally importantly, Sahni (p. 86) goes on to write the following:

> My excavations here have revealed several thousands of pieces of polished and unpolished Chunar sandstone representing a portion of the debris of two Asokan pillars, which had been battered to pieces, probably by the Huns in the 6th century AD. These pieces included one large fragment from the junction of the upper polished and lower rough surface of the shaft of one of these pillars and another from the summit with the tapering hole which held a long and stout copper bolt to support the capital. One or two tiny pieces broken from a figure of lion show that the columns were as usual crowned with statues of one or the other four noble animals of the Buddhist texts ... The present excavations establish the former existence of two Asokan pillars at Bairat ...

Falk (2006) in his discussion on Bairat ignores these finds and observations of Sahni who excavated this site on behalf of the Jaipur (princely) State government. Those who are familiar with the manifold significance of Sahni's work in the history of Indian archaeology cannot peremptorily brush aside his field-observations, and we on our part would accept his judgement on the Bairat archaeological situation at its face-value.

At this point, we may draw attention to the find of a decorated stone umbrella and its long, decorated stone shaft, both in the ruins of Deur Kothar and Panguraria. The Deur Kothar examples were kept in the Archaeological Survey of India store room/museum at the site when we saw them in 2000, and we found the Panguraria specimens in the custody of the Archaeological Survey of India watchman in a neighbouring village called Budhni. The Panguraria stupa is most likely to be Asokan whereas the Deur Kothar stupa also goes undoubtedly back to the same period. The direct Asokan association with the Deur Kothar stupa is somewhat in doubt because the inscription written in Asokan Brahmi on the fragments of one or more polished monolithic sandstone pillars at the site is supposedly by a Buddhist monk. Deur Kothar has also revealed a stone stupa railing which, unlike the Bharhut stupa railing or other famous stupa railings of the period, was not ornamented in detail but certainly carried some simpler decorative motifs like lotus and water vessel. The early stage of the stupa embellishment tradition can be seen in the Mauryan period stupa remains of Deur Kothar and Panguraria, and from this point of view, there was no break or dichotomy between the art traditions of the Mauryan and Sunga periods.

Different parts of the Malwa plateau are easily accessible from Bairat. R.C. Agrawal (1962) noticed Bharhut-type stupa remains in a *chhatri* or mausoleum at Lalsot. These remains were apparently carried to Lalsot from somewhere else and incorporated in the mausoleum of the much later Rajput phase. However, the Dausa-Lalsot area apparently falls on an early trade route which in this case can easily go to Sawai Madhopur-Shivpuri-Jhansi sector, or from Lalsot, one can also travel to Morena, Gwalior, Datia and Jhansi. Secondly, from Bairat one can pass through the Jaipur area to reach Tonk, Bundi and the ancient city of *Madhyamika* or Nagari between Chitor and Kota. From the Kota sector, Mandasor in Madhya Pradesh is also easily accessible. The tie-up of Bairat is with the Delhi sector, and through Bairat one can take a direct route to Malwa.

III. AFGHANISTAN

III.1. Shahr-i-Kuna or Old Kandahar

III.1.1. Kandahar Graeco-Aramaic Bilingual Inscription

This inscription was discovered in 1958 and its Greek and Aramaic texts have been translated by various scholars including J. Filliozat (1961-62). It was found engraved on a block of rock in the area of Shahri-Kuna or Old Kandahar, south of the road to Herat via Girishk. Filliozat's translation of the Greek text is as follows:

> Ten years having elapsed (from his installation), King Piodasses has shown mankind (the way to) Piety. And since then he has rendered mankind more pious, and everything is thriving on the whole earth. And the king abstains from animals (i.e. meat), and all men including the king's huntsmen and fishermen have stopped hunting. And those who could not control themselves have ceased to do so as far as they could. And (having become) obedient to father and mother and to the elders, contrary to what happened before, they will, henceforward, by thus acting, lead a better and in every way more profitable life.

The same scholar's translation of the Aramaic version is as follows:

(Line 1) Ten years having elapsed (?), it happened (?) that our Lord Priyadarsi, the king, became the institutor of Truth.

(Line 2) Since then, evil diminished among all men, and all the misfortunes (?) he caused to disappear;

(Line 3) and upon all the earth (there are) peace (and) joy. And furthermore, (there is) this about food: for our Lord, the king,

(Line 4) a few (animals) are killed; seeing this, all the men ceased (killing animals), even (?) those who catch fish (i.e. the fishermen);

(Line 5) these men are subject to prohibition. Similarly, those who were without restraint have ceased

(Line 6) to be without restraint. And (there reigns) obedience to one's mother and to one's father and to old people

(Line 7) according to the obligations set on everyone by fortune. And there is no Judgement for all pious men.

(Line 8) This (i.e. the practice of the Law) has been profitable for all men and shall be still profitable.

This bilingual edict's similarity to Rock Edicts I and IV is unmistakable, and this is no doubt a concisely expressed version of the two, without being a word-for-word translation of them. Old Kandahar was the site of Alexandria of Arachosia which was established by Alexander. The Graeco-Aramaic edict was intended for Asoka's Greek (*Yonas*) and *Kamboja* (Iranian origin) subjects. The Kambojas are supposed to be the Iranian autochthons of the region where the Greek colonies were established.

III.1.2. Kandahar Greek Inscription

This inscription was found in 1963 in the ruins of Shahr-i-Kuna or Old Kandahar. The stone on which it was engraved is a rectangular block of porous limestone (45 cm high, 69.5 cm wide and 12-13 cm thick). D. Schlumberger and E. Benveniste (1967-68) translated it as follows:

> ... Piety and self-control in all schools (of thought). Now he is most master of himself who controls his tongue. And may they neither praise themselves nor blame other (schools) about anything; for this is vain, and it is better to praise other (schools) and to abstain from blaming them in any respect. In so doing they will extol themselves and gain the favour of the other (schools); in transgressing this, they will harm their reputation and estrange other (schools). They who praise themselves and blame other (schools) behave in a rather conceited way; in striving to outshine others they rather do harm to themselves. It is fit that people respect each other and accept each other's teachings. In so doing they will grow in knowledge, transmitting to each other whatever each of them knows. And there should be no hesitation in saying so to those who act accordingly, so that they will ever keep on living piously.
>
> In the eighth year of his reign Piodasses overwhelmed Kalinga. One hundred and fifty thousand persons were captured and deported, a hundred thousand others were killed and about as many died. Just as he had given orders to abstain from (consuming) living beings, he has been zealous in organizing Piety. And this he took with even more grief: the

> brahmans and sramans and all others who lived there (in Kalinga) practising Piety, – those who lived there had to mind the king's interests, to revere and respect master, fathers and mothers, to love and refrain from deceiving friends and companions, to treat as gently as possible slaves and servants, – if, of all those who thus behaved someone died or was deported, this to others felt it as a personal sorrow, and the king was deeply afflicted thereby. And, as amongst all other nations there are ...

This incomplete edict incorporates the greater part of the 12th major rock edict and the beginning section of the 13th rock edict. Obviously, two blocks of inscribed stone are missing, one containing the beginning of the 12th rock edict and another containing the rest of the 13th rock edict. Further, the Greek text is not "so much a translation, as a free and sometimes shortened adaptation from one of the Indian texts, faithful to the spirit and general meaning of Asoka's proclamation rather than to its wording" (Schlumberger and Benveniste 1967-68, p. 195). The Greek text displays correct and fluent literary Greek style of the period and it has been claimed that both language and writing "testify to the unity and vigour of Greek culture in the 3rd century BC" in this region.

The inscribed block deserves attention for another reason. According to Schlumberger and Benveniste (1967-68, p. 196), this is the first example of an Asokan inscription engraved on a stone wall which possibly was a retaining wall rather than a freestanding wall.

III.1.3. Kandahar Aramaic Inscription

Engraved on an irregularly shaped (24 cm wide, 18.5 cm high and 16 cm thick) block of limestone, this inscription in Aramaic script came to be known in the scholarly world in 1964 and came reputedly from the ruins of Old Kandahar or Shah-i-Kuna. Along with an inscription, also in Aramaic script and associated with Asoka, from the eastern Afghanistan area of Lamghan or ancient Lampak, which was reported by W.B. Henning in 1949 and known by 1932, this belongs to a special class of inscriptions, as S. Shaked (1969) emphatically pointed out. They are both bilingual inscriptions, but "the two languages are mixed, each short section in one language is followed by one in the other language. The two languages involved, both written in Aramaic characters, are Aramaic and Middle Indian (Prakrit). The text, as produced by B.N. Mukherjee (1984, p. 41), is as follows:

(Practice) [of Dhamma] – (so) it is said – to (?) ... and (or and which is) goodness[.] Whatever ... – (so) it is said – the world [has] to [follow] totally [and] the world has imitated – (so) it is said – ... and (they) have been caused to increase and [will continue to] be caused to increase for [i.e. in respect of] obedience totally ... – (so) it is said –, for [in respect of] obedience to precious [i.e. venerable] persons ... by proper regard (or respectful behaviour) to the aged ... to weak (persons) [and] to slaves.

Mukherjee's comment is that "the person or persons responsible for drafting the text of the inscription consulted and translated and transliterated portions of the Prakrit text of PE VII", although it was not followed in meticulous detail.

Thus, there are three Asokan inscriptions from Kandahar, all from the old part of the city or Shah-i-Kuna. The location of Kandahar immediately signifies movement (from the subcontinental side) through the Bolan pass. More than that, on the southern side, the Bolan pass was accessed from the side of Sind – from the Sibi plain which adjoins the Indus. Thus, in the Asokan or Mauryan scheme, the lower Indus valley or Sind was a major early historical area. Equally importantly, Kandahar plays a special role in the communication geography of Afghanistan. From Kandahar, the road goes to Farah in the west and from Farah to Herat. From Herat, the northern Afghan plain of Balkh or the area near Mazar-i-Sharif is easily accessible, but more significantly, Herat gives access to northeast Iran in the area of Meshed which lies on the route passing through northern Afghanistan, following closely the foothill zone of the Elburz mountain range. From Kandahar, one can also follow the Helmand valley to Zabul or Seistan area of Iran, thus joining the route going through southern Iran. This route eventually reaches the southern section of the Zagros range, passing through the areas of Bam, Kirman, Fars plain and eventually Luristan. Across the Zagros in the modern Ahvaz area, the route soon crosses over to the Basra area of modern Iraq, just as the northern Iranian route reaches the Iraqi plain through the defile of Behistun. The fact that Kandahar figured prominently in the Asokan scheme is a clear indication of the general significance of the links of contemporary India with West Asia in general. This is something which is also indicated by the references to the North African and Mediterranean kings in the edicts.

One may also be aware of the possibility that the lower Indus valley or Sind need not be the only spring-board of movements to Kandahar. The problem is that the early historic phase is a little known phase in the archaeology of Sind. It is just possible that during this phase the Bolan was not the only major route to reach Kandahar from the Indian side. Akra in Bannu is a proven major early historic city-site of the region, and it can be argued that during the Asokan times, Akra was mediating goods between Mauryan India and Kandahar through the Tochi-Kurram valley.

III.2. Lamghan / Pul-i-Darunta

Darunta is clearly marked a little to the west of Jalalabad on a detailed map of eastern Afghanistan. Jalalabad is reached from Peshawar by following the Khyber route. Darunta lies near the confluence of the Laghman and Kabul rivers. The province of Laghman (modern capital: Mehtarlam) lies basically along the Laghman river, which is joined upstream, successively, by the Alingar and the Alishing rivers. Geographically, the province of Laghman occupies a significant position because it is possible to have access to a number of areas from here. Kapisa, of which Begram was the centre, lies a little to the northwest of Lamghan or ancient *Lampaka*. Begram lies in a tributary valley of the Panjsher whereas Kapisa as a whole falls in the Panjsher valley. The Panjsher joins the Kabul river to the west of the Panjsher-Kabul confluence. From Begram, the route goes across the Hindukush to Kunduz from where the Oxus valley and the Kokcha valley, a tributary valley of the Oxus, are both accessible. Another route from Begram goes to the Mazar-i-Sharif area via Aibak and Kholm. From Mazar-i-Sharif, Balkh is approachable and so is a large segment of Central Asia including Uzbekistan and Turkmenistan. The fact that Asokan inscriptions have been found in the Lamghan sector is a conclusive proof of the fact that the Khyber pass route was being used during the Asokan times to reach Central Asia through Begram.

III.2.1. Lamghan Sultan Baba Ridge Inscription

This inscription on a vertical slab of stone near the top of the hill, locally called Sultan Baba, contains 6 lines of Aramaic letters. In B.N. Mukherjee's version, it is translated as follows:

(Lines 1-3) In the year 16, king Priyadarsi scattered abundantly (i.e. dispersed) and pushed out of (or expelled from) the prosperous (population) the lovers of what is hunting of creatures and fishes and what (i.e. that which) is worthless (or empty) work.

(Lines 3-5) 300 'bows' (measure) this mountain named Tdmr. This road is Krpty (Karapathi), (so) it is said. (From here) the garden is more than 120 (bows distant). Trt' is (from) here 100 (bows distant). The height (of the mountain is) 80 (bows) (or 'Trt' is (from) here (distant by) 100 in addition to 80 (bows).

(Line 6) With the judge (named) W'su.

III.2.2. Lamghan Sam Baba Ridge Inscription

About 2 km from Sultan Baba, there is a cliff called Sam Baba. The 10-line Aramaic inscription here was reported in 1973. B.N. Mukherjee's translation is as follows:

(Lines 1-5) In the month (of) Elul (Ululu) (of) the year 16 king Priyadarsi scattered abundantly (i.e. dispersed) (and) pushed out of (or expelled from) the prosperous (population) (those who) rush (after) what is hunting of fishes and creatures (and) the lovers of what (i.e. that which) is worthless (or empty work).

(Lines 5-8) 500 (?) 'bows' (measure) this mountain named 'hwty. This road (is) Krpty (Karapathi), (so) it is said. Towards the garden (the distance is) 300 (bows). Trt' is (from) here 13 (bows). The height (of the mountain) is 200 (bows) (or 'Trt is (from)here 13 (bows) in addition to 200 (bows).

(Lines 8-9). The scribe with (i.e. together with) Wsu the judge (and) the pure (one).

(Line 10). Whsu, the dispenser of meritorious work, the governor, the pure (one) (and) (settler of guilt and punishment?)

There are overwhelming similarities between these two inscriptions. They begin with Asoka's stoppage of the slaughter of animals and fishes at the expiry of 16 years after his coming to power. The Sam Baba edict also draws attention to his displeasure with the people who did worthless or empty work. In the second section, both inscriptions put forward certain measurements, but the places mentioned still remain to be satisfactorily identified. Some scholars postulate a reference to the Royal Road to West Asia in this section, but the issue is not yet settled. The 'judge' Wsu/Whsu was mentioned as the executor of the royal dictates or as the Mauryan governor of the region. There is a reference to the scribe in the second edict but he is not mentioned by name.

It is probable that Lamghan was a part of the Kamboja territory which figures under the rubric *Yonas* and *Kambojas* in the Asokan edicts, the *Yonas* falling under the territory of Kandahar. Mukherjee further points out that the unit of measurement mentioned as 'bows' is identical with *Dhanus* or 'bow' mentioned in certain ancient Indian texts as a measure of length.

III.2.3. The Third Asokan Inscription (in Aramaic) from Laghman

Found inscribed in Aramaic on a stone fragment (10"x8") in the neighbourhood of Pul-i-Darunta, Laghman, it was noted first in a Persian language periodical in 1932. It was discussed in detail by W.B. Henning in 1949 since when it has been been studied by several scholars, Mukherjee among them. The translation that one finds in Mukherjee (1884, p. 30) is as follows:

Line 1. (No?) living being (is to be) fattened (with other living being?)...

Line 2. ... To be to people (i.e. existing people)...

Line 3. ... To be seen – it is said – not (good) ...,

Line 4. (...increase) of this object (i.e. practice of Dharma) – it is said (caused) to increase...,

Line 5. ... To see, to be seen – it is said ...,

Line 6. ... Of (meaning 'by') the Beloved of the Gods (when) consecrated (for eight years) – it is said ....,

Lines 7-8.... In (outlying) towns – it is said (.) (All these instructions) were set (or put) to write (or writing on pillar(s) (so that) they were (i.e. would be) made known (to) whoever were (i.e. would be) descendants(.)

The interesting part of this Aramaic inscription is that it contains some Prakrit words found in several Asokan rock edicts and pillar edicts. The pillar edicts represent PE V and PE III, and the relevant rock edicts are RE IV, RE V, RE IX and RE XIII. Thus, the inscription is more Indo-Aramaic than exclusively Aramaic.

IV. THE TAXILA PILLAR INSCRIPTION IN ARAMAIC

L.D. Barnett (1915) published it first, and in his letter (quoted by Barnett) to Barnett, John Marshall, the excavator of Taxila, writes that "the inscription was carved on an octagonal pillar of white marble"and "it was discovered in a house of the first century BC, and must have been buried in its present worn and broken condition, before the beginning of our era". The fourth edition of Marshall's *A Guide to Taxila* (1960) contains the following observation by him (Marshall 1960, p. 74):

> The record is fragmentary, but there is enough to indicate that the pillar was set up in honour of a high official named Romedote at the time when the crown-prince Asoka, here referred to by his well-known title of Priyadarsi, was governor of Taxila on behalf of his father Bindusara.

The translation by Mukherjee (1984, p. 26) seems to differ substantially from what was inferred by Marshall.

(Lines 1-6). ... for the creations of Law, unto the non-injury to (the creatures) worthy of that which (is) the non-injury and to his (i.e. one's own) father (and) the aged good obedience(.)

(Lines 6-7) This (and) that (i.e. various kinds of practice of Law (have) good (or many (fold) or much) increase.

(Lines 8-12) This document (or (this) good document) exists (until) our lord Priyadarsi dies ... and also (until after) his son ... belonging to our lord Priyadarsi(.)

V. THE BUNER/TAKHT-I-BAHI STONE SLAB INSCRIBED IN ASOKAN BRAHMI

This inscription in Asokan Brahmi occurs on a 24 cm high and 14 cm wide (about 3 cm thick) piece of dark schist and has only three lines of letters visiblc. K.R. Norman (1988) reads them as *nampiye piya bhisitename ye setama,* which exactly agrees with portions of the first three lines of PE VI:

> *(deva)nampiye piya (dasilajahevamaha duvadasa vasaa) bhisitename (dhammalipilikhapita lokasa hitasukha) ye setama (pahatatamtam-dhammavadhipapora).*

The words which figure both in this slab and the full version of PE VI are underlined in the above extract.

The example does not come from a known context. It came from a private collection in Karachi and was originally acquired in Buner or Takht-i-Bahi. It seems to be better known as the Buner slab. Doubts have been expressed (cf. Falk 2006, p. 291) about the genuineness of this find, especially because the script used is Brahmi and not Kharosthi, as it should be in the northwestern region. It is not that forgeries are unknown in the world of subcontinental antiquities, but forgeries are generally inspired by the strong commercial value of the original items. In this case, the profit motif of the private collector in question cannot be said to be high, and on the whole the Buner slab may be given the benefit of the doubt.

If the specimen comes from Buner, that will mean that it lay on the route which went northeast from Peshawar to Chitral-Gilgit and eventually to Central Asia. The Asokan period link with the region in question has also been suggested by the locations of Shahbazgarhi and Manserah edicts. If the specimen comes from Takht-i-Bahi in the Peshawar plain, one need not be surprised by the occurrence because, as we have seen, Asokan edicts occur near Jalalabad which is only a little beyond the Khyber pass near Peshawar. The only reason why this specimen can be considered suspect because this shows the use of Brahmi in what is essentially a non-Brahmi area. However, there can always be exceptions. One recalls the occurrence of a Kharosthi inscription of c.3rd century BC at Khaniara in a valley below the modern town of Dharamsala in Kangra, which does not otherwise belong to the Kharosthi belt of inscriptions.

VI. BARABAR HILLS

The three cave inscriptions of Asoka in this complex of hills about 25 km to the north of Gaya occur in the three caves locally known as Sudama, Visva Jhopri and Karna Chopar. The most famous of the Barabar hill complex of caves, the Lomash Rishi cave which shows a row of elephants along the architrave of its entrance door, does not bear any Asokan inscription, although there is no doubt its being Mauryan because of the polished character of the straight walls of its outer room. The Karna Chopar cave shows a single vaulted room with a plain but polished interior. The inscription (Hultzsch 1925, p. 181) states that "when king Priyadarsin had been anointed nineteen years, this cave in the very pleasant Khalatika mountain was given" by him "for shelter during the rainy season". Whether this was given exclusively to the Ajivikas, the sect established by the Buddha's and Mahavira's contemporary Makkhali Gosala, is not clear but there is no doubt about its being intended as a place where the monks, the Ajivikas or not, would spend the monsoon months. The three other caves have a larger outer room with vaulted roof and a circular inner room with hemispherical domed roof. In the case of the Sudama cave, the interior is plain but highly polished. In the case of the Visva Jhopri cave, the outer room is polished throughout but the inner room is rough and unfinished. In the case of the Lomash Rishi cave, the inner room is unfinished and so also are the floor and the roof of its outer room. The Sudama cave or, as the inscription calls it, the Banyan cave (*Nigoha-Kubha*) was given to the Ajivikas by 'king Priyadarsin (when he had been) anointed twelve years'. The inscription in the Visva Jhopri cave states that when King Priyadarsin had been anointed twelve years, this cave in the Khalatika mountain was given to the Ajivikas by him.

These are straightforward donatory records but what is interesting is that in the case of two of these Asokan caves – the Visva Jhopri and Lomash Rishi caves – there is much which is unfinished. The Visva Jhopri cave, in fact, bears one of the inscriptions. This simple fact suggests that the task of engraving inscriptions at particular places was not undertaken under close royal supervisions. The task was, apparently, entrusted to the royal officials who for various reasons did not think it fit to complete the caves meant for the Ajivika or other categories of monks.

5

The Seven Pillar Edicts and Various Related Issues

The pillars which bear Asoka's inscriptions form a distinct category of material remains in Indian archaeology. They are made from a single block of stone, freestanding and not based on any platform or supported by any other way at the ground level. The shaft rises straight from the ground and tapers up to an inverted lotus capital. The base of the inverted capital is a rope-like plain or adorned circle which gives way to a round or rectangular abacus above. The sides of the abacus can be plain or carry a frieze adorned with animals and 'wheels of law'. Single animals (cf. a bull, a lion and an elephant) or addorsed lions are at the top of the column, seated or standing firmly on the abacus. Occasionally, there can be bead-and-reel motifs immediately below the inverted lotus capital, and variations can also be observed in the frieze on the sides of, or around, the abacus. The capital portion is hewn out of a solid block of stone and joined to the column by a copper bolt, a specimen of which has been found at Rampurva.

The monolithic columns such as these do not occur in any other phase of Indian history. The examples (cf. Latia near Banaras), where the capital is not a piece separate from the column but only a continuation of the same, cannot be put in this category. In such cases, the capital and other components were hewn out of the same piece of monolithic rock. There is also no question of a Mauryan column having a base, at least at the ground level. Further, the Mauryan columns were never divided into separate

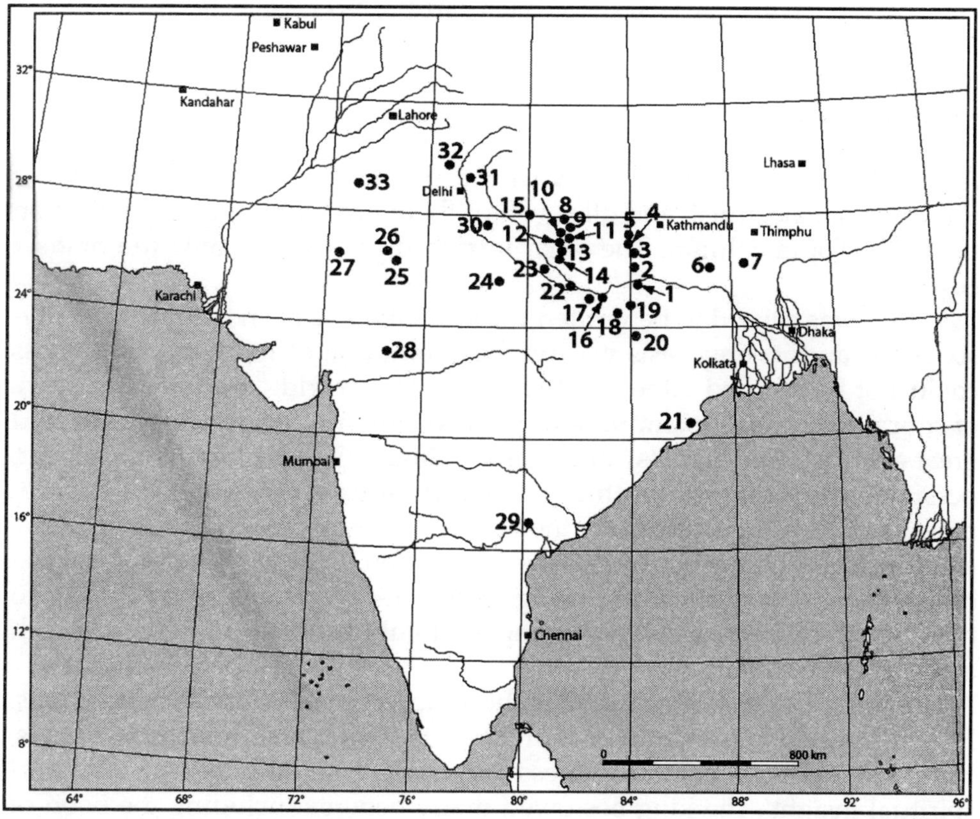

Map 4. Major sites mentioned in Chapter 5. 1. Pataliputra, 2. Kolhua, 3. Lauriya Araraj, 4. Lauriya Nandangarh, 5. Rampurva, 6. Sikligarh, 7. Mahasthangarh, 8. Tilaurakot, 9. Rummindei, 10. Gotihawa, 11. Nigliva, 12. Bansi, 13. Bhagalpur (opposite Khairadih), 14. Khairadih, 15. Ayodhya, 16. Varanasi, 17. Sarnath, 18. Ahraura (Belkhara), 19. Prahladpur, 20. Bakraur, 21. Bhuvaneswar , 22. Allahabad (Queen's edict, Kausambi edict), 23. Kausambi, 24. Deur Kothar, 25. Sanchi, 26. Udayagiri (Gwalior), 27. Sodanga (Ujjayini) 28. Bhopal, 29. Amaravati, 30. Sankisa, 31. Delhi-Meerat, 32. Delhi-Topra, 33. Hissar, Fatehabad.

segments and then joined together. This does away with the claim of the pillar fragments found on the top of a hilly plateau overlooking Chunar being components of Mauryan pillars. It is likely that the Chunar examples were either dressed cylinders of stone, which were fashioned into sculptures at the Gupta and post-Gupta period sculptural workshops at Sarnath or shafts of oil-presses, the like of which can still be seen in the Banaras countryside.

I. THE CONTENTS OF THE SEVEN PILLAR EDICTS (AFTER HULTZSCH 1925)

I.1. Pillar Edicts I-V

All these seven edicts begin with the preamble: "King *Devanampriya Priyadarsi* speaks thus" and all seven of them are found engraved only on the Delhi-Topra column. The other inscribed pillars bear only the first six edicts.

PE I was caused to be written when Asoka had been anointed twenty-six years, and its emphasis was on the promotion of morality. Happiness could not be secured either in this or the next world "without great love of morality, careful examination, great obedience, great fear of sin and great energy". His "agents" of all ranks – high, low and middle – strove to persuade even the unmindful or fickle persons to go along the path of morality. The same was true of the king's *Mahamatras* (or 'judicial officers') employed among the borderers. The instruction to these agents and judicial officers was "to protect according to morality, to dispose according to morality, to cause pleasure according to morality and to guard their speech according to morality".

Stating in the beginning that the practice of morality is meritorious, PE II lists the components of morality: "few sins, many virtuous deeds, compassion, liberality, truthfulness and purity". In addition to the 'gift of spiritual insight', the king bestowed many benefits including the boon of life on 'bipeds and quadrupeds', including birds and aquatic animals. This particular edict was put up in order that people might conform to its injunctions and ideas for a long time.

PE III points out that, while people are aware of the virtuous deeds done by them, they do not own up their performance of evil deeds which are basically caused by fierceness, cruelty, anger, pride and envy. The royal aim was to make people perform deeds which would lead to happiness both in this and the other worlds.

The focus of PE IV, issued twenty-six years after the king had been anointed, is the action of the class of officers known as the *Lajukas* and some aspects of judicial proceedings. Empowered by the royal order to act fearlessly and confidently to administer both punishment and reward to, and act in the interest of the welfare and happiness of, the "many thousands of men" they were supposed to look after, the *Lajukas* could be compared to intelligent nurses employed to effectively look after children. They should be impartial both in judicial proceedings and the awards of punishments. Even for those already convicted and even condemned to death, there should be a respite of three days so that appeal could be lodged by their relatives to the *Lajukas* to rescind their order, and even if such appeals were unsuccessful, the convicted ones could distribute gifts or undergo fasts to attain merit and thus attain happiness in the next world. The aim was to promote moral practices such as self-control and the distribution of gifts among people.

The interpretation of this edict has drawn some comments from K.R. Norman (1975) who doubts if Asoka could maintain death sentence as punishment in view of his belief in the sanctity of life.

PE V, issued twenty-six years after the king had been anointed, lists the birds and animals which were declared inviolable by him: "parrots, *mainas*, the *aruna*, ruddy geese, wild geese, the *nandimukha*, the *gelata*, bats, queen-ants, terrapins, boneless fish, the *vedaveyaka*, the *Ganga-Puputaka*, skate fish, tortoises and porcupines, squirrels (?), the *srimara*, bulls set at liberty, iguanas (?), the rhinoceros, white doves, domestic doves, (and) all the quadrupeds which are neither useful nor edible". She-goats, ewes and sows which had cubs or were in milk were made similarly inviolable. The cubs below the age of six months were inviolable. Male chickens or cocks were not to be castrated, and husks containing living beings were not to be burnt. Fire could not be set to forests either to burn them down needlessly or to kill the living beings in them. Living animals were not supposed to be fed with other living animals. Fish was inviolable and not meant to be sold on some specific days of the calendar ("the three *Chaturmasis* and on the *Tishya* full-moon during three days, viz., the fourteenth, the fifteenth and the first *tithi)* and "on every fast-day". No animal in the 'elephant-park' and 'the preserves of the fishermen' was supposed to be killed on the same days. Again, bulls must not be castrated on "the eighth *tithi* of every fortnight, on the fourteenth, on the fifteenth, on *Tishya*, on *Punarvasu*, on the three *Chaturmasis* and on festivals". He-goats, rams, boars and whatever other animals are castrated must not be castrated 'on *Tishya*, on *Punarvasu*, on the *Chaturmasis*' and the horses and bullocks were not to be branded 'during the fortnight of every *Chaturmasi*'.

According to this PE, the king ordered the release of prisoners twenty-five times since he had been anointed.

I.1.1. Notes on the Birds, Fishes and Animals Mentioned in PE V

The identification of birds, fishes and animals, which has been quoted above, is based on Hultzsch. However, identifications such as these are always fraught with problems, and unanimity of opinion is seldom possible.

For instance, K.R. Norman (1967) decided to identify the birds and animals mentioned in this PE quite differently. While there is no dispute regarding parrots and *mainas, aruna* has been taken as an adjective of the ruddy geese or *Chakravaka*. Norman interprets *Nandimukha* as a kind of water-bird and *Gelata* could mean, according to him, reddish duck or pink-headed duck. 'Terrapins' and 'bone-less fish' in Hultzsch's translation could mean, according to Norman, turtles and tortoises, whereas *Jatuka ambakipilaka,* translated as bats and queen-ants by Hultzsch could stand, according to Norman, for the water-bird 'bronze-winged jacana'. The other items in Norman's list are water-snakes, Gangetic dolphins, sea-cows, pangolins, snakes, black cobra, lizard, house-lizard or gecko and white pigeon.

Norman argues that instead of Hultzsch's 'random list of animals' one gets, if one follows his identifications, a kind of systematic list: "(a)two talking birds whose names are frequently linked together; (b) a series of aquatic birds including a water-haunting bat; (c) a series of aquatic animals, (d) a series of reptiles, legged and legless"; and "(e) three birds of the pigeon/dove family". One wonders, however, why snakes and even black cobra should be put in the list of 'inviolable' animals by Asoka or if he really had wanted to put up a systematic list.

Far more important than the controversial identifications of the specified members of the animal, bird and fish kingdom, was the royal concern with what may be interpreted in the modern context as conservation laws.

In the case of fish, this concern was analysed marvellously clearly by Sundar Lal Hora (1950). He begins by arguing that the species of fish referred to in the Pillar Edict V included the following:

1. *Anathikamachhe* = sharks, boneless fishes.
2. *Vedaveyake* = eels, fishes easily eluding grasp.
3. *Gamgapuputake* = porpoise, fish-like animal with lumpy body.
4. *Samkujamachhe* = skate or ray, fishes moving by contracting and expanding their bodies.
5. *Kaphatasayake* = globe fish, fish-like porcupine and feigning death when in danger.

Hora points out that there is even in modern times "strong prejudice against eating the flesh of the five varieties of animals enumerated above. There are, however, sound reasons in certain cases. For instance, globe fishes and their allies are poisonous and should not be eaten. Unless properly treated, the flesh of sharks, rays, and skates is bitter to taste and gritty on account of the deposition of uric acid crystals in their flesh" (Hora 1950, p. 49).

Hora also believes that the correct translation of the edict's relevant term *Tisu Chatummasisu* should be "third *Chaturmasi*". This should not mean 'three *Chaturmasis*', as has been generally supposed. In this he follows the opinion of B.M. Barua:

> Asoka's expression *tisu chatummasisu* cannot but mean the three full moon days that occurred in *Asadha, Karttika,* and *Phalguna,* at the end of the three four-monthly seasons and were observed in the Middle Country as holidays.

According to Hora, this is the correct interpretation of the dates mentioned in PE V. Otherwise, the injunction does not make much sense in the light of the present-day knowledge of fisheries of the Indian rivers. Assuming that in ancient times the Indian annual calendar commenced in the month of *Agrahayana* (November-December), the third four-monthly period (*Sravana* or July-August, *Bhadra* or August-September, *Asvina* or September-October, and *Kartika* or October-November) would cover the whole of the rainy season.

"If my contention is correct that the catching of fish was prohibited during the third *Chaturmasi* on the 14th and 15th day of the moon and the first day after the full moon, then the close periods are based on a remarkable insight into the breeding habits of the common food fishes of the fresh waters of India. The most important groups of fishes are the Carps, such as Catla (*Catla catla*), Rohita (*Labeo rohita*), Mrigal (*Cirrhima mrigala*), Calbaus (*Labeo calbasu*), etc.; Silond (*Silonia silondia*); Pangas (*Pangasius pangasius*), Vacha (*Eutropiichthys vacha*), etc., and the Hilsa (*Hilsa ilisha*). All these fishes breed in the rainy season when the rivers are flooded. Usually the heavy breeding occurs during July and August, but depending on the early or late rains, the breeding may start in June or may last up to September also. One further thing which has come to light in recent years, though it has not yet been firmly established, is that the breeding is influenced by the phases of the moon or in other words there is a lunar periodicity in the reproduction of the principal freshwater fishes of India. The principal fishery of Hilsa, for instance, is round about the full moon and the new moon periods and the breeding of Carps, so far recorded or observed, has also been round about the same periods and the eighth day" (Hora 1950, p. 51).

Hora (1950, p. 53) sums up Asoka's fishery laws as follows:

1. No fish should be caught on the 14th and 15th day of the moon and the first day after the full moon during the period of the third *Chaturmasi*. This will mean 12 days.

2. No fish should be caught on the 14th and 15th days of the moon and the first day after the full moon of the month of *Pausha* (December-January) = 3 days.
3. No fish should be caught on the fast days – *Amavasya* or the day before new moon and the *Ashtami* or the eighth day during every fortnightly period of the moon = 12+24 = 36 days.
4. No tank fish (animals in the preserves of fishermen) should be taken during the aforementioned days.

The total number of days on which fish could not be caught thus amounted to 51 days in a year, according to Hora's calculation. However, B.M. Barua calculates that the total number of such days in a year would be 72 days. This was "calculated at the rate of 3 days in every lunar half-month, viz., the first, the eighth, and the full or new moon" and including the three *Chaturmasi* and *Taisha* full moon days in the list of full moon days throughout the year.

Hora points out that besides the principal food fishes, there are other varieties which do not breed during the rainy season but at other times of the year. According to him, Asoka spread prohibition in driblets over the whole year and thus assured that no undue hardship was caused to his fish-eating subjects. Barua has also pointed out that Asoka's injunction broadly follows the restriction on the slaughter of animals in Kautilya's *Arthasastra* (XIII.5). According to Kautilya, the king should prohibit in a conquered territory the slaughter of animals for half a month during the period from July to September, to which he should add four nights on full moon days and one night to mark the royal birth anniversary or the date of the royal conquest of the concerned territory. Thus, in PE V Asoka was not laying an injunction which was way beyond the general practice in ancient India and his concern with non-violence or the killing of living beings does not seem to be the only guiding spirit in this case.

Hora's emphasis was only on fishes, but by prohibiting animal slaughter in the rainy season and certain other days of the year, Asoka's laws foreshadowed in a way some of the corresponding laws of British and later India when hunting was generally prohibited and the forests 'closed' in the rainy months. In fact, 'gun licenses' in the Indian countryside used to specifically mention the birds and animals which could not be shot in their breeding seasons. Possibly they do so even now.

I.2. Pillar Edicts VI-VII

PE VI, issued twenty-six years after the king had been anointed, mentions that visiting people personally was his 'principal duty' and that all sects had been honoured by him with honours of various kinds. He directed his attention to all classes of people – not only his relatives but also those near and far. The purpose was to bring happiness to them. The 'rescripts on morality', which he issued after he had been anointed twelve years, aimed at promoting the welfare, happiness and morality among people.

PE VII, which is available only in the Delhi-Topra version, was issued twenty-seven years after the king had been anointed. It begins by saying that, although the kings in the earlier times had tried to promote morality among their subjects, there was no adequate progress of morality. To overcome this, the king *Devanampiya* issued proclamations on morality, and ordered instructions in morality to be given by his agents who were concerned with people and given the duty of exhorting them to the paths of morality and explaining morality to them. The *Lajukas*, who were supposedly occupied with "many thousands of men", were mentioned first as these agents. For the same purpose, the king set up pillars on morality, issued proclamations on morality and appointed *Mahamatras* of morality who had manifold tasks in relation to the adherents of various religions and faith: the affairs of the *Samgha* or the Buddhist church and of the Brahmanas, *Ajivakas* and *Nirgranthas* or Jainas, and also of various other sects.

The *Mahamatras* and many other royal officers were occupied with the delivery of gifts made by the king and his queens and *harem* to the worthy recipients both in the royal court and the provinces. They were also entrusted with the task of delivering similar gifts made by his sons and other queens' sons.

Morality comprised compassion, liberality, truthfulness, purity, gentleness and goodness. Through the propagation of morality, the people had been made to progress by offering obedience to mother and father, the elders and the aged. They were also made to progress by practising courtesy to the Brahmanas and Sramanas, the poor and the distressed, and even to the slaves and servants.

The progress of morality was achieved both by imposing moral restrictions and bringing about conversions. The moral restrictions were less significant in comparison with conversions. The king's injunction regarding the inviolable status of certain animals is an example of moral restrictions but there are also cases of many other moral restrictions which were imposed by the king. By conversion, the progress of morality was promoted more widely or considerably because it led to the people abstaining from hurting living beings and from killing animals.

The king hoped that his injunctions would last as long as his sons and great-grandsons would reign or the sun and the moon would shine.

Happiness in this and the next worlds would result from following these injunctions.

This 'rescript on morality' was caused to be written when the king had been anointed twenty-seven years, and for their long-lasting duration, such 'rescripts on morality' should be engraved where stone pillars or stone slabs are available.

II. THE LOCATIONS OF ASOKAN PILLARS IN THE ACCOUNTS OF FA-XIAN AND XUANG-XANG (HIUEN-TSANG)

Fa-Xian visited India in AD 399-414 and Zuang-Zang in AD 629-645, leaving behind in their narratives references to columns which distinctly recall those built by Asoka and were in fact stated by the Chinese pilgrims to have been erected by him. We are indebted to V.A. Smith (1909c) for bringing out the significance of these records in the study of the present distribution of Asokan pillars.

II.1. THE TESTIMONY OF FA-XIAN

Fa-Xian mentioned three Asokan pillars, one in Sankisa and two in Pataliputra. In Sankisa, where the Buddha descended from heaven by a ladder, Asoka had built a temple, and behind this, he erected a stone pillar with a lion on the top of it. According to Smith's calculation of the height mentioned by Fa-Xian, the pillar was "equivalent to 40 or 50 English feet in height". To the south of a stupa and monastery complex built by Asoka about half a mile to the south of Pataliputra, there was a stone pillar which was 14 or 15 cubits in circumference and more than 30 cubits high. It contained an inscription which stated that Asoka donated *Jambudvipa* or his entire kingdom to the general body of monks and redeemed it by giving money three times.

Near this monastic complex in Pataliputra, Asoka had also built a city called *Ne-le*, near which there was a more than 30 feet high pillar with a lion sitting on the top. This pillar carried an inscription giving the date of the building of *Ne-le*.

II.2. THE TESTIMONY OF XUANG-XANG

In the course of his travels, Xuang-Xang saw no less than 15 Asokan pillars. There was one in Sankisa or Kapitha, with a crouching lion on the top. The east gate of the Jetavana monastery in Sravasti had two Asokan pillars, one on each side of the entrance and both 70 feet high. The one on the right side of the gate was surmounted by a sculptured wheel and the one on the left was surmounted by a bull. The third Sravasti pillar reputedly lay to the northwest of Jetavana, but, as Smith points out, there seems to be a confusion about the relevant passage of Xuang-Xang. The 30 feet high fourth pillar lay in front of the stupa dedicated to the memory of Krakuchhanda or one of the past Buddhas, about 10 miles to the south of Kapilavastu or modern Piprahwa. At the birth place of another past Buddha, Kanakamuni, which was 6 miles to the northeast of Karkuchhanda's place, there was another Asokan pillar, about 20 feet high and crowned by a lion. The Rummindei or Lumbini pillar had a horse on the top but its shaft was broken by lightning. At Kusinagara there were two pillars, one by the side of the temple containing the recumbent image of the dying Buddha and the other at the spot where the Buddha's mortal relics were divided among themselves by eight kings. Both of them reputedly carried inscriptions about the events they were supposed to commemorate. There was a pillar to the northeast of Banaras, to the west of the Barna or Baruna river. The pillar to mark the spot where the Buddha had first turned the wheel of the law in Sarnath was about 70 feet high. To the east, possibly in the area of modern Chhapra, there was a stone pillar surmounted by a lion in front of an Asokan stupa. The pillar was recorded as 20 feet high but this may be due to the fact that it had got partly buried. To the north of the 'monkey tank' at Vaisali, there was a 50-60 feet high pillar surmounted by a lion. Like his predecessor Fa-Xian, Xuang-Xang also had seen two Asokan pillars at Pataliputra, apparently both previously observed by Fa-Xian. Xuang-Xang's fifteenth Asokan pillar stood beside a stupa near the *Karanda Venuvana* or lake at Old Rajagriha. This had the figure of an elephant at the top and was about 50 feet high.

A few places like Krakuchchhanda's town, Kanakamuni's town and the pillar-bearing site supposedly in the Chhapra area remain unidentified and no pillar has yet been found in Rajgir and Sravasti. Smith has offered convincing grounds to argue that the Lat Bhairo column in Banaras incorporates the surviving part of the Asokan column which was deliberately burnt down during a particularly virulent Hindu-Muslim riot in 1809.

On the whole, the collective testimony of Fa-Xian and Xuang-Xang is unequivocal and also remarkably interesting in the sense that it shows the original distribution of the Asokan pillars much more extensive than what it is today. Smith points out that with the exception of the column at Sankisa in the Farukhabad district of the Doab, "all the monuments described stood in Magadha or the neighbouring regions, the home provinces, within easy reach of Pataliputra, the capital, and not too remote from the sandstone quarries of Canar (Chunar) in the Mirzapur District".

Although Smith's observation is true in the light of the Chinese pilgrims' accounts, those accounts are not necessarily the exclusive or even the primary basis of our understanding of the distribution of Asokan columns. This will be obvious in the light of a close examination of their surviving material relics. Two cardinal features of the Chinese accounts are the frequent references to the inscriptions on them and the animals on their tops. The contents of the inscriptions remained unspecified and there is no way of infering that they contained mostly the royal injunctions on morality and the ways to propagate them. The references to the animals on the top, including a horse at Rummindei, are in a sense more interesting because they invariably establish a link between the Chinese pilgrims' accounts of the pillars and their surviving remains. The reference to the horse at Rummindei, which has not yet turned up in the archaeological excavations at the site, amplifies the surviving archaeological evidence of these pillars.

III. ASOKAN PILLARS AND BELL-CAPITALS

There is no inscription on some pillars which have been unquestionably accepted as Asokan because of their context and associated bell-capitals with standing or fallen animals. The Kolhua pillar of Vaisali and the pillar with the bull capital at Rampurva are the principal examples of this feature. At some places, currently there is no pillar but there are bell-capitals which indicate the presence of pillars, although, in view of the Kolhua and Rampurva examples, there is no assurance that these pillars were all inscribed. Similarly, fragments of pillars with Asokan edicts have been reportedly discovered at Amaravati and in the area of Buner. Although these two finds are not beyond dispute, they may be brought under the purview of the present discussion. Similarly, at Deur Kothar near Rewa, stone pillars of indisputably Asokan type occur in the Mauryan context and bear, at least in one case, an inscription engraved in Asokan Brahmi. The implications of this discovery deserve careful consideration. Claims of the existence of Asokan pillars can be made at Sikligarh in Purnea, Bhagalpur on the bank of the Ghaghra in Uttar Pradesh, and the bank of the Garra river, also in Uttar Pradesh. Similar claims are also possible in the case of the following pillars: Lat Bhairo in Banaras, the Prahladpur pillar now in Banaras and the Bakraur pillar now in Bodh Gaya. Whether there are Asokan pillars in Bhopal and Bhuvaneshwar deserves examination too. The degree of authenticity of all these claims has to be discussed. Thus, the general issue of Asokan pillars is undoubtedly more complex than is usually thought, and the related issue of the historical-geographical significance of their locations may be equally complex too.

III.1. Pataliputra

The modern Patna locality where a large number of Asokan or at least Mauryan pillars have been found is Kumrahar which has four major phases of excavation (1892, 1896-97, 1913-15 and 1951-55). In 1892, L.A. Waddell came upon a fragment of a 'colossal Asokan pillar' 12 feet below surface in the northwestern portion of the site, and in 1896-97 P.C. Mukherji found many fragments of such pillars near the Kallu and Chaman tanks. The latter noticed that these stone fragments were invariably found in a blackish layer composed of 'ashes, embers and bits of lime' and suggested 'deliberate destruction by vandals'. In 1913-15, D.B. Spooner found traces of 72 pillars spaced about 14 to 15 feet apart and a series of wooden platforms parallel to the rows of pillars. Below the Gupta period ruins of c.4th-5th century AD, Spooner encountered a thick layer of ashes and below this, a clay/silt deposit which contained cylindrical shafts of the ash of the upper deposit and fragments of pillars. These shafts were also spaced 14 to 15 feet apart. Virgin soil lay below this deposit. In 1951-55, A. Altekar and V. Misra (Altekar and Misra 1959) excavated 8 more pillars of the Hall proper and 4 pillars possibly belonging to the porch of the Hall. The pillars were found to stand on wooden basements, each 4 feet 6 inch square and placed on a 6 inch thick clay deposit. These pillars were 32.5 feet high, of which 9 feet were buried inside the plinth. The buried portion also was polished.

Outside Kumrahar, a pillar was reported from Bulandibagh (Patil 1963, p. 393), and although an Asokan pillar was reported from the compound of a mosque in Patna in 1999 (Falk 2006), there is as yet no positive proof.

No pillar reported in Pataliputra is inscribed. There is also no typical Asokan pillar capital here.

III.2. Kolhua

Although the Kolhua pillar in the close vicinity of the ancient city of Vaisali has been known since the late 18th century, it is only comparatively recently that it has been excavated up to its base and that its contemporaneity with a Mauryan stupa nearby has been established (Gupta 1979-80). Along with its lion capital seated on a rectangular abacus, this pillar is 14.6 m high. The remains of the stupa have yielded a fragment of a stone umbrella and pieces of a relic casket, all bearing typical Mauryan polish. Although the column carries no Asokan inscription, there is no reason to doubt its authenticity as an Asokan pillar.

III.3. Lauriya Araraj

The village of Rahariya or Radhia is about 2.5 miles to the west of the Araraj pillar which derives the second part of its name from the temple of *Araraj-Mahadeo* which lies about a mile to its northeast. The town of Betiah in Champaran lies to its northwest and can be approached from the Pipra ghat crossing of the Gandak, which can be reached in its turn by travelling from Vaisali via Kesariya. There is a well-known major stupa (recently excavated) at Kesariya. There is no reason to call it Radhia pillar, as it was named in the late 18th century. The village in which the pillar is located is *Lauriya*. However, the name *Radhia* has still a relevance. Under this rubric, a miniature painting of the Ms Sanskrit Add. 1643, a manuscript of the Sanskrit *Astasahasrika Prajnaparamita* in the Cambridge University collection shows a vihara or monastery, a stupa and behind them, a pillar surmounted by the bird *Garuda*. The manuscript is dated AD 1015. (Bendall 1883, pp. 151-152; Foucher 1900, p. 55, Pl. I, no. 5). This led V.A. Smith to infer that the Lauriya Araraj inscribed column was surmounted by Garuda.

According to A. Cunningham (1877, pp. 39-42), this is 36.5 feet high, with a base diameter of 41.8 inch and a top diameter of 37.6 inch. In 1871 (Cunningham 1871, p. 67), he estimated its weight, including the portion below ground as 40 tons. In 1877 he thought that this weight was about 30 tons. The Asokan inscription on the pillar is in two columns, one facing the south comprising the first four edicts and that facing the north comprising the edicts V and VI. The name *Lauriya Araraj* was given to the column by Cunningham.

III.4. Lauriya Nandangarh

The site lies to the northwest of Betiah, and there had been a confusion about its name too. Known in the late 18th century as Mathia pillar, this was named Lauriya Navandgarh or Nonadgarh or even Naonadgarh by Cunningham (1871) who thought that the neighbouring complex of mounds was known as Navandgarh. There is no 'fort' nearby and the high mounds that one could see close to it some years back are all individual mounds of uncertain periods, although the most prominent one, which shows a terraced temple, is not earlier than c.9th century AD or thereabouts. By the time these mounds came to be excavated early in the 20th century, the name was changed to Nandangarh.

The Lauriya Nandangarh pillar is the only surviving complete and standing inscribed column of Asoka. During a visit in the rainy season a few years ago, I found the base of the pillar waterlogged and was told by the local people that this state of affairs was a comparatively recent development. Unless the situation is closely examined by the Archaeological Survey of India, who looks after it as a protected monument, and measures are undertaken to put a stop to this waterlogging, the base of the pillar is likely to get weakened, and some day the pillar will fall. There is a photograph of the pillar in its waterlogged condition which may be seen in my *The Oxford Companion to Indian Archaeology* (Chakrabarti 2006).

Cunningham (1877) notes that the pillar is "much thinner and lighter in appearance than those of Araraj and Bakhra". The Kolhua pillar was earlier known as the 'Basarh-Bakhira' pillar. The total height of the pillar, inclusive of its single-lion capital is, according to him, 'rather more than 39½ feet'. The name of the Mughal emperor Aurangzeb is engraved on the pillar and it appears that the Mughal army on its return journey from Bengal after the expedition against Shuja, a contender for the Mughal throne, took a cannon shot against the pillar, the mark of which can be seen just below the capital. The mouth of the seated lion is wide open but partly broken. Interestingly, Cunningham saw the pillar being worshipped. A man, two women and a child 'set up a small flag before the pillar, and placed offerings of sweetmeats around it'.

III.5. Rampurva

There are remains of two pillars at Rampurva ("39½ miles to the north of Betiya, 20½ miles to the north-north-east-half-north from Laoriya Naonadgarh" and 4 miles to the south of the first range of hills – Someshwar range – at the border of Nepal and India, cf. Carlleyle 1877-80), both found associated with animal capitals. The one with the lion capital is inscribed but the one with the bull capital is not so. The site on the eastern bank of a small river called the Hariora or Hariora was discovered by A.C.L. Carlleyle and although the 'bell-shaped capital' of one pillar was still at the site, the animal itself was missing. This pillar was found buried in a slanting position, showing only a portion of the capital above ground. About 850 feet south of this pillar there were two mounds, 370 feet apart, and occupying the central position between these mounds was the stump of the second Rampurva stone pillar. He found its surviving portion 6 feet high and 9¼ feet in circumference. Carlleyle laid trenches on either side of the northern pillar ('the circumference of the lowest exposed part 11 feet and near the top about 8 feet'), which led to the discovery of the Asokan inscription in two parts on the opposing sides of the pillar.

In 1880-81, Cunningham deputed one of his assistants, H.B.W. Garrick, to the site for photography (Cunningham and Garrick 1883, pp. 110-117). Garrick disconnected the capital from the shaft and consequently discovered the copper bolt which fixed the capital to the shaft.

> I managed to disconnect this huge capital from the shaft of the pillar. The method adopted for fastening these two masses of stone together was a solid barrel-shapen bolt of pure copper, measuring 2 feet ½ inch long and 4-5/16 inch in diameter at centre; it tapers slightly towards the ends where its diameter is 3-5/8 inch. The bolt projected exactly half its length, or 1¼ inch, from the shaft, and the projecting portion received the capital; both ends of the bolt were beautifully fitted into the stone, thus dispensing with any cement substance to hold it.

In the post-Garrick phase, A.H. Longhurst argued that the remains of pillars at the site indicated the existence of two pillars, and to settle this question, D.R. Sahni (1907-8) excavated the site in November 2007-January 2008.

At the depth of 7 feet below surface, Sahni found evidence of a floor of the Asokan period and at the same level he found a terracotta ring-well comprising 9 rings, each of which was 4.5 inch high. The pillar in the north rested, edge-wise, on a stone slab which was 1.75 feet thick and 7.75 feet wide. There was also support of *Sal* wood stakes. The pillar measures 44 feet and 9¼ inch long, exclusive of the capital. The diameter is 3 feet at the top and 4 feet at the base. The lion capital of this pillar was found on the brick platform of the Asokan period and save for the loss of the upper jaw, it was undamaged.

The southern pillar lay 900 feet to the south of the northern one. The brick plinth on which it rested measured 11½ feet from east to west and 9 feet from north to south, and had a brick floor 2 feet below it. The surviving stump was found to be 12½ feet high, and the missing upper portion of the shaft lay on the floor, about 3 feet away to the east. This carried a socket-hole (6 inch in diameter and about 1 foot in depth) at the upper end to hold the bolt which fixed the capital. The bull capital was located at the same level. The bull itself is 4 feet high and the capital as a whole 6 feet 9 inch. The estimated total length of the shaft was more than 40 feet, exclusive of the capital. There was no evidence of structures in the two mounds to the south of the northern pillar.

Sahni's comment (Sahni 1907-8, p. 188) on the overthrow of the two Rampurva columns is important.

> Their destruction evidently took place at a very early date. This is especially manifest in regard to the southern pillar, for its broken shaft and capital were lying on the brick paving around the column, which is the earliest construction on the spot. The northern column would seem to have stood much longer in position, though here too the separation of the crowning figure from the column must be assigned approximately to the same period as the demolition of the southern column. No clue was found as to the causes of their destruction, but it may be presumed that it was brought about by inundation.

III.6. The Historical-Geographical Significance of the Locations of the Kolhua, Lauriya Araraj, Lauriya Nandangarh and Rampurva Pillars

The modern route to Vaisali from Patna passes through the Hajipur area and that the same was the case in the ancient context is also shown by the find of a bell-capital of the Mauryan period found at Salempur near Hajipur. The capital found in 1918-19 by H. Pandey "consists of two pairs of bulls seated back to back, on a plain square abacus, with a square block above the animals, which is adorned with the honeysuckle ornament" (Patil 1963, p. 508). This has been illustrated in S.P.Gupta's *The Roots of Indian Art* (Gupta 1980), p. 82, Plates 50 b, 51b, as being from Hajipur. The present measurement of the capital which has the heads of the bulls missing is 36x75x44 cm. Gupta lists it as "late Mauryan" without showing any reason. This, of course, is not the usual Asokan bell-capital which is part of a free-standing pillar but a capital which was at the top of a pillar supporting a structure. Now that a Mauryan stupa at Kolhua has been found to be contemporary with the Kolhua pillar, one has to say that this pillar came up as a part of a monastic complex. This direct monastic association may be one of the reasons why the Kolhua pillar does not carry any pillar edict. There is, however, no doubt about the general significance of the Vaisali area in the ancient context: its location in a crucial segment of north Bihar giving access to the areas further north and east. One of the northern alignments led by Kesariya, a place which has an association with the Buddha in the early Buddhist tradition and was later the site of a grand brick stupa, to the Gandak crossing at Pipra Ghat and beyond that, to Araraj, Nandangarh and Rampurva. The geographical significance of this alignment in relation to Nepal or, more specifically, the Kathmandu valley with which Asoka has a strong association in the local tradition, was long realized by scholars.

This is how Carlleyle (p. 54) described the alignment of these pillars:

> ... four different pillars of Asoka are now known to be situated along the line of the old north road which led from Magadha to Nipal, or from the Ganges opposite Pataliputra or Patna, through Basarh or Vaisali, and Kesariya, in a northern or rather north-north-westerly direction, keeping at a moderate distance to the east of the Gandak, to the Tarai and hills of Nipal.

He, in fact, expected "to find another pillar, or else a rock-cut inscription, still further north somewhere in the Nipal Tarai". His map showing Rampurva puts it straight on the old track leading to Nepal.

The modern route of the region to Nepal passes by Raxaul and Birganj, both of which lie to the east of Betiah. We have elsewhere noticed that this modern route passes through a low-lying area and was certainly avoided in the ancient times or even in pre-modern times when Sugouli or Betiah was the preferred stopping point on the Indian side for Nepal. This is the general direction which was outlined by Colonel Kirkpatrick's (1811) *An Account of the Kingdom of Nepal, being the Substance of Observations Made during a Mission to that Country in the Year 1793 by Colonel Kirkpatrick.* Chapter 1 describes the route from 'Munniary to Hettowra', which went through the 'Cheeriaghaty hills', Muckwanpore Valley and fort of Muckwanpore, and Hettowra. Chapter 2 describes the route from Sugouli/ 'Segouly' to Hettowra: Segouly > Boori Gunduck river > Tillawe river > fort of Ultown > Beheera Nullah > Goorpussra > forest > Nagsoti and Bechiacori rivers > Bechiakori hills > Purrewabheer > Joona river > forest of Dumwa > Kuora river > Hettowra. Kirkpatrick's focus was on the transport of British goods both to Nepal and Tibet. From Sugouli to Hetaura, the pack bullocks or carriages would carry goods in four or five days and from Hetaura to Kathmandu the hill porters would carry the goods in three or four days.

> At Kathmandu, the merchants or caravans will disperse. Those having goods intended for the Laehassen or eastern market, would convey them by porters to Listee, the Nepal frontier town on that side, and only three days distance from Kooti, a considerable town of Tibet. This journey may be performed with ease in eight days. The Nepal mart or entrepot for supplying Diggercheh or Teeshoo Lumboo and the adjacent parts would be Dholaka, which is stuated below the pass of Phullak, whence Tibet may be entered with greater ease than by Kooti. Dholaka is not above five

> easy days journey from Kathmandu. The merchandise intended for middle Tibet, or that part of Tibet lying directly to the northward of Nepal, would be transported to Russooa, the frontier town of Nepal in that quarter. This would take seven or eight days. The articles designed for the supply of the north-west parts of Tibet, would have to proceed to Joomlah, or rather to its capital, Chinachin. Chinachin is pretty near a month's journey for a caravan from Kathmandu, to the northwest of which it lies. This is the frontier station of Nepal in the Taklaghar quarter. Taklaghar is a town of Tibet of considerable note. It is about 12 journies from Chinachin, but much nearer to the borders of the Joomlah district. Chinachin might also be approached by way of Almorah; but to take this route, merchants would have to advance far up into Rohilkhand, it would not answer, probably, so well for the staples in question as the Kathmandu road: though, doubtlessly it would seem to be the properest channel for the exports of the Vizier's country, and perhaps of Benares (Kirkpatrick 1811, pp. 373-374).

Vincent Smith (1909, pp. 77-78) underlines the extensive character of Mauryan presence in the Kathmandu valley: the tradition of the erection of stupas by Asoka and the laying out of Patan by him, among others. The network of routes that we have described on the basis of Kirkpatrick seems to suggest the general significance of Nepal in the Asokan scheme of things, and on this basis it is possible to argue that trade links with Tibet were also parts of this scheme. There is as yet no specific archaeological evidence of the Mauryan presence in Nepal beyond the Tarai, but one may in this context point out the location of an early Buddhist stupa near Tanakpur, an entry point both to Nepal and the Himalayas on the Indian side. In a different context. I have argued that the archaeological sites in the Pilibhit and other districts which border the Rohilkhand section of Uttar Pradesh with Nepal underscore the possibility of close trade links with Nepal through this sector. Thus, beyond the line of four Asokan pillars in north Bihar, there is a possible extensive network of links with Nepal and Tibet in the Mauryan context. There is also no doubt that the present Patna-Rampurva alignment played a major role in this regard. .

It is interesting to reflect that Carlleyle was more aware of the significance of this alignment than many of his contemporary scholars. He pointed out that, across the first line of Indo-Nepal hills, there were three passes across the second line of hills called the Sidra range: the Churia ghati pass or the western pass, the Thori ghati or the central pass which is the most difficult one and runs along the Kudi river, and the Goramasaon pass or the eastern pass. He expected to find "another inscription of Asoka somewhere in or just beyond one or other of these three passes".

IV. THE PATALIPUTRA-MAHASTHANGARH ALIGNMENT AND SIKLIGARH PILLAR

The ancient road from Pataliputra to Mahasthangarh in the Bagura district of Bangladesh passes along the northern bank of the Ganga till it reaches the Kandaran-Bangarh section of Dinajpur in modern West Bengal. It crosses the Purneah-Katihar section of Bihar before entering West Bengal. The site of Sikligarh which has a high mud fortification wall around it and the fragmentary stone column outside, which is remarkably similar to an Asokan column, have been known since the days of Francis Buchanan since the early 19th century. It may be noted that there is no archaeological indication of the date of the mud rampart of the fortified section. Our brief exploration of the area failed to yield even a single diagnostic sherd. The area is generally devoid of brickbats and pottery. A detailed report on the surviving part of the pillar was published by L.A. Waddell in 1890/91. Three years before this date, the Collector of the district had it excavated around the base. Since then the pillar has been standing at an angle of about 65 degrees.

> As the appearance of the monolith was suggestive of its being probably an edict pillar, and its greater portion was buried indergground, I had it excavated. The operation showed that the pillar had originally been implanted for over half its length in a foundation of irregular layers of brick and mortar ... The pillar retained its smooth and polished surface throughout its extent, except in a few portions where this surface has scaled off ... The most careful search all over the pillar, however, failed to find any trace of an inscription. The basal extremity of the pillar was sharply truncated across and rested in the sand; and here immediately under the pillar was found the gold coin of the Indo-Scythic character ... The upper extremity of the pillar is perforated by a hole (12 inch deep, and in diameter 5½ inch at the top and 3½ inch at the bottom) which evidently formed the socket for the stem or bolt of a crowning ornament; ... Local tradition alleges that the shaft was formerly surmounted by the figure of a lion but that this was removed many hundreds of years ago, no one knows where (Waddell 1891, p. 244).

The total length of the surviving portion is 19 feet 11 inch, of which 7½ feet is above ground. The diameter at 3 feet from the top is 112½ inch. The gold coin recovered from below the pillar was issued by the Kushan king Vasudeva.

Waddell has given a sketch of the pillar, which suggests that it was broken into two long before the present time. The coin was put below the portion that was put in the ground at that time. The second century AD coin of Vasudeva approximately suggests the period before which the pillar was not vandalised. The diameter of the column, the quality of its stone and its polish clearly drive home its Mauryan character. Besides, the presence of a hole which shows the presence of a socket to hold the stem of a bolt seems to categorically demonstrate the truth of this assertion. Geographically, its position on the Pataliputra-Mahasthangarh road does not undermine the hypothesis of its Mauryan character. There are, apparently, some brick structures around the pillar. If excavated, these structures will throw light on their character. One need not be surprised if these ruins represent a monastic complex. The fortified area itself should be excavated. At present, the sensible observation is that the Sikligarh pillar was set up during the Mauryan period and pulled down as early as the post-second century AD.

V. RUMMINDEI, NIGLIVA AND GOTIHAWA

These three sites are located in an archaeologically rich area of the Nepalese *Tarai*, none of them far from the fortified early historic city-site of Tilaurakot where the mud fortification dates back to c.600 BC and makes it a major early historic city site of the sub-continent. The basic antiquity of Tilaurakot may be a few centuries earlier, considering that the Painted Grey Ware has been reported from the site and that the antiquity of the NBP-bearing level at Gotihawa is c. 800 BC. The most notable site across the border in India is Piprahwa, famous not merely because of the late nineteenth century discovery of a soapstone relic casket containing, according to one of the readings of the inscription inscribed on it, the corporeal relics of the lord Buddha but also because of the find of the Buddhist monastic seal of Kapilavastu in an excavated monastery. Also on the Indian side is Bansi, where an Asokan lion capital was found and suggested that it lay at the approach to Lumbini and Kapilavastu from the side of Pataliputra. The region as a whole has figured prominently in the sub-continent's archaeological map since the late nineteenth century, not the least because of the unwarranted confusion about the location of Kapilavastu, the capital of the Buddha's father Suddhodana of the Sakya clan.

V.1. RUMMINDEI OR LUMBINI

In his prefatory note to P.C. Mukherji's *A Report on a Tour of Exploration of the Antiquities in the Tarai, Nepal, the Region of Kapilavastu; during February and March, 1899* (Mukherji 1901), Vincent Smith (in Mukherji 1901, pp. 6-7) had no doubt about the identity of Rummindei with 'the Lumbini garden of Buddhist tradition':

1. The names Rummeindei and Lumbini are 'practically identical'.
2. The 'river of oil' which flows past Lumbini to the southeast in Xuang-Xang's account is the modern 'Tilar Nadi' or the river of oil.
3. The 'bathing tank' mentioned by Xuang-Xang was 25 paces to the south of the nativity tree and according to Fa-Xian, it was 20 paces to the south. The distance between the small nativity temple and the modern pond which lies to the south of the temple is about 25 paces.
4. According to Xuang-Xang, the horse-topped pillar which was erected by Asoka close to the spot where the gods received the infant Bodhisattva was struck by lightning and, during the time of his visit, lay on the ground, split in the middle. Currently, the Asokan pillar stands close to the nativity temple and is also split in the middle, possibly because of being struck by lightning.
5. The nativity group of sculptures still exists at the position 'assigned by tradition to the nativity tree'.

As Smith puts it, "the site of Lumbini garden is therefore fixed with absolute certainty. It is interesting to note that the testimony of the Asokan pillar at the site, which specifically mentions Lumbini as the birth-place of the Buddha, is only one of the pieces of supporting evidence, according to Smith, all the other pieces being textual. To us, the evidence of the pillar alone would have been conclusive.

The first phase of archaeological work at Lumbini was done by the Nepalese general Khadga Shamser and the Archaeological Survey of India representative A. Fuhrer in 1896. The second phase of work was done in 1899 by P.C. Mukherji, another Archaeological Survey of India representative. About a mile north of the Pararia village of the Bhagavanpur *tehsil*, there was a stretch of 'very high ground' measuring about 440 yards north-south and 220 yards east-west and possessing some tanks in its western and southern peripheries. About 500 feet to the north of this ground, there is another rectangular plot of elevated ground (300 feet x 400 feet) which was surrounded by a wide ditch and had access in the southeastern section.

> This is the sacred site of Rummindei, who is known throughout the Tarai as a local goddess of some celebrity. The Paharies, hill-men, call her Rupa-dei. She is believed to grant the prayers of her devotees, who bring her offerings of eatables, goats and fowls that are sactificed and fed here with great ceremony (Mukherji 1901, p. 34).

The Rummindei is represented by a collection of ancient sculptures which are now kept in a modern shrine with earlier origins. About 100 feet south of the temple is a small tank and the temple has in its close vicinity a few small mounds.

The Asokan pillar lies about 45 feet to the northwest of the Rummindei temple. The upper portion of the shaft is missing along with the animal on the top of the bell-capital. The latter is also partly damaged but shows a hole (5 inch in diameter and 1 foot deep) for the copper mortice to attach the capital to the pillar.

The brick-railing around the pillar was traced to some depth, the most important find in this context being a pavement at a depth of about 6 feet. The earlier background of the Rummindei temple was clear from the remains of a *Saptaratha* brick temple below it and miscellaneous sculptures including one of *Hara-Gouri* and a large one of *Mayadevi* represented as holding the branch of a tree at the time of her delivery.

Mukherji traced the remains of a few stupas in the general area: "vestiges of some eight stupas were already discovered, and basements of some more were traced." The site was found full of ancient ruins and wherever he excavated, the walls of ancient structures were brought to light.

The post-Mukherji work at Lumbini has been discussed in detail by T.N. Mishra (2004). In 1933-39, the Nepalese general Kaisher Shamsher excavated many stupas and monasteries at the site, but not always in an acceptable manner. In 1962, Debala Mitra excavated the area of the pillar. In 1970-71, N.R. Banerji and B.K. Rijal excavated in the old village area of Lumbini (600m x 300m) bringing out a cultural sequence from the NBP phase to c.8th century AD. In 1974-83, B.K. Rijal identified many large and small *Chaityas* in and around the Lumbini nativity site. One of the most important discoveries was made in 1975 when, at a distance of about 30 feet to the north of the Asokan pillar, an oblong burnt brick shrine (15′4″ x 12′5″) was found with a square *Chaitya* of the Mauryan period over it. In 1984-86, T.N. Mishra investigated the nativity mound, highlighting its cultural sequence from the NBP phase to c.13th century AD. There were also three monasteries and 13 large and small stupas in this area. The total height of the Asokan pillar was found to be 30′ 10″ and it was found to rest on a flat basement stone. In 1993-95, S. Uesaka and Japan Buddhist Federation and B.K. Rijal further explored the nativity temple and found two phases of outer walls built around it. In the first phase, the wall measured 26m x 21 m whereas in the second phase, it was 30 to 20 cm shorter. The outer walls were built by using 14 square box-chambers rammed with clay. This phase of the temple goes back to the NBP period. The chronology of the successive phases of the temple is as follows: phase 2: c. 200-100 BC; phase 3: early Gupta period, c. AD 350; phase 4: 7th-8th century AD. It is thus absolutely clear that the structural activity at Lumbini did not begin with Asoka's visit to the site and as some Nepalese scholars have emphasized, there was a persistent Nepalese tradition about its religious sanctity as the birth-place of the Buddha.

The text of the Lumbini/Rummindei pillar inscription (after Hultzsch 1925, p. xxii-xxiii, 164-165):

(A) When king Devanampriya Priyadarsin had been anointed twenty years, he came himself and worshipped (this spot), because the Buddha Sakyamuni was born here.

(B) (He) both caused to be made a stone bearing a horse (?) and caused a stone pillar to be set up, (in order to show) that the Blessed One was born here.

(C) He made the village of Lummini free of taxes, and paying (only) an eighth share (of the produce).

In this inscription, the text *silâvigadabhi-cha* is subject to different interpretations. G. Buhler (1898-99, note 4, p. 5) wrote that the translation of *vigadabhi* was not certain. "It may be a word governing *Sila* and a technical term of unknown meaning". Vincent Smith (1905) admits that the difficult word is *Vigadabhi,* which has been variously interpreted as 'horse', 'she-ass', 'big sun' and 'railing' or 'enclosure'. He follows Richard Pischel's translation of it "as an adjective meaning 'flawless', or without defect, qualifying *Sila*". His translation of the inscription is as follows: "His Sacred and Gracious Majesty the King, having come in person twenty years after his coronation, did reverence (*saying*), 'Here was Buddha born, the sage of the Sakyas'. And he caused a faultless block of stone to be prepared, and set up a stone-pillar (*made from it*), (*saying*), 'Here was the Venerable One born'. And he made the village of Lummini revenue-free, in its entirety". The debate did not end here. In 1914, J. Charpentier (1914) translated the inscription in the following fashion: "His Majesty King Priyadarsin came here himself twenty years after his anointment, and, worship having been performed, because here was born Buddha the saint of the Sakyas he had a slab of stone bearing a horse made and a stone pillar raised up. Because here was born the venerable one the village of Lummini was made free from religious taxes and entitled to the grain-tax for eight years."

Another debated term is *Athabhagiye* or Sanskrit *Ashtabhagiya.* The term literally means 'eight shares (of land)', but here the term eight may also mean completeness, and if so, the term *Ashtabhagiya* here "should be interpreted as meaning that the grant covered the whole of the lands; that is to say, that a village was regarded in ancient times as a unit of eight parts, not of sixteen, as is now usual". The term thus means "in its entirety".

V.2. Nigliva/Nigali Sagar

This site is located in an area of rather closely packed archaeological sites, beginning with Tauliva or Taulihawa. Mukherji (1901, pp 18-19) had no doubt that it was an extensive site containing, among others, one or more temple ruins. Tilaurakot, a rectangular fort site (1600 feet x 1000 feet) surrounded by a ditch on the bank of the Banganga river, lies about 2 miles due north of Tauliva. Mukherji himself explored miscellaneous structural ruins within the fortifications, and more recent work has firmly established its character as a major fortified settlement of c.600 BC and later, complete with guardrooms and planned streets. The Painted Grey Ware found in its lowest level underlines the antiquity of occupation in the general area around 1000 BC, if not still earlier. At Chitra-dei across the river, Mukherji excavated what he thought was 'the biggest temple' he had yet discovered in Tarai. About 2 miles north of Tilaurakot lay Sagarwa or Sagarhawa where Mukherji had observed a number of stupa and monasteries. A temple was observed at Bikuli, about 3 miles north-northeast of Sagarwa.

Nigali Sagar or Nigliva is about a mile-and-half east of Sagarwa and noted for Nigali Sagar, a large east-west tank about a mile south of the village. The two portions of an Asokan column, known locally as *Loriki-Nigali* or 'smoking pipe', were observed on the western embankment of this tank. The upper part of the pillar is 14'-9-1/2" long.

> The top of the pillar has a diameter of 2', above which a smaller drum rises 2-1/2". In the centre of this is a hole, 4" in diameter, and 1'-4" in depth, in which was fitted the copper mortice of the capital, which is now missing. The lower portion of the pillar is about 10'... its upper diameter 2'-4".. (Mukherji 1901, p. 30).

Araura-kot is about 1500' to the southeast of Nigali Sagar and a rectangular fort (750'x600') with mud fortifications on two sides and brick fortifications on the other two sides. There was a surrounding ditch and traces of two gates, one each on the west and the east.

According to Mukherji, the Asokan pillar fragments were not *in situ*. He points out that when it was excavated earlier by L.A. Waddell, "the broken bottom was exposed, where no foundation or basement was discovered". He could not also find the traces of any stupa in the immediate neighbourhood. The stupa, alleged to be present by A. Fuhrer earlier, was not in existence.

Hultzsch's translation (Hultzsch 1925, pp. 165-166) of the Nigali Sagar edict is as follows:

(A) When king Devanampriya Priyadarsin had been anointed fourteen years, he enlarged the stupa of the Buddha Konakamana to the double (of its original size).

(B) And when he had been anointed (twenty) years, he came himself and worshipped (this spot) (and) caused (a stone pillar to be set up).

Buhler (1898-99) infers that the stupa of Konakamana, as it was enlarged for the second time under Asoka, is likely to predate his reign. His comments on what it implies in the mythology and chronology of Buddhism are interesting:

> Konakamana or Konagamana belongs to the long series of purely mythical predecessors of the historical founder of Buddhism. The mythology of Buddhism must not only have been developed, but the myths must have been fixed locally, before it could occur to the Faithful to build stupas in honour of their heroes. It seems difficult to believe that all these developments could have been accomplished in a short time. As they had been completed in the first half of the third century BC, it becomes probable that the origins of Buddhism lay very much earlier and that, therefore, it is impossible, as some scholars have done, to fix the *Nirvana* in 350 BC or in 325 BC. The remoter date, cir. 477 BC is also, on this consideration, the more probable one. (Buhler 1898-99, p. 2)

V.3. Gotihawa / Gutiva

About 4 miles to the southwest of Tilaurakot is the site of Gutiva which had in the centre of the village in Mukherji's time (Mukherji 1901, pp. 31-32), "a large brick stupa, 68 feet in diameter, and still about 9 feet in height .... 32-1/2 feet from the outer rim of the Stupa stands the lower portion of an ancient pillar of the Priyadarsi style, of which the upper portion is gone. Only a small portion is visible above the ground, which is known as *Phutesvara* Mahadeva, "the broken lord".

The pillar stood on a large granite slab (7'x 5'8-1/2"x10") and was found to be made of "hard sandstone of a yellowish colour, as is the case with all constructions of a similar shape" (Mukherji 1901, pp. 31-32). Below the pedestal was brick masonry, as the bedding for the pedestal and pillar. Of the three fragments of the pillar lying in the village, one was a portion of the bell-shaped base of the capital. These fragments were locally called *Gutis,* from which the name *Gutiva* is derived.

In G. Verardi's excavations, the Gotihawa stupa was found to have a long history. Period I dated from about 800 BC and was associated with the NBP, corded ware, etc. Period II saw the building of the stupa in the 3rd-2nd century BC, although the date may be earlier. The stupa was enlarged in its phase 3 of the 1st-2nd century AD. In phase 4 (4th-5th century AD and later), the stupa was abandoned and there are signs of non-Buddhist occupation in the area.

V.4. Observations on the Archaeological Contexts of Rummindei, Nigliva and Gotihawa

All these three Asokan pillars stood in an area and topography of rich archaeological heritage. Not merely these three but all the other related sites listed and explored since the 19th century must be said to lie in a comparatively limited geographical area, the distance between Tilaurakot and Lumbini being not more than 27 km. The sites of Tauliva, Tilaurakot, Nigliva and Araurakot lie, in fact, close together, within only a few kilometres of each other. Tilaurakot is a large fortified site and although not on the same scale, Araurakot also is fortified. Moreover, the area seems to be crowded with temples, stupas and monasteries, apparently with long histories of occupation. At Lumbini, the archaeological discoveries have been complex. The history of the nativity temple going back to the Asokan period, if not earlier, is exciting in its own term. The c.800 BC antiquity of the NBP at Gotihawa puts the NBP of the region in the main stream of its development in the central Ganga plain. Some of the discoveries elsewhere in the general region, although a little outside the area of Tilaurakot-Gotihawa-Lumbini, seem to be exciting too. Although not yet published or analysed clearly, Nepalese scholars can now think about these discoveries in terms of the ancient kingdoms of the Sakyas and the Koliyas. For instance, the Rohini river is supposed to demarcate the Sakya and Koliya kingdoms. The heart of the Koliya country seems to be Devadaha at Panditpur, Bajiria village in the Nawalparsi district. Here, a 700 m long perimeter wall and a canal for channelling water from the Rohini have been reported. Although a clear assessment of the archaeological wealth of the Nepalese *Tarai* has to wait for a better availability of the relevant publications, there is little doubt that this section of Tarai has emerged to be one of the major early historic zones of the central Ganga plain. The fact that Asoka decided to have three of his pillars, two of which were inscribed recording his visits to the area, erected in this part was possibly due not merely to its great religious significance in Buddhist history but also to the significance of the region as a whole.

Our understanding of the archaeology of the region has also been complicated by the issue of the identification of Kapilavastu. The issue has been debated for long, Vincent Smith's exposition being one of its early definitive expositions. Smith did not believe that the ancient Sravasti stood at the site of modern Sahet-Mahet, although the inscription found in the Jetavana monastery area of Sahet-Mahet, by virtue of its mention of Jetavana in this regard, leaves no doubt about the authenticity of the identification of Sahet Mahet with the ancient Sravasti. Smith put more store by the literary data, especially the bearings given in the records of Fa-Xian and Xuang-Xang, than by the evidence of archaeology or of inscriptions.

> Personally, I have no doubt that the true site of the city (of Sravasti) has been approximately fixed at the point where the Rapti issues from the hills northeast of Nepalganj railway station. I venture to think that I have succeeded in demonstrating that Sahet-Mahet on the borders of the Gonda and Bahraich districts in Oudh cannot possibly be Sravasti (Smith 1901, pp. 7-8; for his detailed discussion, Smith 1898, 1900).

Regarding the identification of Kapilavastu also, Smith puts exclusive stress on its bearings given by Fa-Xian and Xuang-Xang, which leads him to believe that Kapilavastu lay about 9 miles west of Lumbini, according to Fa-Xian but about 15/16 miles in the westerly direction, according to Xuang-Xang.

> Let the reader now take a pair of compass with Rummindei as a centre and describe to the west an arc with 9 miles (or 50 *li*) radius. That arc will cut the group of ruins near Piprava and will not intersect any other ruins. *Prima facie*, therefore, Piprava is the Kapilavastu of Fa-hien. ... If the reader again takes up the compass, and in accordance with Hiuen Tsiang's indication, describes an arc on the map of 14 miles radius (= 15 or 16 by road), he will find that the arc cuts through Tilaura-Kot, which is the central mass part of a great mass of ruins extending for miles. *Prima facie*, then, the Tilaura-Kot group of ruins is the Kapilavastu of Hiuen Tsiang (Smith 1901, p. 10).

He goes on to emphasize the extensive character of Kapilavastu ruins as described by Xuang-Xang: a circuit of two-and-a-half miles for the royal precincts and numerous ruined monasteries. "Proposals to identify any individual small section of the ruins, such as Tilaura-Kot or Araura-Kot, with Kapilavastu as a whole exhibit a misunderstanding of the premisers" (Smith 1901, p. 11). Further, he comments that "the area bounded by Lori-ki-Kudan, Gutiva, Tilaura-Kot, Sagarwa, Nigliva and Araura-Kot is amply sufficient to provide room for all the objects described by Hiuen Tsiang as existing in his time, and the remains are sufficiently numerous. Tilaura-Kot occupies the centre of the position, and is clearly the citadel of the ruined city" (Smith 1901, p. 12).

Smith's assertion (Smith 1901, p. 10) that "Piprava is the Kapilavastu of Fa-hien, whereas the city round Tilaura-Kot is the Kapilavastu of Hiuen Tsiang" has a major implication for the indisputable archaeological identity of Piprahwa as Kapilavastu. The epigraphical evidence here is definitive and came from the cells and the verandah on the northern side of its eastern monastery. As K.M. Srivastava, the excavator writes:

> In 1973, the cells and the verandah on the northern side of the eastern monastery yielded terracotta sealings with the legend *Kapilavastu*. The sealings have not been found in a hoard but occurring at different levels and spots ranging between 1.05 and 1.75 m in depth. The legend on the sealings in Brahmi characters of the 1st-2nd centuries AD can be classified into three groups. One of them reads *Devaputra-vihare Kapilavastu-bhikkhusanghasa* and the second *Maha-Kapilavastu-bhikkhusanghasa*, while the third carries names of monks, one being *Sarandasa*. In 1974, the lid of a pot carrying the inscription of the first group was also found. The inscription on the sealings and the lid was the deciding evidence in the identification of Kapilavastu (Srivastava 1989, pp. 345-346).

What is interesting is that Piprahwa remained under occupation till the 3rd century AD when it experienced severe burning and was abandoned. The point is that in the 4th century AD, Fa-Xian could visit Piprahwa because its adjacent settlement site of Ganwaria was inhabited till at least 4th century AD.

According to the normal epigraphical dictates, Piprahwa was no doubt Kapilasvastu. Whether it remained under this name only till the 4th century AD and the name got transferred to the Tilaurakot area by the 7th century AD when Xuang-Xang visited it is impossible to say.

Tilaura-Kot has certainly thrown up a problem. This problem is rooted in the archaeological character of the site which encompasses not merely its fortified section but also its precincts covering a large area. Piprahwa is too far to be considered a part of this area. Araura-Kot also is a fortified site. The presence of two fortified sites – Tilaura-Kot and Araura-Kot – at this spot seems to underscore a special significance for this area of the

Sakyas. Moreover, if the first rampart of Tilaura-Kot dates from c. 600 BC, as it has been alleged, the site seems to be a *Mahajanapada* period site in the beginning. Although the area of the Mallas, Sakyas and Koliyas is not textually known to belong to the *Mahajanapada* complex, the antiquity of the fortifications at Tilaura-Kot suggests otherwise. The Malla-Sakya-Koliya territory of the early Buddhist literature has so far lain in the shadow of the far larger territory of Kosala, but the accumulated archaeological evidence seems to call for a fresh assessment of its significance.

VI. THE BELL-CAPITAL OF BANSI AND THE PILLAR OF BHAGALPUR

Bansi (27-10-47 N/82-55-48 E) is presently in the Siddharthanagar district of Uttar Pradesh and known for its Asokan bell-capital (now kept in the Lucknow museum), which was recovered from the side of a tank by the side of the road which comes from Kopia and goes to the Bansi market on the way to Piprahwa and Lumbini. The lotus capital shows a partly defaced abacus and the remains of the legs of a lion on its top. The abacus carries the honey-suckle motif around it. Although S.P. Gupta (p. 27) reports the stump of an *in situ* Asokan pillar in the area, I was unable to locate it. However, the villagers pointed out the place from where the capital was recovered. The capital is undoubtedly Asokan and of good quality.

The case of the Bhagalpur pillar is complex. Bhagalpur (Survey of India toposheet number 63 N/16; 26-12 N/83-52 E) is near a ferry point on the northern bank of the Ghaghra, with the excavated chalcolithic and later site of Khairadih directly opposite on the southern bank. The temple-mound of Bhagalpur also seems to have similarly high antiquity. The pillar, which lies behind the modern Secondary School of the place, is a monolithic sandstone pillar with clear traces of a circular abacus. H.B.W. Garrick (Cunningham and Garrick 1883, pp. 130-131; pls. 30, 31) found the overall existing height 17'3-1/2" and the diameter 1'6". An inscription of c. 11th/12th century AD is engraved on the lower portion of the pillar. Although none of the earlier scholars hinted at the Mauryan identity of this uninscribed monolithic pillar, I would put it in the Mauryan category because columns of this type are not known to exist later.

The Bhagalpur pillar and the Bansi capital mark the alignment of the most direct route between Pataliputra and Lumbini. Pointing out that the Rampurwa pillars point towards the Kathmandu Valley and not towards Lumbini because there is a massive and difficult range of the Nepal Siwaliks between the Bhikna Tori pass beyond Rampurwa and Lumbini, I argued that "a straighter and easier route to Lumbini from Pataliputra must have existed during the early historic period". I wrote the following:

> The first sign-post after Pataliputra in this regard is Masarh because this yielded the fragment of an Asokan pillar capital ... Proceeding beyond Masarh, the Lumbini route had to cross the Ganga at some point. Now, a little before Buxar there was a major ferry point across the Ganga, and the modern railway bridge to the Ballia side follows broadly this ferry alignment. If this was a ferry point in the ancient context, there should be an ancient site on the other side of the Ganga in this direction. Pakka-Kot clearly fits the bill of such an ancient settlement. Beyond Pukka-Kot, the two sites of Tika Deori and Lakhneswar Dih, both on the Chhoti Saryu, deserve notice. Both are early historical sites, and taken together with Pukka-Kot, suggest the general significance of this sector in the early historic context. The next fixed point, before one crosses the Ghjaghra at Turtipar, is Khairadih, a major early historical settlement. On the other side of the Ghaghra is Bhagalpur where a standing, broken and presumably Mauryan pillar (uninscribed) can still be seen.
>
> Having crossed the Ghaghra at Khairadih, the route possibly followed for some time the alignment of what is locally known as 'Ram-Janki road' along the Ghaghra towards the west. At some point, it branched off the Ram-Janki road (according to the local tradition, this was the route followed by Ram and Janaki to reach Ayodhya from Mithila) and moved towards Kopia which is a fortified early historic city-site, passing Sohgaura, an indisputably Mauryan administrative centre on the way. The fixed point in the direction of Lumbini beyond Kopia is Bansi, which yielded a fragment of an Asokan pillar capital. The place where this fragment was discovered lies a little outside the modern Bansi bazaar, which still remains the most convenient stopping place before proceeding to modern Birdpur, Kapilavastu and Lumbini.
>
> Thus, at every stage of my suggested Pataliputra-Lumbini road, there are clear archaeological sign-posts, and having travelled all along this way, I am in a position to claim that this was the most direct route that Asoka could have adopted for going to Lumbini. There were two major river-crossings on the way, one over the Ganga a little to the east of Buxar, and the other over the Ghaghra at Turtipar/Khairadih (Chakrabarti 2001, pp. 242-243).

VII. AYODHYA

The inverted lotus capital that one now finds these days as the base of the Sivalinga in the Nageshwar Nath Siva temple of Ayodhya is the positive proof of the former existence of an Asokan pillar in Ayodhya, although

Xuang Xang does not mention it, despite mentioning the erection of a stupa at the site by Asoka. There is a mound behind the temple, and it is probable that the capital came from there. The importance of Saketa or Ayodhya on the southern bank of the Sarayu or Ghaghra is well understood. Across the river, the capital of Kosala, Sravasti, lay within easy distance. Ayodhya gave access to a number of areas: Rohilkhand, along the southern bank of the Ghaghra to the west; Banaras via Akbarpur and Jaunpur; Mirzapur and eventually Central India and the Deccan via Jaunpur. The early Buddhist literature testifies that the movements of monks between this place and Sravasti were frequent. From Sravasti, there is also a straight route to the Nepalese Tarai. The find of an Asokan capital in Ayodhya, in fact, underscores the significance of the place.

VIII. VARANASI: LAT BHAIRO

Xuang Xang reported both an Asokan stupa and an Asokan capital to the northeast of the capital and on the west side of the Baruna or Barna river, the northern one of the two tributaries of the Ganga (*Baruna* and *Asi*) in Banaras. The stupa was about 100 feet high and in front of it was a pillar of polished green stone, "clear and lustrous as a mirror in which the reflection of the Buddha was constantly visible" (Smith 1909, p. 337). Smith (1909, p. 338) points out that the stupa and pillar "should be sought in the space between the northeastern corner of Benares and the mile-long section of the Barna's course which runs nearly due north and south. In no other locality could the monuments be said to stand to the west of the Barna river". Depending mostly on the authority of M.A. Sherring's account of Banaras (1868), he points out that the Lat Bhairo pillar (encased in a copper sheath; currently 7-8 feet in height and 3 feet in thickness) stands to the north of the Kapalmochan tank and is the remnant of an ancient pillar which was destroyed in the Hindu-Muslim riots of Banaras in 1809. Smith further points out that an account of these riots was compiled on the basis of official documents by Phil Robinson (1865; for a modern discussion, Visuvalingam and Chalier-Visuvalingam 2006). "The Lat was destroyed on the 21 October by a mob of Muhammadan weaver and others who heaped up inflammable materials round the monument, which was rubbed from top to bottom with spirits and gunpowder and sprinkled with water to make the stone crack" (Smith 1909, note 1, p. 338). According to Robinson (1865), the existing stump, set up in June, 1810, does not occupy the original site. Smith, however, does not think that the base portion of the pillar was removed anywhere and according to him, "it occupies its original position".

That Lat Bhairo stood on a direct old route between Banaras and Sarnath has been pointed out by a number of scholars including F.O. Oertel who undertook excavations at Sarnath in 1904-05:

> Starting from the centre of Benares near the Pachgangaghat, where Aurangzeb's mosque now rises on the ruins of an ancient temple, this road led due north past Lat Bhairo and crossed the Barna river at Purana Pul, by bridge, some remains of which can still be seen a little distance above the viaduct of the metre gauge railway to Ghazipur.

There was a Mughal period bridge with three spans at this spot till the end of the eighteenth century, but when it got damaged due to floods, the then Resident of Banaras, Jonathan Duncan, pulled it down and used the stone for a new bridge over the Barna.

Falk (2006, pp. 166-168) considers the idea of Asokan origin of Lat Bhairo disputable. He cites the opinion of R. Heber (1828) who wrote about its 'exquisite carvings'. However, Heber depended on the report by Mr. Bird who was then the magistrate of Banaras and the 'carvings' of Bird's report might also have meant engraved letters. The French jeweller J.B. Tavernier in 1665 found the column 32 to 35 feet high and thick enough for three people to put their hands around it. Its material was sandstone and it was surmounted by a ball and below the ball it was encircled by large beads.

Till the copper sheath is removed from the pillar and it is properly inspected, there is no way one can be dogmatic about its Asokan identity. However, the known fact that before the riots of 1809 it was a monolithic stone column which was more than 30 feet high lends some strength to the belief that it was indeed set up by Asoka.

IX. SARNATH

The inscribed Asokan column at Sarnath, located to the south of the Dharmarajika stupa at Sarnath, and its associated lion capital, which later became the national emblem of modern India, were found in 1904-05 during F.O. Oertel's excavations at the site. The circumstances of the discovery are interesting. The stump of the column protruded slightly above a concrete terrace which may be called the upper concrete terrace. At a depth of 5′8″ below this terrace, there was a brick floor, and "in this floor were found, embedded in their original positions, parts of six stone railing posts and two cross-rails ornamented with rosettes". The railing posts were uninscribed. The foot of the column was reached 17′ below the upper concrete terrace and it was found resting on a large flat stone (8′x6′x18″).

It has been estimated that the shaft of the column was 27-1/2′ from the original floor level and that it tapered from 2′4″ in diameter at the bottom to 1′10″ in diameter at the top. About 12-1/2′ more lay unpolished below the ground. The lion capital, which was found detached from the column but lying near it, was 7′ high. Several fragments of a stone wheel found in the same area testify that the lion capital was topped by a stone wheel.

Oertel (1904-05, p. 68) observed that "the column must have been battered down and violently thrown against the shrine. Two of the lion heads of the capital, which apparently struck the building, were broken and pieces of the shaft were lying scattered around".

The Sarnath pillar inscription reads (after Hultzsch 1925, pp. 161-164):

(A) Deva(nampriya) ...
(B) ... Pata(liputra)...
(C) ... the Samgha (cannot) be divided by any one.
(D) But indeed that monk or nun who shall break up the Samgha, should be caused to put on white robes and to reside in a non-residence.
(E) Thus this edict must be submitted both to the Samgha of monks and to the Samgha of nuns.
(F) Thus speaks Devanampriya.
(G) Let one copy of this (edict) remain with you deposited in (your) office; and deposit ye another copy of this very (edict) with the lay-worshippers.
(H) These lay-worshippers may come on every fast-day (*posatha*) in order to be inspired with confidence in this very edict; and inevitably on every fast-day, every *Mahamatra* (will) come to the fast-day (service) in order to be inspired with confidence in this very edict and to understand (it).
(I) And as far as your district (extends), dispatch ye (an officer) everywhere according to the letter of this (edict)
(J) In the same way cause (your subordinates) to dispatch (an officer) according to the letter of this (edict) in all the territories (surrounding) forts.

Addressed probably to the *Mahamatras* of Pataliputra, this edict has a few problematic issues. One is the translation of *Samsalanasi Nikhita*, which, according to Hultzsch, should convey the sense of 'deposited in your office'. *Nikhita* has been used in the sense of 'depositing' but should *Samsalana* or Sanskrit *Samsarana* mean anything as specific as 'your office', although Hultzsch accepts the version that it may designate some locality.

V.A. Smith (1909, p. 70) also translates it as 'office' – in fact, as 'head office'. The 'fast-days', according to Sircar (1965, p. 65, note 2), comprise the full-moon day, the fourteenth day of dark fortnight, and the eighth days of the bright and dark fortnights. These are days of religious contemplation for the Buddhist monks and lay worshippers alike, and on the two *Upasotha* days of the fourteenth and the fifteenth, the monks gather in the monastery for the *Patimokkha* to be read out section by section to them. Regarding the 'territories surrounding forts' (in 'J'), Hultzsch (1925, p. 164, note 1) argues that this seems to refer to outlying jungle tracts, possibly those in the Nepalese terai, which were not 'fully pacified, but were held by means of military posts. This is a purely subjective speculation. Smith (1909, p. 70) points out that the word for 'district', *Vishaya,* signified in later times the area 'now known as *Pargana*' and may have had the same meaning in Asoka's time. Each *Vishaya* was under the administration of a *Vishayapati* and each garrison or fortified place (*Kotta*) was commanded by a governor. The royal orders were conveyed to such districts and forts by the responsible local officials. Again, Smith speculates that the Sanchi, Allahabad-Kausambi and Sarnath pillar edicts, all of whom were concerned with the possibility of schism in the Buddhist congregration, were possibly inscribed at the same time. It is probable that all these edicts are later the six pillar edicts of Asoka, which were all issued in the 27th year of his reign or after twenty-six years of his coronation. According to Smith, "it seems reasonable to suppose that the orders in these documents resulted from the deliberations of the Council of Pataliputra vouched for by literary tradition. On this supposition the date of the Council will fall between 243 and 232 (BC), the date of Asoka's death".

IX.1. A Second Pillar at Sarnath(?)

The postulate has been offered by H. Falk (2006, p. 211) on the basis of H. Hargreaves' finds at the site (Hargreaves 1914-15). Attention to these finds has been drawn by a number of scholars including S.P. Gupta (1980) but their implication regarding the existence of a second pillar at Sarnath has so long been ignored. West of the Mauryan and later stupa area, a 25″ square section was found 'closely packed' 'to a depth of 2′6″ with "stone fragments, the debris of monuments ranging from Maurya times to the 1st century BC".

These fragmentary remains include human, semi-human and animal figures, railings, cross-bars, and copings, capitals with volutes, neckings of polished capitals of Indo-Persepolitan type inscribed with Mauryan Brahmi characters recording the gifts of inhabitants of Ujjain and Pataliputra, and part of the rim of a large wheel resembling that which crowned the lion capital of the Sarnath pillar. Some of the monuments, of which these formed part, had undoubtedly been wilfully destroyed while others, especially railing pillars, had clearly suffered the ravages of fire (Hargreaves 1914-15, p. 111).

Hargreaves believes that this material was collected elsewhere at the site and deposited where he found them. The date of the deposition, according to him, is "assignable to a post-Kushan date and one, very probably, not late in the Gupta period". In his list of these objects 'capitals' are specifically mentioned, and under '105' the following entry occurs:

Fragments of Indo-Persepolitan bell capitals. Large proportion retains original polish. Some calcined. Bead and reel and cable mouldings. Diameter varies from one foot upwards (Hargreaves 1914-15, p. 117).

Falk (2006, pp. 211-212) has apparently traced some of these fragments to the reserve collection of the Indian Museum in Kolkata and argued them to be parts of the same capital and attached abacus. According to his measurements, this capital, i.e., the capital of the postulated second pillar "seems to have been larger than the famous one in the site museum" of Sarnath. The illustration published by Falk (2006, Fig. 18, p. 213), which shows the petal ends of 'accession number 9490' of the Indian Museum, leaves no doubt that this fragment belonged to an Asokan bell-capital.

The trace of a second Asokan column at Sarnath is no doubt important, although one wonders why none of the two Chinese pilgrims, Fa-Xian and Xuang Zang, mentioned only one column at the site.

X. PRAHLADPUR

Along with the pillar from Latia, which has been included by Falk (2006, pp. 234-235) in his list of 'non-Asokan pillars', the Prahladpur pillar has been known from the early days of Asokan research, although, like the Latia pillar near Zamania south of the Ganga, the Prahladpur pillar, also south of the Ganga and not far from Zamania, is uninscribed. The Latia pillar can straightaway be put out of consideration in the present context because its capital and the crowning portion have been fashioned out of the same monolithic piece of stone that the pillar is made of. A better explanation is provided by Falk's reference to J. Williams who considers this an example of a Gupta period *dhvajastambha*.

The Prahladpur specimen, removed from its original site to the grounds of the Sanskrit College of Banaras, whose building was designed by Markham Kittoe, is a much stronger candidate for Mauryan affiliation. The fact that it carries later inscriptions including some in shell script and one in Gupta script is not a strongly relevant argument against its being Mauryan, because these inscriptions could have been added or inscribed much later. The pillar originally rested on a base-slab and the upper rim of the shaft is rounded. The latter implies that this carried, in all likelihood, an abacus above with a capital on its top. The total surviving length is about 10.98 m, with the diameter tapering towards the top. Falk's objection to the idea of its being Mauryan is based on the fact that wherever it has been damaged, the inside colour is reddish. The point is that we do not know enough of the stone of Asokan columns to argue that the sandstone used for them was invariably uniform in all respects.

Prahladpur, as the excavations at the site (Narain and Roy 1968) have shown, has a black-and-red ware antecedence. Bairant in the same area is a major fortified early historic site. Prahladpur is also a ferry point, and on the other side of the Ganga is the area of Saidpur-Jahuraganj, an area of considerable early historic and earlier remains. More importantly, if one came through the Robertsganj section from the Deccan and had decided to bypass Banaras on the way to Bihar or the Ghazipur section of Uttar Pradesh, one could travel straight to the southern side of the Ganga in Chandauli and move from there. The ferry point at Prahladpur took one to the northern bank of the Ganga east of Banaras, and the Buxar section of Bihar was also not far off from places like Zamania and Dildarpur in this section.

It may be emphasized that the Banaras area as a whole was at the crossings of various routes, the most important of which was the complex of routes towards the Deccan, going either through Ahraura or through Mirzapur. The Ahraura egress was linked with Bihar and the Mirzapur egress was linked through Jaunpur and Ayodhya with Sravasti. But routes came to Banaras also from many places in eastern UP.

XI. BELKHARA (AHRAURA)

This pillar stands near the bank of the Garra river near Ahraura. The location is on the way from Ahraura to Likhuania, from where the road ascends to Sukrit on the way to Robertsganj and the Son crossing for the Surguja section of Central India. Till the beginning of the railways, there was a brisk trade between Ahraura and Surguja, and the local revenue collector of Ahraura was powerful enough to build a fort between Ahraura and Sukrit to monitor this trade. There is ample archaeological evidence at Likhuania and in the adjacent areas to suggest that this was an old route, part of the Deccan routes complex from Banaras to the Deccan. On the pillar at Belkhara, I wrote the following in 2001 (Chakrabarti 2001, pp. 239-240):

> Not far from the Ahraura bazaar and near the village of Belkhara, there is a broken round monolithic pillar with a small Ganesa image attached to its base and two inscriptions on its body. The Ganesa image was added later and the inscriptions also could have been incised later. One of the inscriptions need not be earlier than the eleventh-twelfth century AD. The second inscription belongs to an uncertain category. According to local reports, the pillar was removed from the Garra Dam when this dam was being built around 1954 and placed at its recent spot which is not far from the original spot now submerged in water. This pillar appeared to be Mauryan. Cunningham (1880: 128-30) noticed the pillar at Belkhara and dated the eleventh-twelfth century AD inscription on it to AD 1196. His measurement for the broken pillar is 11 ft 7 inch long and 15 inch in diameter. According to Cunningham's reading of the inscription, the pillar was erected by the mason Jaluna in AD 1196. What deserves notice, however, is that round, monolithic and polished pillars of this type were not made in ancient India after the Maurya period and that Cunningham might have got carried away by his reading of the inscription which was most likely engraved much later than the initial establishment of the pillar. Despite such a weighty opinion as that of Cunningham in this matter, the possibility of Mauryan affiliation of this pillar should not be ignored.

Considering the intrinsic significance of the Ahraura zone and considering that a Minor Rock Edict occurs at Ahraura itself, the Belkhara pillar which significantly resembles Mauryan period pillars, dates probably from that period.

XII. BAKRAUR

An inscription of the ninth century AD during the reign of the Pala king, Devapala (AD 815-855) identified the ruins of the stupa at Bakraur near Bodh Gaya as the site of the house of Sujata who offered sweetened milk and rice to the Buddha meditating below the Bodhi tree. K.M. Srivastava's excavations of the stupa established its multi-stage history which continued possibly from the pre-Christian period to the 9th/10th century AD. It has been known as a site since the early 19th century and was also noted in some detail by Cunningham (1871) who found two pieces of a broken stone pillar near the ruins of a brick stupa. The main portion of the surviving pillar was removed to Gaya town in the beginning of the 19th century and removed again in the first three or four decades of the 20th century to the bank of Mucilinda tank to the south of the Bodh Gaya temple. This portion is about 16′ high and the diameter is a little more than 2 feet 4 inch. There is no report of an inscription here. Falk (2006, p. 229) points out that the dimensions are comparable to those of Asokan pillars. The supposition is strengthened by Xuang Xang's report that there was a pillar by the site of a stupa across the Niranjana river at Bodh Gaya.

XIII. BHUVANESVARA: BHASKARESVARA AND RAMESVARA TEMPLES

Whether or not in its original position, the Mauryan identity of the stone column serving as the phallus of Siva in the Bhaskaresvara temple of Bhuvanesvar, which was estimated to be about 40′ high early in the 19th century, cannot be seriously doubted. A stone lion and a bell-capital were recovered at some distance from this temple. The latter pieces were not found together or even at the same spot but came from the vicinity of the Ramesvara temple which is far from Bhaskaresvara. The quality of these pieces in view of their suggested Mauryan affiliation has been doubted, but considering that the Mauryan art tradition admitted a great deal of diversity, the objections to their being Mauryan on the ground of quality, are not particularly valid. On the other hand, in view of the strong Mauryan association with Orissa, the location of a Mauryan pillar outside the fortifications of the early historic city of Sisupalgarh is not an improbability.

XIV. ALLAHABAD

The Allahabad pillar located inside the fort overlooking the junction of the Ganga and Yamuna is 35 feet high, with a lower diameter of 2 feet 11 inch and an upper diameter of 2 feet 2 inch. These measurements without taking the height of the now-missing portion of the capital into consideration were published by Cunningham in 1877 (Cunningham 1877, p. 37). Cunningham writes that the abacus survived, although he does not say if his measurement of the height of the column included that of the abacus. It is unlikely to have been the case.

> The circular abacus, however, still remains with its graceful scroll of alternate lotus and honeysuckle, resting on a beaded astragalus of Greek origin. This was once surmounted by the statue of a lion; but the lion must have disappeared many centuries ago, as when the pillar was re-erected

> by Jahangir in AD 1605, it was crowned by a globe, surmounted by a cone, as described and sketched by Padre Tieffenthaler in the middle of the next century. It then stood in the middle of the fort (Cunningham 1877, p. 37).

Cunningham, in fact, offers an account of the number of times this pillar was thrown to the ground and later erected on the basis of James Prinsep's analysis of the locations of the various inscriptions engraved on it. Prinsep comments that the pillar was "overthrown some time after its first erection by the great Asoka". According to him, this is proved by the insertion of several names in a script which may be called intermediate between the Asokan and post-Asokan forms. Regarding one of these names, he comments:

> Now it would have been exceedingly difficult, if not impossible, to have cut the name No. 10 up and down at right angles to the other writing, *while the pillar was erect,* to say nothing of the place being out of reach, unless a scaffold were erected on purpose, which would hardly be the case, since the object of an ambitious visitor would be defeated by placing his name out of sight and in an unreadable position. The pillar was erected as Samudra Gupta's arm, and there it probably remained until overthrown again by the idol-breaking zeal of the Musalmans; for we find no writings on it of the Pala or Sarnath type (i.e., of the tenth century), but a quantity appears with plain legible dates from the Samvat year 1420, or AD 1363, down to 1660 odd, and it is remarkable that these occupy one side of the shaft, or that which was uppermost when the pillar was in a prostrate position. A few detached and ill-executed Nagari names with Samvat dates of 1800 odd show that ever since it was laid on the ground again by General Garstin, the passion for recording visits of piety or curiosity has been at work (Prinsep 1838, cited by Cunningham 1877, p. 38).

Cunningham made some calculations on his own: seven dates from AD 1240 to 1341; five ranging from AD 1407 to 1438; twelve ranging from AD 1444 to 1527; three ranging from AD 1575 to 1583; and three of AD 1807.

> These dates, combined with the total absence of any medieval Nagari inscriptions, are sufficient to show that the pillar was standing out of the reach of pilgrims' scribbling from the time of the Guptas until that of the early Musulman kings of Delhi. There are then twelve dated inscriptions coming down to near the death of Muhammad Tughlak. There is not a single record of the time of Firoz Tughlak which leads me to suspect that he may have re-erected this pillar with its globe and cone, like those of the *Zarin Minar*, or Golden Pillar, at Delhi. But if he did set it up, it must have been thrown down again during the troubled times of his immediate successors, as the dates begin again in AD 1407 and 1408. It was next set

> up by Jahangir in AH 1014, or AD 1605, to be pulled down by General Kyd in AD 1798. It was once more scribbled upon in AD 1807, and finally in 1883 it was set up as it stands at present (Cunningham 1877, pp. 38-39).

The idea that the Allahabad pillar which, as we have noticed, has had a singularly checkered history, was brought from its original position in Kausambi to Allahabad was nothing but a suggestion of Cunningham. It was not based on any proof. Because the short Asokan edict engraved on it is an order for the *Mahamatras* of Kausambi, "it seems probable that this pillar may have been originally erected in that city, and afterwards removed to Prayag or Allahabad" (Cunningham 1877, p. 39). In that case, he further argued, that it was 'highly probable' that it was brought to Prayaga by Firoz Tughlak "whose removal of the Siwalik and Mirat pillars to Delhi gives countenance to this suggestion". Another argument was that the Chinese pilgrims Fa-Xian and Xuang Xang did not report any Asokan pillar at Prayag.

As far as we can judge, there is nothing in the records or the actual circumstances to suggest that the Allahabad pillar was brought from elsewhere. Prayag's position as a pilgrimage centre is well known, and so is its position in relation to the route to Central India and the Deccan through the Baghelkhand or Rewa plateau. The location of an Asokan pillar in this sector cannot be an improbability. Besides, its specific location in the fort area which overlooks the Ganga-Yamuna confluence seems to make sense in view of the holiness of the place.

The six pillar edicts are neatly engraved in continuous lines around the column and have been damaged both by the peeling off of the stone in some places and the cutting of the inscription of the Mughal emperor Jahangir on a great portion of the third and fourth edicts. This section is followed downwards by the famous inscription of Samudragupta. Two short Asokan inscriptions figure towards its right. Their names, 'Queen's edict' and 'Kausambi edict', were given by Cunningham. As one of them refers to Asoka's queens, Cunningham calls it 'Queen's edict'. The second one refers to the *Mahamatras* of Kausambi and thus he calls it 'Kausambi edict'. The texts of these two inscriptions are as follows:

XIV.1. The Queen's Edict (after Hultzsch 1925, pp. 158-59)

(A) At the word of Devanampriya, the Mahamatras everywhere have to be told (this).

(B) What gifts (have been made) here by the second queen (viz.) either mango-groves, or gardens, or alms-houses, or whatever else, these (shall) be registered (in the name) of that queen.

(C) This (is) (the request) of the second queen, the mother of Tivala, the Kaluvaki.

It has been added (Hultzsch 1925, p. 159, note 9) that *Kaluvaki* is probably the name of the queen's family and may be connected with the Vedic *Gotra* of the *Karus*. One is not sure if 'alm-house' connotes the proper sense of *Danagriha* of the original – literally the house for the distribution of gifts.

XIV.2. The Kausambi Edict (after Hultzsch 1925, pp. 159-160)

(A) (Devanam)priya commands (thus).
(B) The Mahamatras at Kosambi
(C) ... is made united.
(D) ... should not be received into the *Samgha*.
(E) And also that monk or nun (who) shall break up the *Samgha*, should be caused to put on white robes and to reside in a non-residence.

Hultzsch (p. 160, note 5) refers to a passage from Buddhaghosha's *Samantapasadika,* where Asoka is stated to have given white robes to the heretical monks whom he expelled.

XV. KAUSAMBI PILLAR

Of the pillar fragments noted by Cunningham at Kausambi, the longest one was put up at the original spot by D.R. Sahni in 1922. There is no inscription of Asoka on the surviving part, although some later inscriptions from the Gupta period onwards are there. Falk (2006, p. 176) draws attention to a fragment of a monolithic stone pillar in the Allahabad museum and argues against its Mauryan affiliation. As it is part of a monolithic stone pillar with a hole on top for the fixing of a capital above, it is, in all probability, a Mauryan piece. In that case, the possibility of the existence of more than one Mauryan pillar at Kausambi is undeniable. Considering the significance of Kausambi as an ancient city, it is not an unlikely situation.

The significance of Allahabad and Kausambi in the communication links of the Gangetic plain and of this plain with Central India and the Deccan is not always appreciated. The route from Banaras to Allahabad/ Prayag is marked by a chain of sites along the north bank of the Ganga, and beyond Allahabad, this chain goes in the direction of the Kanpur-Mathura region. Equally importantly, a route goes from Allahabad along the northern bank of the Yamuna to the Garhwa-Shankargarh sector via

Bhita, and a route from Kausambi crosses the Yamuna in this sector and links up with the route which comes from Allahabad. The combined route then goes in the direction of the Vindhyas and Rewa (Baghelkhand). This is an arterial line towards the Deccan, and overlooking one of the spots where the route from Garhwa-Shankargarh ascends the Vindhyan scarp is the major stupa site of Deur Kothar at the edge of the Rewa plateau.

XVI. DEUR KOTHAR

Although excavated in 1999-2001, the stupa and monastic complex of Deur Kothar lies mostly unpublished. The main stupa at the half-a-kilometre-long site directly overlooks the Sohagi Ghat ascent of the Vindhyas and has in addition 3 small brick-built stupas, 29 or 30 small stone-built stupas, 63 rock-shelters, out of which six rock-shelters contain pre-Buddhist and Buddhist rock-paintings and painted inscriptions, and a number of both stone-built and brick-built monasteries. The traces of stone-built paths is clearly visible within the complex where one can also detect stone balustrades and uprights of stupa railings and pieces of stone carrying early Brahmi inscriptions. The excavations of the main stupa and the importance of these excavations and the site as a whole have been discussed by me (Chakrabarti 2005, pp. 73-74) elsewhere.

> The body of the main brick-built stupa was circled by a single-brick wall, and the 10-18 cm wide space between them was filled up by a thick infill of compact clay. The stupa complex was surrounded by a stone railing which has survived in the form of stone copings and railings. Some of these railings bore decorative motifs and donors' inscriptions. On the western and southern sides of the stupa, there were monolithic staircases with six steps at the ground level to approach the body of the stupa, and although their traces on the other two sides have been found destroyed, such steps may be presumed to have existed on the north and east sides as well. There was certainly a *harmika* – or a stone enclosure with stone railings on four sides and a stone-built umbrella with a long shaft in the centre – on the top of the stupa, because fragments of such an umbrella have been found in the excavations. There was also a stone-paved floor what has been called a 'flagstone flooring' around the stupa complex.
>
> The western section of the stupa periphery had a stone pillar which was identical with the Mauryan period stone pillars found elsewhere. Parts of the round abacus of this column have been found. This pillar was found in fragments overlying the stone flooring which was contemporary with the stupa complex. The foundation pit of this pillar contained ashy soil and glazed nodules which may be interpreted as products of burning.

> The results of the excavations of the main stupa at Deur Kothar are significant in the early historic archaeology of India for a number of reasons. First, this is the first Mauryan period stupa which has yielded the evidence of decorated stone balustrades, thus proving that this feature of the early Buddhist stupas, which one generally associated with the Sunga period, had a Mauryan ancestry. This shows that there is no dichotomy between the Mauryan and Sunga art styles; on the contrary, there was a continuum of both style and motifs. Secondly, whatever has been illustrated of the decorations of the Deur Kothar railings shows designs (cf. lotus placed in a vessel) sculpted in low relief, suggesting the beginning of this style which got elaborated in the Sunga period, in the Mauryan period itself. Thirdly, this element of continuum is also clear from the occurrence of a number of donative inscriptions found engraved on the railings. This categorically demonstrates that there is no longer any reason to hold that the Maurya art was only a court art and not supported by the donations of the people. Fourthly, the fragments of the Mauryan pillar which have been found show that this pillar, which is absolutely identical with the type of column on which Asoka had his pillar edicts engraved, did not bear any royal edict. On the contrary, the six-line inscription written in Mauryan Brahmi on this particular Mauryan pillar, although not yet properly edited and published, suggests that the erection and dedication of this stone pillar at this place were caused by a Buddhist monk (*upasaka*) and his disciples. Finally, the fact that the fragments of this pillar directly overlay the stone-paved floor contemporary with the stupa shows that the destruction of the pillar happened not very long after the stupa and the pillar came into existence. On the basis of the present evidence, one tends to agree with the view of the excavator that the destruction of the pillar, and perhaps the stupa which does not have any post-Mauryan vestige, can be related to the textual tradition about the hostility of the first Sunga king, Pushyamitra Sunga, towards Buddhism.

The great significance of the find of this inscribed 'Mauryan' column in the context of a Mauryan period stupa at Deur Kothar has not yet been properly appreciated in Indian archaeology. It is an inscribed 'Mauryan' column – the palaeography of the edict is as Mauryan as any – but the inscription has nothing to do with Asoka or any other Mauryan king. The column is said to have been erected by a group of Buddhist monks.

XVII. SANCHI

A local landlord tried to cut up the Sanchi pillar and use the shaft in a sugarcane press (Marshall 1918, pp. 90-91). The inscribed stump remained in its original position, which is near the southern gateway of the main stupa. The estimated total height of the pillar is 42 feet. Its bottom rested directly on the bed-rock and was circular and hammer-dressed up to a height of eight feet from the bottom. Above this height, it was chiselled and polished. The base was found embedded in a packing of heavy stones which was retained in position by massive wall. A layer of earth and small debris overlay this packing and was topped by a six-inch-thick layer of *bajri* or broken brick which extended over the whole area round about the stupa. The *bajri* layer also marked 'the dividing line between the rough-dressed base and polished section of the shaft above' (Marshall and Foucher 1983 reprint, p. 26).

Sanchi Inscription (Hultzsch 1925, pp. 160-161)

(A) .....

(B) (cannot) be divided.

(C) The Samgha both of monks and nuns is made united as long as (my) sons and great-grandsons (shall reign and) as long as the moon and the sun (shall shine).

(D) The monk or nun who shall break up the Samgha, must be caused to put on white robes, and to reside in a non-residence.

(E) For my desire is that the Samgha may be united (and) of long duration.

The translation offered by N.G. Majumdar (in Marshall and Foucher 1983 reprint, p. 287) is somewhat different: "The (split-up) Samgha, both of monks and of nuns, has been made one united whole. As long as (my) sons and great-grandsons (shall rule) and the moon and the sun (shall shine), the monk or nun who creates a division in the Samgha shall be made to put on white robes and to reside out of the (Samgha) residence. For what is my desire? ... That the Samgha as a united (body) may long endure."

In his notes on this inscription, Majumdar points out that "there was ample provision in the Code of the Buddhist Samgha for dealing with *Samghaveda,* which in the *Patimokkha* is reckoned as one of the Thirteen Minor Priestly Offences" and finds it strange that this needed royal injunctions issued from at least three major places – Allahabad-Kausambi and Sanchi. He further analyses the relevant Buddhist texts and finds that the punishment of residing outside the residence earmarked for the monks was considered punishment enough for the monks guilty for such offences. He did not have to put on white robes. This was a new measure meant for adding extra humiliation for the guilty monks. Majumdar suspects that these measures, if promulgated by the Church, might have been flouted. The Church seems to have appealed to the highest authority for enforcing it on the monks. "It seems as if a serious cleavage had already occurred, and the Church had to provide for effective safeguards against its recurrence in future" (Majumdar in Marshall and Foucher 1983 reprint, p. 286).

XVIII. UDAYAGIRI (GWALIOR MUSEUM)

The Mauryan identity of this lion capital (4 lions shown seated back to back) from Udayagiri in the outskirts of Vidisa near Sanchi (now in Gwalior) was pointed out by J. Williams (1973). This follows the Mauryan type of capital in all other respects except the human figures on the abacus which have been clearly rendered in the style of Gupta art of c. 6th century AD. The standing figures represent the signs of the zodiac whereas the seated figures represent *Adityas* or sons of Aditi, who are associated with the sun. Williams calls it a 'recut' Asokan capital and offers another example of this type from Khairadih. A *Surya* image from Khairadih (now in the Lucknow museum), dated c.8th century AD, "retains one bead and reel from a border below, and on the back of the *Prabha-mandala*, a rounded polished surface which appears to be part of the original animal" (Williams 1973, p. 239). It is interesting to recall in this context that opposite Khairadih, across the Ghaghra, we have argued that the pillar at Bhagalpur is of Mauryan affiliation. Regarding the Udayagiri capital, J.C. Harle (1974, p. 41) accepts Williams' position and deals at length with the iconography of the Gupta period figures on the abacus.

Williams (1973, plate 11) also publishes the illustration of a single-lion capital from Udayagiri and dates it to the Sunga phase and later. The abacus, as seen in the plate, shows a winged lion followed by a bull. Again, this capital follows the Mauryan model and hints at the possibility of more than one Mauryan pillar at Udayagiri near Vidisa. The capital is unlikely to belong to the Sunga phase for the simple reason that no specifically Sunga context is yet known to have yielded this type of capital.

XIX. BHOPAL(?)

The capital of this pillar (Falk 2006, p. 22) is integral with the pillar itself and there can be no question of its being Mauryan. To us, this seems to be Latia-like pillar.

XX. SODANGA (UJJAYINI)

In 1989, V.S. Wakankar found a statue of elephant with Mauryan polish at Sodanga which lies about 15 km to the northeast of Ujjayini. Its trunk is partly broken. Later, Rahman Ali and others of the Vikram University, Ujjayini, picked up a lotus capital from the close vicinity of a stupa at

Sodanga. This stupa, which has a stone circular wall around, goes back to the Mauryan period. The first occupation of the site dates from c.600 BC. The pillar itself is missing. The lotus capital measures 2.54 m in diameter and 66 cm in height. The elephant figure measures 123x65x50 cm (length, height and width).

The most famous Asokan period stupa at Ujjain is the Kanipur stupa lying a few km to the northeast. According to local tradition, this was the stupa built by Asoka in honour of his queen Devi who was reputedly from a Vaisya family. This stupa (107 m in diameter and more than 30 m high), excavated by M.G. Garde in 1938-39, is also known as *Vaisya Tekri*. Rahman Ali and others (2004) refer to another Asokan stupa near the modern Ranjit Hanuman temple, about 1.5 km from Sodanga.

The location of Sodanga is interesting. It lies on the Ujjain-Nagda road. As I wrote elsewhere:

> Ujjain-Nagda-Ratlam-Baroda alignment is the modern alignment between Ujjain and Gujarat, and considering the open nature of the topography and the importance of the Chambal crossing at Nagda, as shown by the chalcolithic and later period mound at Nagda, it is reasonable to infer that this alignment was significant in the ancient context as well (Chakrabarti 2005, p. 106).

Ujjain or the ancient city of Ujjayini holds a nodal position in the communication network of Malwa: between Ujjain and the Narmada on the way to the Deccan, between Ujjain and Gujarat, between Ujjain and Rajasthan, especially Ajmer on the way to Delhi, and between Ujjain and Vidisa. That Asokan remains have been located at Ujjain is only something historically and geographically natural.

XXI. AMARAVATI

It is a fragmentary inscription engraved on a sandstone block (10 inch long and 17 inch high), possibly part of an Asokan pillar. There is some trace of 'Mauryan polish' on the inscribed face of the slab which is said to be fine-grained quartzite of the Nallamalai range. The inscription has been analysed line by line by Sircar (2000, pp. 118-122), and in each line he finds words which occur elsewhere in indubitable Asokan inscriptions. For instance, "the second line reads *(dha) kho likhite* (*me*) in which *dha* seems to be the second letter of *idha* so that the sentence stands for Sanskrit *iha khalu likhitam maya,* 'indeed (it) has been written here by me'. The style of the sentence is no doubt clearly Asokan and all the four words are found in Asoka's edicts" (Sircar 2000, p. 120). Sircar's careful conclusion at the end is as follows:

> We have seen that the palaeography and language of the inscription under study do not go against its ascription to the Maurya emperor Asoka and that, on the other hand, its style seems to be perfectly Asokan while its contents remind us of some of the known edicts of Asoka. The ideas suggested by the words of the inscription are similar to those peculiar to the records of Asoka and have not yet been noticed in any other inscription. The use of the First Person singular is also rare in royal records excepting those of Asoka. These facts, when considered along with others that the inscription was engraved on a sandstone pillar like those of Asoka, that the pillar bore the so-called 'Mauryan polish' and that the record has to be assigned to the Maurya age on grounds of palaeography, indeed make it very probable that the epigraph belongs to Asoka ... (Sircar 2000, p. 121)

In view of the general significance of the Krishna Valley in Andhra and the great significance of Amaravati both as a Buddhist centre and an urban centre, the presence of an Asokan inscription at the site is not something aberrant in the archaeological record.

XXII. SANKISA

Sankisa lies to the west of modern Farukhabad in Uttar Pradesh and has been known as Sankisa of the Buddhist and other early literatures of India for a long time. The credit of first identifying this site goes to Cunningham who discovered a Maurya elephant capital here in 1862-63. The pillar is missing. About 400 feet to the north of the *Bisari devi* temple mound, he found an elephant capital, with the face and the tusks of this standing elephant missing.

> The capital itself is of the well known bell-shape, corded or reeded perpendicularly, with an abacus of honeysuckle similar to that of the Allahabad pillar. The figure of the elephant is by far the best representation of that animal I have ever seen in any Indian sculpture. The veins of the legs are carefully chiselled, and the toes of the feet are well and faithfully represented, but the loss of the trunk prevents us from forming a decided opinion as to its excellence as a work of art. If we may judge from the position of the legs, the animal was most probably represented as standing still with his trunk hanging down. The stone is a fine-grained sandstone of reddish hue, and has been very highly polished. The bell-capital is low, its breadth being greater than its height, in which particular it resembles the Asoka pillar of *Navandgarh Lauriya,* to the north of Bettiah. Taking all these circumstances into consideration along with the superior execution of the work, I feel satisfied that this capital is of the same age as the well-known Asoka pillars of Allahabad and Navandgarh (Cunningham 1871, pp. 274-275).

Pl. I. Surya Image from Khairadih.

Pl. II. Attendant Deity of the Surya Image from Khairadih.

Pl. III. A View of the Head of the Surya Image from Khairadih.

Pl. IV. Another View (from the Opposite Side) of the Head of the Surya Image from Khairadih.

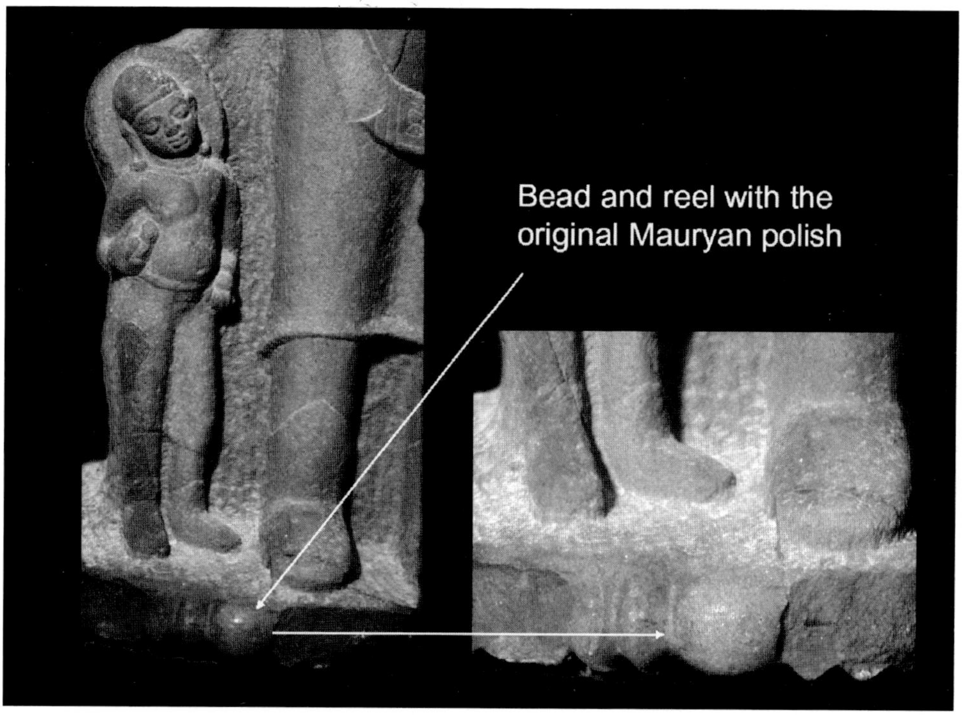

Pl. V. Bead and Reel Motif on the Surya Image from Khairadih.

Pl. VI. The General View of a Neolithic Site in Andhra in the Area of the Edicts.

Pl. VII. The General View of the Valley below the Yerragudi Hill.

Pl. VIII. Location of the Asokan Inscription at Yerragudi.

Sankisa lies on a major axis of the Ganga plain, the axis which traverses the area from Mathura to Kanauj and beyond. Sankisa is also a holy spot for the Buddhists because here the Buddha descended from the *Trayastrimsa* heaven. Regretfully, the associated pillar has not yet been traced. Regarding the quality of the elephant capital, it has to be admitted that sculpturally it is somewhat heavy and somewhat ill at ease on the top of the abacus. Falk (2006, p. 207, fig. 6) argues that the pillar was slender in relation to its heavy top. The Chinese pilgrims report a lion, instead of an elephant, on the top of the Asokan pillar at Sankisa, but there is no assurance that their observations are correct in all cases.

XXIII. DELHI-TOPRA AND DELHI-MEERAT

An inordinate amount of literature on these two inscribed pillars has been concerned how Firoz Shah Tughlak transported them to Delhi and re-erected them. In the Archaeological Survey of India *Memoir* on Firoz Shah Kotla (page 1937), there is a translation of the relevant extracts [Folios 91(b) to 105(b)] from *Sirat-i-Firozshahi,* a Persian manuscript dated 1002 Hijri in the Oriental Public Library of Bankipore, Patna, by M.H. Kuraishi. Shams-i-Siraj, the author of *Tarikh-i-Firozshahi* and a contemporary of Firoz, wrote his account of the transportation of the pillar from Topra drawing, apparently, from his memory, because when it was transported, he was twelve years old. One regrets that the identity of Topra is not yet certain. In 1871, Cunningham pointed out that the pillar was brought to Delhi from a place variously called *Topur, Topra, Toparsuk, Tohera, Tawera* and *Nahera.* It was "on the bank of the Jumna, in the district of Salora, not far from Khizrabad, which is at the foot of the mountains, 90 *kos* from Delhi". Cunningham argued that the distance from Delhi and the position at the foot of the mountains pointed out the present Khizrabad on the Yamuna, just below the spot where the river issues from the lower range of hills. At Khizrabad, the pillar was taken to Delhi by boat and the village from where it was originally brought was "perhaps the present *Paota,* on the western bank of the Yamuna, a few miles to the northeast of Khizrabad". What is somewhat problematic is that Cunningham emphasized in this context the significance of the area around the ancient city of Srughna which has, in fact, in its vicinity an Asokan period stupa. The site of Srughna is no doubt important (cf. Chakrabarti and Saini 2009) but it throws no light on the exact location of the Asokan pillar which now stands in Firoz Shah Kotla of Delhi. In 1877, Cunningham (1877, p. 34) reiterate his opinion, but in 1882 (Cunningham 1882, pp. 78-79) he change his opinion and opened that Topra, a village on the direct line between Ambala and Sirsawa (on the other bank of the Yamuna) was the place from where the pillar was transported to Delhi. To the east of the village, he points out the bricks of the pre-Christian era embedded in two mounds. It is this identification which has subsequently been accepted by people including the present author. However, strong doubts persist because the place is considerably away from the Siwaliks. Locationally, Paota or Paonta Sahib, a Sikh religious spot, on the bank of the Yamuna near the modern Saharanpur-Kalsi alignment, possibly makes more sense, although it must be confessed that I have not yet surveyed the Paonta Sahib area. If one proceeds from Kalsi towards the ancient Srughna, one of the ways to approach it is to follow the course of the Yamuna. Paonta Sahib lies at a crossing which gives access to the Sadhora area.

Cunningham (1877, p. 35) estimates the total height of the pillar to be 42 feet 7 inch, of which 35 feet are highly polished. Its upper diameter is 25.3 inch and its lower diameter 38.8 inch. One has to accept that along with Kalsi, the Delhi-Topra pillar indicates the general significance of the Siwalik area in the Mauryan scheme of things.

The exact spot in the Meerat area from where the Asokan pillar now standing on the ridge at the back of the Delhi University was transported to Delhi, also by Firoz Shah Tughlak, is totally unknown, there being no indication, not even a remote one, in this regard. This column seems to have had an interesting history – broken into fragments due to a gunpowder explosion during the reign of Farukhseer (AD 1713-1719) of the Mughal dynasty early in the 18th century, the shifting of these fragments to Calcutta and their subsequent return to the standing form in the present position.

Did this pillar stand somewhere near Meerat on the way to Hastinapur? From Meerat, there is a straight route to the Siwaliks near the modern Najibabad area, from where a road goes to Pauri via Kotdwar. There are archaeological sites of the pre-Christian era in the Najibabad sector, giving an indication of the ancient importance of this access route to the Himalayas.

XXIV. HISSAR AND FATEHABAD

The Mauryan significance of the pillar, now embedded in the floor of a mosque inside the Hissar fort, was first argued in the 7th volume of the *Journal of the Asiatic Society of Bengal* (Brown 1838) but it was soon doubted by scholars including James Prinsep and Cunningham (1875, pp. 140-142). Its indisputable Mauryan identity in the form of rather damaged but still clear letters had to wait for the epigraphist B.C. Chhabra's publication in 1964 (Chhabra 1964). The upper half of the pillar is now found inside a mosque in Fatehabad, which, like the Hissar fort, was also constructed by Firoz and his son in the 14th century. According to Chhabra, the lower part of the Hissar pillar fragment is badly damaged but one can discern here and there patches of Mauryan polish and traces of old inscriptions, one in early Brahmi and the rest in the Gupta period script. The Arabic inscriptions now completely cover the fragment which survives inside the Fatehabad mosque, leaving behind very few traces of Mauryan polish. However, "still from the proportions and the peculiar Chunar stone one can easily recognize it as being Asokan" (Chhabra 1964; for a good documentation of these pillar fragments, Falk 2006, pp. 169-170, 173-174).

There is no reason to assume that the pillar fragments were shifted to Hissar and Fatehabad by Firoz and his son because the Delhi-Topra and Delhi-Meerat pillars were transported to Delhi by Firoz. The Fatehabad fragment was likely to have been moved from Hissar to Fatehabad by Firoz's son because he established Fatehabad. The Hissar fragment's original position was likely to have been in the Hissar area itself.

The chain of sites extending in the direction of Pakistani Panjab through Rohtak, Hansi and Hissar makes us believe that this was one of the arterial lines to the northwest in early historic (and both earlier and later) India. Rohtak or ancient Rohitaka was a major city and both at Hansi and Hissar, there are traces of major historical occupations. This route crossed over to the Ajudhan and Dipalpur segments of modern Pakistan on the way to places such as Multan, Dera Ghazi Khan and Dera Ismail Khan. This could eventually end up in Afghanistan, especially in the Kandahar sector. Akra, at the mouth of the Tochi-Kurram Valley, in Bannu was likely to have been a major trade entrepot of the period, receiving on the one hand the trade goods coming from as far as the Delhi-Mathura sector via Rohtak, Hansi and Hissar. The Rohtak-Hansi-Hissar-Abohar-Fazilka alignment led to Bahawalpur on the one hand and Multan on the other. In any case, the location of an Asokan pillar along this route is a distinct theoretical possibility, and there is no reason to deny the significance of the Hissar location in the distribution of the Asokan pillars.

6

Summary and Discussion

We have discussed the locations of all the Asokan edict-bearing sites and the sites where Asoka's presence can be inferred with varying degrees of certainty and possibility. We have not found a single case where the possibility of Asokan presence needs outright denial. Apart from the 'Lumbini edict' reported from Bhuvaneswar, we have not found a single plausible case of forgery, and even in the case of this particular Bhuvaneswar find, one wonders whether it was a forgery or the result of copying the Lumbini edict as a ritual activity. Despite Falk's claim that the slab inscribed with parts of PE VI in a Karachi private collection – the so-called Buner slab – is a forgery, we find no possible reason to consider it a forgery. In a number of cases, the pillars or the pillar fragments which have survived are only doubtfully Asokan. The Belkhara pillar fragment from near Ahraura and the pillar known as *Bhim-ki-Chhari* or 'Bhima's cane or stick' at Bhagalpur on the opposite bank of the Ghaghra at Khairadih belong to this category. In both cases, however, I have pointed out at length the geographical importance of their locations, although that does not necessarily warrant Asokan presence there. One of our major points of argument has been that monolithic columns of stone with a separable section for capitals are not known to occur outside the Mauryan context. There have been monolithic columns of stone in the later periods but in all cases their capital-sections are integrated with the body of the column (cf. Kahaun pillar, Latia pillar). Furthermore, the columns considered undoubtedly Mauryan are far from being uniform in their length, diameter or even the degree of their polishing and tapering, as Falk's detailed study (Falk 2006) convincingly shows. The Deur Kothar fragments, for instance, belong to what would otherwise be considered a classic Mauryan column, but, as we have seen, the monk's inscription on it shows that Asoka had nothing to do with it. This find may also support the notion conveyed by the PE VI (line SS in Hultzsch's translation) and MRE-I (line M in Hultzsch's translation) that stone pillars were already present in Asoka's time, i.e., some of them predated Asoka. It is also a well known fact that the quality of the Asokan capitals significantly varied from site to site. The specimens which have been obtained from Sodanga near Ujjain and Sankisa near Farukhabad have, for instance, none of the elegance which the Sarnath quadripartite and the Nageswarnath capital of Ayodhya, for example, possess, but that does not put them outside the Mauryan sphere. The same is true of the capital found in Bhuvaneswar. It looks crude but before one denies it being Mauryan, one has to point out that such lotus capitals have never been found in later contexts. As generic types, such lotus capitals are specific to the Mauryan period alone, and wherever we find them, they have to be placed firmly in the Mauryan sphere. We have no doubt about the Udayagiri find (now kept in Gwalior) being Mauryan, although the sculptures now present in the abacus were later additions. If there is a question mark about the Udayagiri specimen, it needs pointing out that in the form of Khairadi sun image of c. 8th century AD we have a convincing example of how a Mauryan pillar was used to make an image in a much later period.

John Irwin has tried to identify some supposedly pre-Asokan pillars. Without going into the merits of such clear-cut categorisations, we would agree with what Irwin (1974, p. 718) wrote about lumping all Asokan pillars as "uniform products of a single workshop over a period of twenty-five years".

> ...We begin to see them as an odd medley. Some are tall and elegant; others relatively short and clumsy. Some are of one colour and texture of sandstone; some of another. Some are highly polished; some are not. Some have the lower sections of their shafts untrimmed; one is polished right down to the base. Some have projections of one kind, some of another, and some have no projections at all. Some bear insignia on their undersides; others do not. Some had their capitals dowelled one way, some another, and so on. Yet, if all the pillars had been produced by a single generation of craftsmen working at the same quarry, one would expect consistency in the treatment of shafts before any other component.

Falk believes that in addition to the Chunar quarry, extensive use was made of a possible quarry at Pabhosa north of Kausambi. It is certainly possible, and one may even add the name of the Rupbas quarry near

Bharatpur to this list. It appears increasingly unlikely, however, that there was a rigorous homogeneity in the production of pillar shafts.

In a way, the Asokan studies have also suffered because of the cut-and-dried way in which the objects of this period were contrasted with those of the succeeding Sunga period. For instance, the Mauryan art-form was considered something isolated – something imperial and courtly – in contrast with the Sunga period art which appeared not even a century later. The Deur Kothar stupa ornamentations including the railing pillars and coping stones, and the stupa remains of Panguraria including those of Budhni have shown that what emerged full-blown in the stupa art of the Sunga period was only a continuation of the earlier Maurya phase. I particularly recall the delicately ornamented undersides of the stone umbrellas and shafts of the stupas at Deur Kothar, Panguraria and Budhni. Certain dogmatic scholarly positions have also been manifest in the way Hargreaves' find of miscellaneous sculptures from Sarnath was unceremoniously ascribed to an arbitrary 'late Mauryan' period. What is indeed curious is that these objects have seldom made way to the standard scholarly discussions on Mauryan art. This is unfortunate because these Sarnath finds make nonsense of the theory that the Mauryan art was exclusively court-oriented. The Mauryan art was much more diverse than what is usually thought.

The point we are trying to make is that our approach to the Mauryan period in general and Asoka in particular has been impaired to some extent by our own notion of what the different categories of Mauryan objects should be. Once we try to move beyond our dogmas, we realize, as we have realized in this book, that the distribution of Asokan imprints in the subcontinent is much wider than we thought.

We shall never know why the edicts were located at the specific spots they occupied. The general inference that all these spots had already a general attribute of sacredness attached to them has nothing wrong about it, but historically speaking, this does not offer much insight. Nor can we be sure of the premise that a general copy of the edict-type in question went out of the royal court to the concerned officials all over the royal domain, who in turn possibly selected the specific sites and got the class of professional scribes to engrave them. The fact that a professional class of scribes was present in Asoka's India indicates that writing began early enough for a professional class of scribes to emerge by that time. The scribe of the Brahmagiri MRE text, Chapada, wrote his name in Kharosthi (line R of Hultzsch's text), further suggesting that a scribe from the northwest where the use of the Kharosthi script was the general rule did not hesitate to move down to Brahmagiri in the peninsular south and offer his services for executing a royal task. It is generally forgotten that professional scribe groups may still be found in rural India where in the post-offices, courts and land-record offices they are a common sight. They are not government employees with fixed salaries. They offer their services to people for particular tasks, and I find no reason to argue that Chapada of Brahmagiri was an employee of the Mauryan state and not an independent specialist looking for an opportunity to make some money. The fact that Chapada drifted to the south from the northwest means that professional classes could move over long distances in search of livelihood. They did not live in closed political or economic and social landscapes.

The position of scribes in Asoka's domain is also highlighted by the contents of the Sarnath pillar edict where officials are reminded that one copy has been 'pasted up' or inscribed in their 'head office' (*Samsarana*) and "are commanded to send out copies textually correct throughout all parts of their immediate jurisdictions, and to communicate others equally accurate to the governors of garrisons and districts" (Smith 1909b, p. 70). If the interpretation of *Samsarana* as 'head office' or some kind of repository of official documents is true and if the distribution of royal orders in the way in which it is described does not have any element of exaggeration, it must be conceded that the use of written documents was endemic in Mauryan India and that the scribes formed an important professional group of that domain, with possibly some centuries of earlier development. The circumstantial evidence of the inscriptions is enough to demonstrate that Asoka did not 'invent' literacy. The professional class of scribes was there and they were also certainly on the move, selling their services to the royal administrative establishment and the society at large.

When one looks at the whole set of edicts, one realizes that the fact of human movements through the Indian landscape is a common element persisting through them all.

I. MINOR ROCK EDICTS

While approaching the ancient city of Indraprastha or modern Delhi on the bank of the Yamuna from the side of Mathura, a traveller would have no difficulty to take an easy detour to the ridge containing the mother-goddess cult spot of *Kalkaji*, and there, in an open valley below the ridge, he would have noticed the boulder containing the Srinivaspuri/Bahapur version of the MRE-I. Indraprastha would still be more than an hour's walk away. If somebody was keen on moving in the direction of Malwa and beyond from Indraprastha, he would first set out for Bairat or ancient

Viratanagara following the route via Alwar. Before the walls of Viratanagara came into view, he would have noticed by the roadside the rocky cluster with the Bairat version of the MRE-I.

There would be no more MRE-Is over a very large chunk of northern India, but if somebody had come out of the ancient city of Chakranagara in the Yamuna ravines near Etawah and set out in the direction of the Betwa Valley with the aim of travelling through the ancient sites of Ehrich and Tumain towards Vidisa, he would have encountered a large rocky stretch at Gujarra near modern Datia, and that rocky stretch would contain the Gujarra version of the MRE-I. Gujarra also falls on the way from Agra to Jhansi via Bhind and Gwalior.

To make any meaning out of the locations of the other northern MRE-Is – Sasaram, Basaha/Ghurhupur, Ahraura, Rupnath and Panguraria – one will have to begin at the Sasaram end. Routes from both the earlier and later capitals of Magadha, i.e., Rajagriha and Pataliputra, would enter the Kaimurs in the Sasaram-Bhabua sector. The route from Rajagriha would come by Gaya-Bodh Gaya and directly reach Sasaram. It is possible for the route from Pataliputra to follow the Son valley and reach the Bikramganj area first before reaching either Bhabua or Sasaram. The point is that Sasaram in a sense is the starting point of the long trek to the Deccan from Magadha. While moving out of Sasaram in the direction of Bhabua, one sees the MRE-I-bearing 'Chandan Sahid' hill on the right. At Bhabua one takes the path to Chakia across the Karmanasa, and somewhere in the hills in between is the second MRE-I-bearing site of the area, Basaha/Ghurhupur. This stretch contains the ruins of the city-site of Nindaur and can no way be called a 'remote area'. From Chakia one goes either straight to Ramnagar for Varanasi via Sherwan and Bhuili or goes first to Ahraura from where one can either climb up to the Robertsganj plateau for the Son crossing at Agori Khas, from where the route would eventually lead, through Sarguja, to the ancient political unit of South Kosala or the modern Bilaspur-Raipur zone, or go to Varanasi from where another route to Central India and eventually the Deccan through Mirzapur and Rewa would be open. These three MRE-I-bearing sites at relatively short intervals in this section possibly suggest the recognition of the importance of the Kaimurs in maintaining the links of Magadha with Varanasi, Central India and the Deccan. The importance of the Ahraura area has also been proved by the find of a Gupta period fort and tank on the top of the Magan Diwana hill near it.

Rupnath may lie a long way off but belongs to this network. From Mirzapur one travels in the direction of the Vindhyan Rewa plateau or the ancient Chedi country. In the latter, one has to avoid the route from Amarpatan to Bandhogarh to reach South Kosala, and move beyond Satna towards the ancient Tripuri or modern Jubbulpore. In the east-west valley beyond Satna, which is fringed by hills on the north and the south, Rupnath lies at the northern edge and has the ancient city-site of Kakrehta in its vicinity. From Rupnath, the road goes straight to the site of Tripuri on the northern bank of the Narmada.

From Tripuri, the main road alignment towards the Deccan or at least the Andhra coast goes by the Balaghat gap to reach the Wainganga valley which covers the edict-bearing sites of Deotek and Ghugus in the Chandrapur section. The Asokan affinity of Deotek and Ghugus may be debated, but the point is that their locations fall squarely in the alignment of movements from Tripuri to the Andhra coast. This is a positive factor in favour of the argument that these two inscriptions which we have discussed in detail earlier belong to the reign of Asoka. The route coming through South Kosala may also turn towards the Andhra coast through the Chandrapur area, and from the point of view of this possibility also, the finds of Asokan inscriptions at Ghugus and Deotek seem credible enough.

The route which came up to Tripuri via Rupnath might have been in touch with Panguraria by following the Narmada alignment, but for Panguraria a better link-up is with the route coming down the Betwa valley. This lies not far from the Narmada crossing at Hosangabad and has in fact an old crossing of the Narmada at Ninnore in its immediate neighbourhood. There is also a fortified ancient city-site near it at Nadner, which seems to be the place where the prince Samva of the Panguraria version of the MRE-I was likely to have been based. The chief town of the *Monema* country, mentioned in the same edict, if Sircar's version is true, was obviously Nadner.

In Falk's version, the place was visited by Asoka himself in the company of an 'unwedded consort'. One fails to understand why an 'unwedded consort' deserved mention in this version of the MRE-I.

The southern MREs or MRE-IIs lie distributed at rather close intervals at Maski (the northernmost one), Nittur, Udegolam, Gavimath and Palkigundu (the centrally located ones), Brahmagiri, Siddapur and Jatinga Rameseswar (the three southern ones), and Yerragudi and Rajula Mandagiri (the two northeastern ones). Nittur and Udegolam are related to the modern Bellary-Sirguppa road, both lying roughly to the northwest of this alignment which first leads to Sindhnur and then to Maski. Through Lingsugur, Maski is linked with the modern Bagalkot-Bijapur-Solapur alignment which is a major alignment reaching southern Deccan from the Pune area of Maharashtra via Solapur. Gavimath and Palkigundu are around Kopbal, with the area receiving routes from Belgaum-Dharwar, North and South Kanara and the areas lying both to the north and the south. The geo-political importance of the area is amply highlighted because of the location of the Vijayanagar capital Hampi here. The southern MREs of this zone, i.e., Brahmagiri, Siddapur and Jatinga Rameswar are linked primarily with the Mysore-Bangalore-Tumkur-Chitradurg section of Karnataka which, in fact, was a nodal point in the communication network of Karnataka controlling routes coming from the coast and the Belgaum-Dharwar area. One is not sure why there is apparently some kind of urgency in locating these MREs in the landscape within about 150 km radius of Bellary. I can think of two factors. One is the route stretching from this area right up to Solapur in the heart of the Maharashtra Deccan, and the second one is the importance of this area in maintaining links with the Konkan coast, including the north and south Kanara coasts. It appears that the whole stretch of Karnataka was of some fundamental importance to the Mauryan administration, possibly both for its gold and the coastal trade. In this context, it may be worth pointing out that one of the major sources of Vijayanagara wealth was the riches derived from the Indian Ocean trade, and geo-politically, the locations of the southern MREs suggest that the same was true of the Mauryan rule. The locations of Yerragudi and Rajula Mandagiri in two parts of Kurnul to the northeast of Bellary highlight the importance of the alignment which leads up to Raichur and Yadgir, the latter located near the major city-site of the period, Sannati. This alignment is also linked with Cuddapah and Anantapur, the former at the entrance to Tirupati and Tamil Nadu (via Chittoor) and the latter at the approach to Kolar, Bangalore and eventually Dharmapuri (of Tamil Nadu). What is equally important is that the Nandiyal area is easily connected with the alignments we are discussing, and from Nandiyal the mouth of the Krishna valley via the Nandikanama pass is open.

In fact, as one looks at the distribution of the southern MREs one realizes that here the target was to control as much as possible of the vast network of routes leading to various parts of Karnataka, Andhra and Tamil Nadu. Anybody controlling the Tirupati entrance to Tamil Nadu had to be concerned with the state of affairs in this southernmost section of the Indian peninsula. Karnataka seems to be fully under Mauryan control: the Kolar-Bangalore-Mysore belt and the coastal stretch up to south Kanara were certainly within the grasp of the Mauryas directly based both in the Hospet-Hampi-Kopbal area and in the area of Chitradurg (cf. Brahmagiri, Siddapur and Jatinga Rameswar). More interestingly, the Mauryas could link up their control of Karnataka with that of the Andhra coast through the Nandikanama pass and other routes of travel through the Nallamalai hills. I have earlier pointed out that the Bellary area was the cockpit of South Indian history. The later Tamil Nadu dynasties invariably made repeated thrusts to the Bellary region for gaining access to the routes leading to the Konkan coast and other areas in the north and also to the Andhra coast. The powers based in the Bellary region, on the other hand (cf. the Pallavas, Rashtrakutas and others), repeatedly tried to possess as much of the southern peninsula and Andhra as possible. We cannot directly know what was happening in this belt during the time of the Mauryas but the distribution of Asokan MREs certainly suggests that they were keen on maintaining their control of this geo-political segment.

The southern MREs also raise the question of the identifications of Suvarnagiri and Isila. Regarding Isila, I have pointed out that there was no space for a major settlement at Brahmagiri and that this settlement was probably better located near Chitradurg itself. Sannati, a place where a Mauryan official with no less than the rank of a *Kumara* was posted, raises a more serious issue of identification. In view of the fact that Sannati was the largest fortified settlement in the whole of the southern peninsula, I have no hesitation in identifying Suvarnagiri with Sannati. Regarding Sircar's *Monema Desa,* I suggest the area where Panguraria is located, i.e., the area south of modern Bhopal or the area somewhat south of the ancient Vidisa. This area might also have included the area around modern Hosangabad, i.e., the southern bank of the Narmada which in this section is forested, with a road running through it up to the Vidarbha area. This section of the Narmada valley also gave access to the Tapti valley which has been traditionally forded for Maharashtra at Burhanpur, the access to which was protected, at least in the mediaeval times by the fort of Asirgarh.

II. MAJOR ROCK EDICTS AND SEPARATE EDICTS

The edicts in question cover a wide range of locations: Shahbazgarhi, Manserah, Girnar, Kalsi, Sopara, Sannati, Dhauli, Jaugada and the Barabar hills near Gaya. Regarding Shahbazgarhi, we have referred to the results of Ihsan Ali's detailed field-work in the Peshawar plain, and we have further pointed out Ali's observation that the site was oriented towards the Karakoram route leading certainly to central Asia and possibly China. In addition, Shahbazgarhi played a major role in the local communication network: routes to Mardan, Buner, Swat and Malakand Agency and routes to Panjab across the Indus. In the trans-regional network of the subcontinent, it falls on the Peshawar-Charsadda-Mardan-Swabi-Topi-Panjab alignment and on a shorter version of the same route through Lahor (the village of the grammarian Panini in the local village tradition) and Hund. Manserah, as we have earlier noticed, opens up towards Kashmir and Gilgit, but the determining factor of its location was the route to Kashmir from Taxila via Abbotabad. This is the easiest route from the plains to Kashmir, and in the pre-Partition days travellers are known to have used ordinary horse-drawn carriages like *Ekka* on this road. In a sense, there is a linkage between the locations of Shahbazgarhi and Manserah. Between themselves, they demonstrate that in Mauryan India there was no obscurity about the road network which led from the northwest, i.e., Peshawar, to the heart of the Gangetic India on the one hand and to the Karakorams and Kashmir on the other. The fact that the Abbotabad route had primacy in maintaining links between Panjab and Kashmir makes one understand why in the Mauryan scheme Kashmir was important. In the case of Manserah, a little-known observation of Aurel Stein (cited by Smith 1909, p. 127) may have some importance. Stein found traces of an ancient road here leading to a place of pilgrimage now called Breri. Stein considered Breri the Kashmiri equivalent of *Bhattarika-Devi* or *Durga*. In view of the fact that the Karakoram route later acquired a personality of its own because of the plethora of rock-art occurrences and inscriptions along it, it is worth noting that Ali's survey refers to some Achaemenid sites marking the beginning of the Karakoram route. Thus, by the time the Mauryans were ensconced in this region there is a long historical background of this route configuration. The sheer vastness of this configuration needs some emphasis. From Manserah, Srinagar lies a little to the southeast, and through Srinagar Manserah is connected with the Ganderbal-Drass-Kargil-Leh alignment. Chilas and Gilgit beyond Chilas, are approachable from Manserah in two ways, one almost straight northeast to Chilas and the other taking a loop on the west and forming a more roundabout way.

Mingora and the area beyond are within easy reach of Shahbazgarhi, and apart from linking up with Afghanistan, Shahbazgarhi also links up easily with Chitral, and through Mingora, with Chilas as well. I would argue that Central Asia and beyond that, China were within a well-rooted route network of Mauryan India.

Regarding the location of Girnar, it is possible that it gained its importance from its access to the coast and its maritime activities both in the directions of Veraval near Somnath in the south and Porbandar in the west. A convenient model to understand the significance of its location is to look at it in the context of the former princely state of Junagadh, of which Junagadh or the adjoining Girnar was the capital. Among the principal ports of the region were Veraval and Porbandar, the former with coastal sailing up to Mumbai, Goa, Malabar and Cochin on the one hand and with long-distance sailing links up to Karachi, Muscat and Aden on the other. The sailing links of Porbandar were wider, encompassing both Southeast Asia and the African coast within its trading network. The Gulf region was, of course, well within its orbit. If Girnar was the principal city of the Mauryas in the Kathiawar peninsula, one may confidently assert that its importance lay in having access to a vast network of sea routes from the Strait of Malacca to Zanzibar. Among the more direct causes of the importance of Girnar or the ancient city of Girinagara, one may think of its traditional sacred association with such cult-centres as Amba Mata and the life of the twenty-second Jaina Tirthankara, Neminatha. The cluster of eight separate groups of Buddhist caves at or in the vicinity of, Girnar or Junagadh is also indicative of the overwhelming religious significance of Girnar to the Hindus, Jainas and the Buddhists alike. The location of an Asokan edict at Girnar may be an acknowledgement of this sacredness. On a different level, the location of the Sudarsan lake in the periphery of the site must have given an extraordinary additional importance to this location. That the lake is pre-Asokan, dating from the period of his grandfather Chandragupta Maurya, is well known, but the point is that this possibly was one of the largest irrigational projects of Mauryan India. A combination of features such as the access to the Indian Ocean trading network from the Strait of Malacca to Zanzibar, traditional sacredness for the Hindus, Jainas and the Buddhists alike, and the site of a major irrigational enterprise must have made Girnar a place of great significance in the third century BC. It must be emphasized that the early historical personality of Gujarat in general and the Kathiawar peninsula in particular is not clearly understood. The fact that 36 early historical sites have been reported from the Sudarsan lake area suggests the possible density of occupation in Kathiwar of the Mauryan period. One suspects that this was backed by a number of city-sites, of which there is no clear understanding at present. Rather unduly concerned with Red Polished Ware and its possible ramifications, the early historical archaeology of Gujarat has not yet tried to assess its ground carefully, especially the situation in the pre-Kshatrapa period. The NBP is known to occur in Gujarat and should be as old as the Gangetic valley specimens by any reckoning. The fact is that virtually nothing is reported yet about the city-site of Girinagara where the Girnar RE site is located.

Kalsi, or basically the site of a large boulder inscribed with the REs, is a place at the very edge of the Yamuna bed which enters the hills here. It is also at Kalsi that the land begins to rise slowly towards Chakrata. The Yamuna plain here is also hemmed in by the hills rising on the opposite side of the valley. The third century AD ruins of Jagatgram are located in these hills. The routes of the pilgrims travelling up the Yamuna valley to *Yamunotri* or the source of the Yamuna must have passed by Kalsi, and we suspect a political nucleus here covering both this section of the plain and the hilly area further in the interior. However, the only palpable significance that we can make out in the case of Kalsi is that it was one of the principal entrances to the Himalayas which have abundantly drawn pilgrims through the ages. In the modern context, Kalsi is not much of a pilgrim's entrance but the fact that the REs exist here suggest that in the Mauryan period, it was a far more significant place than what is at present. The Doon valleys are also easily accessible from Kalsi, and although these valleys are now full of what is known in modern India as 'English-medium educational institutions' and very little else, it is possible that the access to the resources of the Doon valleys, which are principally timber and rice, was important in the Asokan times.

If the Mauryan possession of Girnar indicates the general Mauryan participation in the Indian Ocean trade from the Strait of Malacca to Zanzibar through the Kathiawar ports, their presence at Sopara in the form of REs greatly strengthens the picture, especially because of the reputation of Sopara in the ancient literary sources. It is also worthy of note that the geo-political zone of the coast where Sopara is located has always been significant in the course of Indian maritime history, Sopara being succeeded by Vasai and Mumbai, both in the same sector. This zone also opened windows on the maritime trade stretching from the east coast of Africa to the Strait of Malacca and including the west coast of India. The historical picture may not be novel but the fact that by the third century BC this picture was clear in its detail seems to give considerable depth and texture to the trade conducted under the Mauryas. The traditional significance of Sopara to the Buddhists is further indicated by B.L. Indraji's assertion that the 'tiny pieces of earthenware' that he found in the relic chamber of the 1st-2nd century AD stupa excavated by him might belong to the Buddha himself. It is possible that Asoka's decision to put up REs at Sopara may partly be due to its unequivocal religious significance.

About Sannati, it is far more easy to be on more secure ground. Without doubt, it is the largest fortified city-site south of the Vindhyas, contains a large number of inscriptions of various periods, and has outside its walls at least three stupas, one of which – the one at Kanganahalli – may justifiably claim, because of its superior quality sculptural resources, to be on the same level as Amaravati. From Paithan or ancient Pratisthana on the upper Godavari, which must have been as much Mauryan as of the Satavahana period, one comes down straight to Ter, the ancient Tagara, and veers further south from this area, with one route going in the direction of Kondapur in the modern Sangareddi district. There is also no difficulty to move from Sannati to the modern Adoni-Pattikonda sector of Kurnul where the edict sites of Erragudi and Rajula Mandagiri are located. From Adoni, one can easily move towards Tamil Nadu and Karnataka. It is also possible to move from Sannati to Alampur on the bank of the Tungabhadra and turn to the inner districts of Andhra. It may be worthwhile to point out that Sannati is not located at the edge of the southern area of the Mauryan control. This control extended to Karnataka and the northern border of Tamil Nadu. The location of the RE-bearing site Erragudi suggests that it gave access to Anantapur, Cuddapah and Chittoor on the way to Tamil Nadu and some northern sections of Karnataka including Bellary, Hospet, etc. The southernmost major settlements which were under the Mauryas were Chitradurg and Vanavasi. Sannati lay well within the geographically secure southern zone of the Mauryan control, and I find it interesting that Sannati is also considerably to the north of the cockpit of South Indian history, i.e., Bellary. Geo-politically, Sannati was absolutely secure, and one understands why it was considered as significant in the Mauryan scheme as Ujjayini, Kosambi and Takshasila. It is interesting that it was also the locale of two Separate Edicts and figures with Dhauli and Jaugada in this regard. Although it is unlikely that Sannati figured in any way in the Kalinga conquest, the location of two Separate Edicts here is surprising.

In remarkable contrast, the Erragudi REs only overlook the main line of communication to Tamil Nadu and Karnataka, especially Tamil Nadu. Unless a major city-site is discovered near Erragudi – and there is a scant prospect of doing so – the site named in the edicts, Suvarnagiri, cannot be place near Erragudi. It can be placed only at Sannati.

Dhauli and Jaugada lie almost at two ends of the coastal sweep of Orissa. I strongly dispute the claim of Dhauli being ancient Tosali. The city-site of Radhanagar near Jajpur was, as I have argued, Tosali. I also suggest that Tosali was the capital of a Mahajanapada period state covering a large section of the Baitarini valley of Orissa, and southwest Bengal. However, Sisupalgarh also was a fortified city-site and so was Jaugada further down the coast in Ganjam. There is no doubt about the inclusion of Jaugada or the ancient site of Samapa in the Kalinga territory, and it appears plausible that Sisupalgarh lay on the way to the eastern part of the Gangetic plain either through the Chhotanagpur platerau or modern West Bengal. This premise seems to be supported by the famous 'lord of Kalinga' inscription of Kharavela in the outskirts of modern Bhuvaneswara. Earlier, I have argued in detail how the battle for Kalinga took place formally in the Kalinga territory and how the Mauryan army was most likely to have followed the later Samudragupta route to the Kalinga coast through South Kosala. It is also possible that Jaugada could be approached straight through the South Kosala route. Regarding the location of Dhauli or Sisupalgarh, we have further noted that from its position at the head of the Mahanadi delta it was conveniently located to maintain links with the hilly region in the interior on the one hand and move up and down the coast on the other. The rich agricultural resource of the Mahanadi delta was also within its easy grasp.

Regarding the geo-political importance of Kalinga, more thoughts are needed. Among other things, it is suitably located to control the area of the Godavari mouth, if not as far as the mouth of the Krishna. The latter also is a distinct possibility, and the Kalinga kings are known to have exercised control as far as the Krishna. We have earlier noted that in an inscription at Guntupalle, the king Sata or Sada of the Mahameghavahana dynasty mentioned in the Udayagiri-Khandagiri cave inscriptions was called the lord of Kalinga-Mahishaka countries and that Mahishaka has been interpreted as the Krishna delta. It has also been argued that the Godavari-Krishna stretch was a major area of sending ships to Southeast Asia. Vengi has been considered an important centre in this regard. It is possible that the annexation of Kalinga was important in the Mauryan framework to safeguard the Mauryan interests in the Godavari-Krishna stretch. The Mauryas were present at Amaravati on the bank of the Krishna, but Amaravati was not a sea-port, and the Mauryans would want to see this sea-board free from the possibility of any inroad from the side of Kalinga whose limits certainly extended well to the east beyond Srikakulam. Kalinga was also located in a section through which the route to the coastal Andhra and other areas of the south from South Kosala and the regions further north would pass.

III. MISCELLANEOUS EDICTS FROM VIDARBHA, BAIRAT, AFGHANISTAN AND THE NORTHWEST, AND THE BARABAR HILLS

The two edicts reported from Ghugus and Deotek, both in the Chandrapur area of Vidarbha, fall, as we have noticed, on a major route going through the Wainganga valley to the Karimnagar section of Andhra. The route might come from the Raipur-Durg-Bhandara section and turn towards Andhra in this segment or might come through Balaghat to reach the Wainganga valley. The route coming from Raipur-Durg-Bhandara also proceeded further west, reaching as far as western Maharashtra. The alignment of the route coming through Balaghat takes one straight to the bank of the Wainganga opposite the fortified and large early historic city site of Pauni. In fact, it is at this point that the Wainganga was crossed to reach the city-site. In view of the geographical significance of the Pauni sector, we have had no hesitation in thinking that the Deotek specimen and the currently untraceable specimen from Ghugus are both genuine Asokan finds. There is, of course, no controversy about the Bhabru edict, and we have seen how it is linked to the route coming from the side of Delhi to reach, in the first instance, Malwa through Rajasthan.

The significance of the northwestern region is highlighted not merely by the Shahbazgarhi and Mansehra REs but also by an Aramaic inscription from Taxila and a fragment of a pillar edict reputedly from Buner or Takht-i-Bahi. We have seen that there is no special reason to consider the Buner/Takht-i-Bahi find a forgery. In fact, in view of the Mauryan familiarity both with the northwest and the areas leading towards the Karakoram route, the probability of its being a genuinely Asokan inscription is almost beyond dispute. Neither should an Asokan inscription from Taxila being in Aramaic be a matter of surprise because 'Romedote', the high official in whose honour the inscription was engraved on an octagonal marble pillar, was possibly an Aramaic-speaking person himself. This inscription is all the more interesting because it was engraved on an octagonal marble pillar and in honour of an official. Both these circumstances are unique and prove that not all the Asokan inscriptions may conform to the types which are generally known.

No less than three inscriptions in two separate scripts (Greek and Aramaic and bilingual Graeco-Aramaic) occur at Kandahar, pointing to the existence of Aramaic-speaking and Greek-speaking Asokan subjects here, but more importantly, they point to the general importance of the Kandahar area itself. In the communication network, the names of the Bolan pass and the Sibi plain (Sind) come readily to mind and underscore the significance of Sind as a whole in this regard. Sind was certainly an important province to the Mauryas. We cannot also put away the significance of the Derah Ghazi and Dera Ismail Khan section in maintaining communication with Kandahar. The Bannu area also must have played a role through its Tochi-Kurram area. In their turn, the Dera Ghazi and Dera Ismail Khan section is linked with Multan, and beyond

Multan, with the route coming to it via Delhi, Hissar and Hansi. The position of the early historic city site of Akra in Bannu may be linked with this issue of access to Kandahar. In Afghanistan itself, Kandahar gives access, through Seistan, to the Baluchistan section of southeast Iran, and through that, to the route which moves through the south Iran plain to the Fars plain where Persepolis is located or to the Gulf region and lower Mesopotamia. From Kandahar, one also moves toward Heart via Farah and Girishk and eventually join the north Iranian route at the foot of the Elburz. This route also led to Mesopotamia through the Zagros belt or towards the Mediterranean through the Caspian shore. The Asokan inscriptions from Jalalabad and Lamghan point to the Mauryan concern with the Hindukush and central Asia. These occurrences also highlight the significance of the Khybar pass during this period. The Hindukush passes and the north Afghan plains must have been as important to the Mauryas as they have been to the countless generations of rulers of the subcontinent. Long before the discovery of the Kandahar and Jalalabad-Lamghan inscriptions, Smith said (1909a, p. 74) that the Mauryan "empire included the famous strongholds of Kabul, Zabul, Kandahar, and Herat, and, and so possessed the the sub-continent's 'scientific frontier', for which "Anglo-Indian statesmen have long sighed in vain". Smith also believes that Kafiristan or northeast Afghanistan was under the Mauryan control.

The locations of the cave edicts in the Barabar hills may be explained more easily by pointing out that the place provided one of the links between Rajagriha and Bodh Gaya and that the place must have had a religious significance. Moreover, as Cunningham pointed out, this lies on the 'high road' between Bodh Gaya and Pataliputra. Otherwise, caves would not have been donated to the Ajivika sect here. There are reports of an ancient settlement in the Barabar hills area, but we cannot vouch for its existence. This seems to be an area where the traditional religious sanctity of its hills overshadowed its importance on the route between Rajagriha and Bodh Gaya.

IV. PILLAR EDICTS

The issue of pillars is more problematic than was once thought. There is no confusion about the pillars which are found inscribed: Delhi-Topra, Delhi-Meerat, Lauriya Araraj, Lauriya Nandangarh, Rampurva lion, Lumbini, Gotihawa, Allahabad, Sanchi, Sarnath, Amaravati and Hissar. Whether in full or in fragments, these have direct Asokan associations. Some fragmentary pillars are assumed to be Asokan without dispute, and in this category, one may put the following: Kolhua complete with the capital but uninscribed, Rampurva bull, Nigliva, and Kausambi. From Nigliva and Kausambi, there is no surviving capital but Kolhua and Rampurva and Sankisa have them, and are in that sense closer to being Asokan. Capitals, integral parts of the Asokan columns occur, without the association of pillars, at Bansi, Ayodhya, Sodanga, Udayagiri, Khairadih, Bhuvaneswar and Sankisa. As far as we can judge, there is every justification to postulate the existence of Asokan pillars at these sites. The monolithic pillars which are now reported from Belkhara (Ahraura), Bhagalpur on the bank of the Ghaghra, Prahladpur, Bakraur, Deur Kothar and Sikligarh are disputed specimens. In the case of Sikligarh, there is convincing argument that it is genuinely Mauryan and was broken in the early centuries AD. The Deur Kothar specimen is genuinely 3rd century BC, but it has been fragmented and the inscription it carries is not Asokan but of the same period. Besides, its capital has not been found. We have put forward strong arguments showing that all the other pillars under consideration stood at important places (cf. Bakraur, Belkhara) and important river-crossings (cf. Prahladpur, Bhagalpur). In addition, inscribed pillar sections or possible fragments come from Amaravati and Buner/Takhi-i-Bahi, and capitals have been reported from Salem between Pataliputra and Vaisali and at Masarh between Pataliputra and Buxar.

We have argued in detail that there is an overwhelming evidence of the association of all the above-mentioned places with routes and river-crossings. Delhi-Topra, even if its present identification with the Topra village near Ambala is true, lies on a route. Sometimes I believe that Paonta Sahib in the same region but beyond the Yamuna in the direction of Kalsi may be a more suitable place for the original site. Regrettably, the Paonta Sahib area has not yet been adequately explored from this point of view either by me or by anybody else. Delhi-Meerat column was located apparently near Meerat on the way to Hastinapur and Nazibabad. This would eventually enter the Himalayan belt beginning at Kotdwar a little beyond Nazibabad. Kolhua, Lauria Araraj, Lauriya Nandangarh and Rampurva lay on the route to the Kathmandu valley through the Bhikna Tori Pass and Hetaura.

Lumbini, Nigliva and Gotihawa, being associated with the life of the Buddha, were objects of journey by itself. We have repeatedly emphasized the significance of Sarnath, Sanchi, Udayagiri near Vidisa, Sankisa, Allahabad, Ujjayini and Kausambi in the route network of the Gangetic India and Malwa. Deur Kothar overlooks the route from the Ganga plain to Central India and the Deccan ascending the Vindhyan scarp at Sohagi Ghat. The significance of the Bhagalpur crossing of the Ghaghra was immense. This must have been the Ghaghra crossing Asoka used while journeying from Pataliputra to Lumbini, and the fact that traces of an Asokan capital have been reported from Khairadih on the opposite bank of the Ghaghra lends credence to our belief. The route coming through the Kaimurs to Chandauli would have crossed the Ganga at Prahladpur to reach directly the modern Saidpur and Ghazipur areas. As the site of the house of Sujata, Bakraur had a sacred status in the history of Buddhism. Belkhara would lead to the top of the Sonabhadra or Robertsganj plateau on the way to the Deccan through the Sarguja plain. Bansi lies at the approach to Lumbini from the Kopia side, a route which Asoka followed. Salem and Masarh were there on the roads between Pataliputra and Vaisali and between Pataliputra and Buxar or Vedagarbhapuri. Sikligarh lies squarely on the road between Patalipura and Mahasthangarh or the ancient Pundranagari in the east. The point is that with their control of the Karatoya plain where Mahåsthangarh is located, the Mauryas would have had interest in the Brahmaputra plain or ancient Kamarupa with which the Karatoya plain has had traditional linkages. Whether there is a suitable literary reference or not, we believe that Kamarupa was under the Mauryan control along with eastern Bengal up to the Chattagram/ Chittagong coast.

Hissar lies well beyond the Gangetic orbit, but when one remembers that a major route went to the Multan area through Delhi-Mathura, Rohtak, Hansi and Hissar, the Asokan inscribed pillar of Hissar falls in place.

Among the various places and groups of people mentioned in the edicts, we have commented in detail on the problems of identifications of Isila, Tosali and Kalinga. Of the identity of the South Indian states and of *Tamraparni* or Sambodhi, there is no problem. The Bhojas have been rightly put by Smith (1909) between the lower sections of the Narmada and the Tapti whereas the Pulindas may belong to some parts of modern Andhra. The Assaka territory comprises the modern Nizambabad-Karimnagar part of Andhra and the area to the south of Nagpur. Pitenikas may be Sanskrit Pratisthanikas and seemingly belong to Paithan on the Godavari. There is no problem to identify the Hellenistic and north African states mentioned in the edicts and there is no problem either about the locations of the Yonas and Kambojas. The Yonas may be securely put around Kandahar whereas the Kambojas may be put in the area of Jalalabad stretching up to northeast Afghanistan. Rashtrikas have been put south of Sopara, i.e., in Maharashtra. The *Nabhas* and *Nabhapamktis* are, in the absence of some later historic references to them, problematic and likely to remain so.

V. HISTORICAL-GEOGRAPHICAL WORLD OF MAURYAN INDIA

In retrospect, the historical-geographical world behind the Asokan edicts surprises us both by their vastness and complexity. Each and every section of the subcontinent seems to be very well-lit and reveals a route network with which we have been familiar in various ways right up to the modern period. This is true not merely of the subcontinent itself but of all the areas outside, with which it has had traditional links – the world of modern Sri Lanka, the world of west Asia, the Mediterranean and north Africa, the world of central Asia beyond the Hindukush and the Karakoram, and the world of Tibet and possibly China (otherwise, why would the Kathmandu valley be part of Mauryan India?). *Suvarnabhumi* or Southeast Asia does not seem to loom large, but the Sri Lankan tradition of his missionary activities there and the Mauryan concern with the occupation of the Godavari-Krishna maritime littoral seem to provide some positive indication, however remote.

There is nothing tentative about Mauryan India. This is an India which had long passed into the historical period. Elsewhere I have argued that the early historic beginning in India was a process which lasted between c.800 and c.500 BC. In the third century BC India, the sub-continent did not belong to diverse stages of socio-economic development. The fact that in some areas the megalithic burial customs were still prevalent does not mean that those areas were not well-rooted in early history; the megaliths simply reflected some local ways of disposing the dead.

The royal call for non-violence, tolerance, concern for all the living beings including fishes and animals, which one hears echoed from the edicts located by the wayside from the Hindukush to Mysore, came not because the monarch had reasons to be apprehensive of great social and economic tensions between his subjects but because he was both a monarch and a monk, trying to put the dark days of the Kalinga war behind him by invoking those simple rules of behaviour with which the people of the sub-continent have traditionally been familiar at the grass-roots level. The level of tolerance, cooperation and respect with which elderly people moving around in the Indian countryside are still greeted may take us by surprise but are nonetheless indications of a simple, ethical code of behaviour which the rural Indians still observe and know by the name of their *Dharma*. Asoka knew his kingdom deeply enough to appeal to his subjects to abide by the precepts of this *Dharma* according to their stations in life and beliefs. A Buddhist monk as well as a king, he would naturally be concerned with the unity and purity of the Buddhist church, but what he preaches as *Dharma* is not specifically Buddhist but is more deep-rooted in the Indian tradition than we occasionally care to admit.

Asoka must have been a man of exceptional mental strength and vision to organize both his administration and missionary activity almost on a superhuman scale without any visible sign of duplicity. The only direct touch that we have with him is through his edicts, and the simple aspect of their locations, the main concern of our book, sheds light on how the vast geographical area he possessed is still with us in the ways people moved from place to place and read, or listened to, the royal messages from the wayside.

Bibliography

Agrawal, R.C. 1962. Unpublished railing pillars from Rajasthan. *Lalit Kala* 11: 60-61.

Ali, Ihsan. 2003. Early Settlements, Irrigation and Trade Routes in Peshawar Plain, Pakistan. *Frontier Archaeology* 1: Directorate of Archaeology and Museums, NWFP, Peshawar.

Ali, Rahman, A. Trivedi, D. Solanki. 2004. *Buddhist Remains of Ujjain Region, Excavations at Sodanga*. Delhi: Sharada Publishing House.

Anand, K. 1995. *History and Archaeology of Buxar, Bhojpur and Rohtas Regions*. Delhi: Ramanand Vidya Bhavan.

Andersen, P.K. 1990. *Studies in the Minor Rock Edicts of Asoka*. Freiburg: Hedwig Falk.

Arunachalam, B. 2002. Use of imagery in reconstruction of the past – a case study of Sopara. *Indian Cartographer*, pp. 342-346.

Banerji, R.D. 1907-08. Patiakella grant of Maharaja Sivaraja (Gupta), Samvat 283. *Epigraphia Indica* 9, pp. 285-288.

———. 1919-20. Neulpur grant of Subhakara, the 8th year. *Epigraphia Indica* 15, pp. 1-8.

Barnett, L.D. 1915. An Aramaic inscription from Taxila. *JRAS*, pp. 340-342.

Barua, B.M. 1946. *Asoka and His Inscriptions*. Calcutta: New Age Publishers Ltd.

Basa, K.K. and P. Mohanty (eds). *Archaeology of Orissa, Vol. II*. Delhi: Pratibha Prakasan.

Bechert, H. 1995. *When did the Buddha Live? The Controversy on the Dating of the Historical Buddha*. Delhi: Sri Satguru Publications.

Beglar, J.D. 1878. *Report of a Tour in Bundelkhand and Malwa, 1871-72; and in the Central Provinces, 1873-74*. Calcutta: Government Printing (Cunningham reports, Vol. 7).

———. 1882. *Report of Tours in the Southeastern Provinces in 1874-75 and 1875-76*. Calcutta: Government Printing (Cunningham reports, Vol. 13).

Bellew, H.W. 1864. *A General Report on the Yusufzais*. Lahore: Government Press.

Bendall, C. 1883. *Catalogue of the Buddhist Sanskrit Manuscripts in the University Library, Cambridge*. Cambridge: University Press.

Bhandarkar, D.R. 1911. *Asoka*. Calcutta: Calcutta University Press.

——. 1929-30. A list of the inscriptions of northern India ... from about A.C. 200. *Epigraphia Indica*. 20, Appendix.

Bhattacharya, N.N. 1991. *The Geographical Dictionary: Ancient and Early Mediaeval India*. Delhi: Munshiram Manoharlal.

Biswas, Dilip K. 1967. *The Legend of Emperor Asoka by J. Przyluski*. Calcutta: Firma K.L. Mukhopadhyay.

Buhler, G. 1877. Three new edicts of Asoka. *The Indian Antiquary* 6: 149-160.

——. 1892. The prasasti of the temple of Lakkha Mandal at Madha in Jaunsar Bawar. *Epigraphia Indica* 1: 10-15.

——. 1894-95. The Siddapur edicts of Asoka. *Epigraphia Indica* 3, pp. 134-142.

——. 1898-99. The Asoka edicts of Paderia and Nigliva. *Epigraphia Indica* 5: 1-6.

Carlleyle, A.C.L. 1877-1880. *Report of Tours in Gorakhpur, Saran, and Ghazipur in 1877-78-79 and 80*. Calcutta: Government Printing (Cunningham reports, Vol. 22).

——. 1878. *Report of a tour in eastern Rajputana in 1871-72 and 1872-73*. Calcutta: Government Printing.

Chakrabarti, Dilip K. 2001. *Archaeological Geography of the Ganga Plain: The Lower and the Middle Ganga*. Delhi: Permanent Black.

——. 2005. *The Archaeology of the Deccan Routes*. Delhi: Munshiram Manoharlal.

——. 2006. *The Oxford Companion to Indian Archaeology*. Delhi: Oxford University Press.

——. 2007. *Archaeological Geography of the Ganga Plain: The Upper Ganga (Oudh, Rohilkhand and the Doab)*. Delhi: Munshiram Manoharlal.

——. 2010. *The Ancient Routes of the Deccan and the Southern Peninsula*. Delhi: Aryan Books.

Chakravarti, N.P. 1948. The minor rock-edicts of Asoka and some connected problems. *Ancient India* 4, pp. 15-25.

Charpentier, J. 1914. A note on the Padariya or Rummindei inscription. *The Indian Antiquary* 43: 17-20.

Chhabra, B.C. 1964. Asokan pillar at Hissar, Panjab. *Visvesvaranand Indological Journal* 2: 319-322.

Chhabra, B.C. and G.S. Gai. 1981. *Inscriptions of the Early Gupta Kings*. Delhi: Archaeological Survey of India.

Court, M. 1836. Extracts translated from a memoir on a map of Peshawar and the country comprised between the Indus and the Hydaspes, the Peucelaotis and Taxila of ancient geography. *JASB* 5: 468-482.

Crooke, W. (ed.). 1920 (original edition of Todd's volume in 1829). *Annals and Antiquities of Rajasthan*, Vol. I. London: H. Milford, Oxford University Press.

Cunningham, A. 1960 reprint. *Bhilsa Topes*. Delhi.

——. 1871. *Archaeological Survey of India: Four Reports Made during the Years 1862-63-64-65*. Simla: Government Central Press (Cunningham reports, Vol. 1).

____. 1872-73. *Archaeological Survey of India, Report for the Year 1872-73*. (Cunningham reports, Vol. 5) Calcutta: Government Printing.

____. 1875. *Report for the Year 1872-73*. Calcutta: Government Printing.

____. 1877. *Corpus Inscriptionum Indicarum, Volume I. Inscriptions of Asoka*. Calcutta: Government Printing.

____. 1880. *Report of Tours in the Gangetic Province from Badaon to Bihar in 1875-76 and 1877-78*. Calcutta: Government of India.

Cunningham, A. and H.B.W. Garrick. 1883. *Report of Tours in North and South Bihar in 1880-81*. Calcutta: Government Printing (Cunningham reports, Vol. 16).

De Smeth, J.B., K.S.P. Rao and R.D. Schuiling. 1985. Gold-scheelite mineralization in the Velligalu schist belt, Andhra Pradesh, India. *Economic Geology* 80: 1996-2000.

Dey, N.L. 1899 (1983 reprint). *The Geographical Dictionary of Ancient and Mediaeval India*. Munshiram Manoharlal.

Elliot, H.M. and J. Dowson. 1867. *The History of India as Told by Its Own Historians*. London: Trubner.

Falk, H. 2006. Asokan Sites and Artefacts. Mainz am Rhine: Verlag Philipp von Zabern.

Filliozat, J. 1961-62. Graeco-Aramaic inscription of Asoka near Kandahar. *Epigraphia Indica* 34: 1-8.

Fleet, J.F. 1904. The date of Buddha's death, as determined by a record of Asoka. *JRAS*, pp. 1-26.

____. 1909a. The day on which Buddha died. *JRAS*, pp. 1-34.

____. 1909b. The origin of the Buddhavarsha, the Ceylonese reckoning from the death of Buddha. *JRAS*, pp. 323-356.

____. 1909c. The last words of Asoka. *JRAS*, pp. 981-1016.

Foucher, A. 1900. *Etude sur L'Iconographie Bouddhique de L'Inde d'apres des Documents Noveaux*. Paris: Ernest Leroux.

Geiger, Wilhelm. 1912 (1986 reprint). *The Mahavamsa or the Great Chronicle of Ceylon*. Delhi: Asia Educational Publishers.

Ghate, Savita. 2007. Geomorphic and environmental changes around Sopara: an early historic port site in north Konkan. *Man and Environment* 32(1): 74-88.

Gommans, J. 1998. The silent frontier of South Asia, c. AD 1100-1800. *Journal of World History* 9: 1-23.

Gupta, K.P. 1979-80. New evidence from Kolhua pillar. *Puratattva* 11: 145-147.

Gupta, P. 1973. *Geography in Ancient Indian Inscriptions*. Delhi: D.K. Publishing House.

Gupta, S.P. 1980. *The Roots of Indian Art*. Delhi: B.R. Publishing Corporation.

Gupta, Vinay K. 2009. *Braj: an Art and Archaeological Study*, Ph.D thesis, National Museum Institute University, Delhi.

Hargreaves, H.R. 1914-15. Excavations at Sarnath. *Annual Report Archaeological Survey of India 1914-15*, pp. 97-131.

Harle, J.C. 1974. *Gupta Sculpture; Indian Sculpture of the Fourth to Sixth Centuries AD* Oxford: Clarendon Press.

Henning, W.B. 1949. The Aramaic inscription of Asoka found in Lampaka. *Bulletin of the School of Oriental and African Studies* 13: 80-88.

Hora, S.L. 1950. Knowledge of the ancient Hindus concerning fish and fisheries of India. 2. Fishery legislation in Asoka's pillar edict V (246 BC). *JASB Letters* 16 (1): 43-56.

Howell, J. and A. Sinha. 1994. Preliminary report on the explorations around Sopara, Surat and Bharuch. *South Asian Studies* 10: 189-199.

Howell, J. 1995. *Excavations at Sannati 1986-1989*. Delhi: Archaeological Survey of India.

Hultzsch, E. 1907-08. Tirumalai rock inscription of Rajendra Chola I. *Epigraphia Indica* 9: 229-233.

——. 1925. *Corpus Inscriptionum Indicarum, Volume I. Inscriptions of Asoka*. Oxford: Clarendon Press.

Indraji, B.L. 1881-82. Sopara. *The Bombay Branch of the Royal Asiatic Society* 15: 273-328.

Irwin, John. 1983. The Lat Bhairo at Banaras (Varanasi): another pre-Ashokan monument? *Zeitschrift der Deutschen Morgenlandischen Gesselschaft* 133: 321-352.

Jain, V.K. 1990. *Trade and Traders in Western India, AD 1000-1300*. Delhi: Munshiram Manoharlal.

Jayaswal, K.P. and R.D. Banerji. 1929-30. The Hathigumpha inscription of Kharavela. *Epigraphia Indica* 20, pp. 71-89.

Kielhorn, F. 1900-01. Two grants of Dandimahadevi. *Epigraphia Indica* 6, pp. 133-142.

——. 1905-06. Junagadh rock inscription of Rudradaman. *Epigraphia Indica* 8: 36-49.

Kirkpatrick, Colonel. 1811. *An Account of the Kingdom of Nepal, being the Substance of Observations Made during a Mission to that Country, in the Year 1793 by Colonel Kirkpatrick*. London: W. Bulmer and Co.

Kittoe. M. 1847. Notes on the viharas and chaityas of Behar. *The Journal of the Asiatic Society of Bengal* (hereafter *JASB*) 16: 272-279.

Lal, B.B. 1949. Sisupalgarh 1948: an early historical fort in eastern India. *Ancient India* 5, pp. 62-105.

Law, B.C. 1943. *Tribes in Ancient India*. Poona: Bhandarkar Oriental Research Institute.

——. 1954. *Historical Geography of Ancient India*. Paris: Asiatic Society of Paris.

——. 1959. *The Chronicle of the Island of Ceylon or Dipavamsa, a Historical Poem of the 4th century AD*. Colombo: The Ceylon Historical Journal, Vol. 7, July 1957 to April 1958, numbers 1-4.

Luders, H. 1912. *A List of Brahmi Inscriptions from the Earliest Times to about AD 400 with the Exception of Those of Asoka*. Appendix to *Epigraphia Indica*, Vol. 10.

Majumdar, N.G. 1935-36. Four copper plates from Soro. *Epigraphia Indica* 23, pp. 197-203.

Majumdar-Sastri, S.N. 1924. *Cunningham's Ancient Geography of India*. Calcutta: Chuckervertty and Chatterjee.

Marshall, J. 1918. *Guide to Sanchi*. Calcutta: Archaeological Survey of India.

_____. 1960. *A Guide to Taxila* 4th ed. Cambridge: Cambridge University Press

Marshall, J. and A. Foucher. 1983 (2nd reprint). *The Monuments of Sanchi*. Vol. I. Delhi: Swati Publications.

Martin, R.M. 1838. *The history, antiquities, topography, and statistics of eastern India*. Vol. I. London: W.G. Allen and Co.

Masson, Charles. 1846. Narratives of an excursion from Peshawar to Shah-Baz-Ghari. *JRAS* 8: 293-302.

MECL (Mineral Exploration Corporation Limited). 2003. *Exploration Report for Gold. Dona East Block Jonnagiri Schist Belt, Kurnool District, Andhra Pradesh*. Nagpur. Unpublished.

Mirashi, V.V. 1960. *Studies in Indology*, Vol. 1. Nagpur: The Vidarbha Samsodhana Mandal.

Mishra, Jitu. 2000. Radhanagar: early historic Buddhism, urban structure and trade. In, Basa and Mohanty (eds.). 2000, pp. 507-550.

Misra, T.N. 2004. Evolution of Buddhism and archaeological excavations in Lumbini. *Ancient Nepal*, pp. 10-18 (available on the web).

Mitra Shastri, A. 1997-98. A (lost?) Asokan edict from Vidarbha. *Puratattva* 28: 55-58.

Mookerji, R.K. 1955 (2nd ed.). *Asoka (Gaekwad Lectures)*. Delhi: Rajkamal Publications.

Mukherjee, B.N. 1984. *Studies in Aramaic Edicts of Asoka*. Calcutta: Indian Museum.

Mukherji, P.C. 1901. *A Report on a Tour of Exploration of the Antiquities in the Tarai, Nepal, the Region of Kapilavastu; during February and March 1899*. Calcutta: Archaeological Survey of India.

Narain, A.K. and T.N. Roy. 1968. *The Excavations at Prahladpur*. Banaras: Banaras Hindu University.

Nath, A. 1995. Antiquities of Graeco-Roman affinity from Adam, an inland mart of central India. *East and West* 45, pp. 149-171.

Norman, K.R. 1967. Notes on Asoka's fifth pillar edict. *JRAS*, pp. 26-32.

_____. 1975. Asoka and capital punishment: notes on a portion of Asoka's fourth pillar edict, with an appendix on the accusative absolute construction. *JRAS*, pp. 16-24.

_____. 1988. A newly found fragment of an Asokan inscription. *South Asian Studies* 4: 99-102.

_____. 1991. Studies in the Minor Rock Edicts of Asoka. *JRAS*, pp. 243-253.

Norris, E. 1846. On the Kapur-di-Giri rock inscription. *JRAS* 8: 303-307.

Oertel, F.O. 1904-05. Excavations at Sarnath. *Annual Report Archaeological Survey of India 1904-05*, pp. 59-104.

Page, J.A. 1937. *A Memoir on Kotla Firoz Shah, Delhi*. Delhi: Memoir of the Archaeological Survey of India 52.

Patil, D.R. 1963. *The Antiquarian Remains in Bihar*. Patna: Kashi Prasad Jayaswal Research Institute.

Pramanik, Shubhra. 2004-05. Significant discoveries around Sudarshan lake, Junagadh. *Puratattva* 35: 179-181.

Prinsep, James. 1834. Note on the Mathiah Lath inscription. *JASB* 3: 481-487.

——. 1835. Further particulars of the Saroon and Tirhoot Laths, and account of two Buddha inscriptions found, the one at Bakhra, in Tirhut, the other at Sarnath, near Benares. *JASB* 4: 124-128.

——. 1837a. Various ancient inscriptions. *JASB* 6: 218-223, 278-288, 663-682, 869-887.

——. 1837b. Interpretation of the most ancient of the inscriptions on the pillar called the Lat of Feroze Shah, near Delhi, and of the Allahabad, Radhia, and Mattiah pillar, or Lat, inscriptions which agree therewith. *JASB* 6: 566-609.

——. 1837d. Note on the facsimilies of the various inscriptions on the ancient column at Allahabad, retaken by Capt. Edward Smith. *JASB* 6: 963-984.

——. 1838a. Discovery of the name of Antiochus the Great, in two of the edicts of Asoka, king of India. *JASB* 7: 156-167.

——. 1836. Various ancient inscriptions. *JASB* 5: 340-349, 482-486, 554-561, 657-661, 724-732, 795.

——. 1837c. Further elucidation of the Lat or Silasthambha inscriptions from various sources. *JASB* 6: 790-797.

——. 1838b. On the edicts of Piyadasi, or Asoka, the Buddhist monarch of India, preserved on the Girnar rock in the Gujerat peninsula, and on the Dhauli rock in Cuttack, with the discovery of Ptolemy's name therein. *JASB* 7: 219-282.

——. 1838c. Examination of the inscriptions from Girnar in Gujarat, and Dhauli in Cuttack *JASB* 7: 334-356.

Prusty, H., P. Mohanty and J. Mishra. 2000. Dantapura, the capital of ancient Kalinga: a reappraisal. In, Basa and Mohanty (eds.). 2000, pp. 651-662.

Rajan, K., Yathees Kumar and Selva Kumar. 2009. *Catalogue of Archaeological Sites in Tamil Nadu*. 2 volumes. Thanjavur: Heritage India Trust.

Ramadas, G. 1917-18. Purle plates of Indravarman. *Epigraphia Indica* 14, pp. 360-363.

Rangacharya, V. 1919. *A Topographical List of the Inscriptions of the Madras Presidency, Vol. III*. Madras: Government Press.

Ravenshaw, C.E. 1839. Notice of inscriptions in Behar. *JASB* 8: 347.

Raychaudhuri, H.C. 1932. *Studies in Indian Antiquities*. Calcutta: University of Calcutta.

——. 1951. The date of Asoka. In, R.C. Majumdar (ed.). *The Age of Imperial Unity*. Bombay: Bharatiya Vidya Bhavan, pp. 92-94.

Robinson, Phil. 1877. The Banaras riots of 1809-1811. *Calcutta Review* 65: 92-119.

Sahni, D.R. 1907-08. Excavations at Rampurva. *Archaeological Survey of India Annual Report 1907-8*, pp. 181-188.

——. 1928-29. The Yerragudi rock edicts of Asoka. *Annual Report, Archaeological Survey of India 1928-29*, pp. 161-167.

——. 1935-36. Excavations at Bairat. *Annual Report Archaeological Survey of India*, pp. 84-87.

Sarma, I.K. 1994. *Parasuramesvara Temple at Gudimallam*. Nagpur: Dattson.

Sarma, I.K. and J.V. Rao. 1993. *Early Brahmi Inscriptions from Sannati*. Delhi: Harman Publishing House.

Sastri, H. Krishna. 1915. The New Asokan Edict of Maski. *Hyderabad Archaeological Series* no. 1. Hyderabad: Govt of Nizam.

Schlumberger, D. and E. Benveniste. 1967-68. A new Greek inscription of Asoka at Kandahar. *Epigraphia Indica* 37: 193-200.

Shaked, S. 1969. Notes on the new Asoka inscription from Kandahar. *JRAS*, pp. 118-122.

Sharma, Aparajita. 2009. A new Asokan inscription from Ratanpurwa. *Sanatan* 20: 10-12.

Sharma, R.N. 1987. 2003. *The Astadhyayi of Panini*. Delhi: Munshiram Manoharlal.

Sherring, M.A. 1868. *Benares, the Sacred City of the Hindus in Ancient and Modern Times*. London: Trubner and Co.

Singh, P., R. Tewari and R.N. Singh. 1999-2000. Explorations in Chaundauli district (UP) 1999-2000: a preliminary report. *Pragdhara* 10: 135-148.

Singh, P.N. and R.N. Singh. 2008. Newly discovered Magan Diwana Brahmi inscriptions near Ahraura, district Mirzapur. *Bharati* 32: 51-56.

Singh, Upinder 1994. *Kings, Brahmanas and Temples in Orissa, an Epigraphic Study AD 300-1147*. Delhi: Munshiram Manoharlal.

Sircar, D.C. 1965. *Select Inscriptions*, Vol. I. Calcutta: Calcutta University.

_____. 1965. *Select Inscriptions*, Vol. I. Calcutta: University of Calcutta.

_____. 1969-70. New Delhi inscription of Asoka. *Epigraphia Indica* 38: 1-4.

_____. 1983. *Select Inscriptions*, Vol. II, Delhi: Motilal Banarsidass.

_____. 2000. Ahraura. *Asokan Studies*. Calcutta, pp. 72-82: Indian Museum.

_____. 1979/2000. *Asokan Studies*. Calcutta: Indian Museum.

Smith, V.A. 1901a. The authorship of Piyadasi inscriptions. *JRAS*, pp. 481-499.

_____. 1909. *The Edicts of Asoka*. London: Essex House Press.

_____. 1909. Identification of the Asoka pillar northeast of Benares city described by Hiuen Tsang. *Zeitschrift der Deutschen Morgenlandischen Gesselschaft*, pp. 337-345.

_____. 1911. The monolithic pillars or columns of Asoka. *Zeitschrift der Deutschen Morgenlandischen Gesselschaft*, pp. 211-240.

_____. 1900. Sravasti. *JRAS*, pp. 1-24.

_____. 1901b. The identity of Piyadasi (Priyadarsin) with Asoka Maurya, and some connected problems. *JRAS*, pp. 827-838.

_____. 1902. Kusinara. *JRAS*, pp. 139-163.

_____. 1909 (2nd ed.). *Asoka, the Buddhist Emperor of India*. Oxford: Clarendon Press.

Smith, Vincent. 1924. *Early History of India*. Oxford: Clarendon press.

Sreenivasachar, P. 1956. *A Corpus of Inscriptions in the Telengana Districts of H.E.H. The Nizam's Dominions, Part III*. Hyderabad: Government of Andhra Pradesh.

Srivastava, K.M. 1989. Piphrawa. In, A. Ghosh (ed.). *Encyclopaedia of Indian Archaeoloogy*. Vol. 2. Delhi: Munshiram Manoharlal.

Strong, J.S. 1983. *The Legend of King Asoka, a Study and Translation of the Asokavadana*. Princeton: Princeton University Press.

Subrahmanyam, B. 1999. *Buddhist Relic Caskets in Andhradesa*. Secunderabad: Ananda Buddha Vihara Trust.

Sugandhi, Namita. 2008. Networks of intention in a peripheral landscape. *Antiquity* 82(317). Project Gallery.

Tewari, R. *et al.* 1998-99. Archaeological investigations in district Mirzapur (Uttar Pradesh). *Pragdhara* 9: 163-223.

Tewari, R. and G.C. Singh. 2000-2001. Exploration in district Mirzapur (Uttar Pradesh): 1999-2000. *Pragdhara* 11: 91-104.

Tewari, R. and R.K. Srivastava. 1996-97. Excavation at Raja Nala-ka-Tila (1995-96), district Sonabhadra (UP): preliminary observations. *Pragdhara* 7: 77-95.

——. 1997-98. Excavation at Raja Nala-ka-Tila (1996-97), district Sonabhadra (UP): preliminary observation. *Pragdhara* 8: 99-105.

Thackston, W.M. 1996. *The Baburnama, Memoirs of Babur, Prince and Emperor*. New York: The Modern Library.

Thaplyal, K.K. 2009. *A New Asokan Inscription from Ratanpurwa*. Varanasi: Jnana Pravaha.

Tripathi, Vibha, P. Upadhyay and O.P. Kumar. 2009. Recently discovered rock edict in Asokan Brahmi at Basaha, district Kaimur, Bihar. *Sanatan* 20: 1-9.

Tripathy, Snigdha. 1997. *Inscriptions of Orissa, Vol. I (circa Fifth-Eighth Centuries AD)*. Delhi: Motilal Banarasidass.

——. 2000. *Inscriptions of Orissa, Vol. II (Inscriptions of the Bhaumakaras)*. Delhi: Pratibha Prakasan.

Tripati, S. and A.S. Gaur. 1997. Onshore and nearshore explorations along the Maharashtra coast. *Man and Environment* 22(2): 73-83.

Turnour, George. 1836. Examination of some points of Buddhist chronology. *JASB* 5: 521-536.

——. 1837a. Account of the Tooth Relic of Ceylon, supposed to be alluded to in the opening passage of the Feroze Lat inscription. *JASB* 6: 856-868.

——. 1837b. Further notes on the inscriptions on the columns at Delhi, Allahabad, Betiah, etc. *JASB* 6: 1049-1064.

——. 1838. An examination of the Pali Buddhistical annals. *JASB* 7: 686-701, 789-817, 919-933, 991-1014.

——. 1837c. An examination of the Pali Buddhistical annals. *JASB* 6: 501-528, 713-737.

Verardi, G. 1995. Excavations at Gotihawa, a note on the results obtained during the first excavastion campaign in Winter 1994-95. *Ancient Nepal* 140, pp. 85-90 excluding illustrations (available on the web).

Visuvalingam, S. and E. Chalier-Visuvalingam. 2006. Bhairava in Banaras: negotiating sacred space and religious identity. In, M. Gaenszle and J. Genganagel (eds.). *Visualizing Space in Banaras*, pp. 95-128. Weisbaden L: Otto Harassowiz.

Vogel, J.Ph. 1929-30. Prakrit inscriptions from a Buddhist site at Nagarjunakonda. *Epigraphia Indica* 20, pp. 1-36.

Waddell, L.A. 1890. Note on the 'Manik-tham' monolith in the Puraniya (Purneah) district (with a sketch and coin). *Proceedings of the Asiatic Society of Bengal*, pp. 243-245.

Walton, H.G. 1911. *Dehra Dun, a Gazetteer, being Vol.I of the District Gazetteers of the United Provinces of Agra and Oudh.*

Watters, T. 1905. *On Yuan Chwang's Travels in India, Vol. 2*. London: Royal Asiatic Society.

Wheeler, R.E.M. 1948. Brahmagiri and Chandravalli 1947. *Ancient India* 4, pp. 180-310.

Williams, J. 1973. A recut Asokan capital and the Gupta attitude towards the past. *Artibus Asiae* 35: 225-240.

Wilson, H.H. 1846. Note by the Director. *JRAS* 8: 308-314.

——. 1850. On the rock inscriptions of Kapur di Giri, Dhauli and Girnar. *JRAS* 12: 153-251.

——. 1856a. On Buddha and Buddhism. *The Journal of the Royal Asiatic Society* (hereafter *JRAS*), 16: 229-265.

——. 1856b. Buddhist inscription of king Piyadasi – translations and observations. *JRAS* 16: 357-365.

Woolner, A.C. 1924 (1993 reprint). *Asoka Text and Glossary*. Delhi: Motilal Banarsidass.

Wright, J.C. 2000. Asoka's 256-night campaign. *JRAS*, pp. 319-339.

Ziauddin, M. and S. Narayanaswami. 1974. Gold Resources of India. *India Geological Survey Bulletin* 38: 1-186.

Index